Safeguarding India's Intangible Heritage

Custodians of Culture

Safeguarding India's Intangible Heritage

Custodians of Culture

DR. AMEEZA ZARRIN
FARHA

GYAN

Published by

GYAN

Gyan Publishing House
5, Ansari Road
Daryaganj, New Delhi-110002
Phone: 011-47034999, 9811692060
E-mail: books@gyanbooks.com

Distribution Network
gyanbooks.com
India, USA, Canada, UK, Australia, France

ISBN: 978-81-212-7137-0 (HB)

First Published, 2023

Printed at: Gyan Press, Delhi.

SAFEGUARDING INDIA'S INTANGIBLE HERITAGE
CUSTODIANS OF CULTURE
Author: Dr. Ameeza Zarrin, Farha

Contents

Preface

India serves as a tribute to the great history woven by millennia of civilization with its rich and diverse cultural tapestry. A wealth of intangible cultural manifestations exist within its boundaries and are just waiting to be discovered and appreciated. This vast country is a reservoir of living heritage that spans time and distance, from ancient customs to contemporary traditions.

The book you hold in your hands, "Safeguarding India's Intangible Heritage: Custodians of Culture" aims to delve into the intricate web of intangible heritage that defines the soul of this incredible land. It seeks to unravel the stories, rituals, art forms, knowledge systems, and practices that have been passed down through generations, shaping the identity of countless communities.

The idea of intangible cultural heritage acknowledges that culture is not just limited to historical monuments and tangible artefacts. It includes the craftsmanship, oral traditions, music, dances, rituals, and indigenous knowledge systems that are essential to the social fabric of a community. This cultural legacy is dynamic and constantly changing, adapting to the changing times while maintaining its core essence.

India's intangible cultural heritage is a tapestry interwoven with diverse threads, reflecting the country's staggering regional, linguistic, religious, and ethnic variations. From the vibrant festivals of north-east to the sacred chants of Varanasi, from Bhand Pathar of Jammu & Kashmir to the classical dance forms of Bharatanatyam, Kathak and martial arts of Kerala, Moreover the centuries-old puppetry traditions of Rajasthan, the age-old craft of Chikankari embroidery from Uttar Pradesh. Each region has nurtured its unique cultural expressions.

This book takes us on a tour of the vast cultural landscapes of India, discovering the rich tapestry of intangible heritage that dwells there. We explore the customs and ceremonies that mark the passage of time, the traditional arts and crafts that demonstrate the artistic ability and inventiveness of craftspeople, and the oral traditions that preserve the knowledge of the past.

Furthermore, this book strives to shed light on the challenges faced by India's intangible cultural heritage in the modern era. The continuation of these priceless traditions is threatened by rapid urbanisation, globalisation, and evolving social dynamics. We must work to preserve and promote intangible heritage's sustainability and recognise its importance.

Present work is a tribute to the custodians of intangible cultural heritage, the often-unacknowledged champions who wholeheartedly dedicate themselves to preserving these traditions for the benefit of posterity. This book also signifies the role of museum in this endeavour, serving as preserver of our intangible heritage by documenting, conserving, and showcasing the diverse expressions of culture, offering a platform for communities to safeguard their traditions and share them with the world.

Acknowledgements

I would like to begin by expressing my profound gratitude to the Most Merciful and Almighty Allah, whose guidance and blessings have illuminated my path throughout the creation of this book. His infinite wisdom and benevolence have been my constant source of inspiration. My deepest appreciation goes to my parents, whose love, support, and sacrifices have been the bedrock of my journey. Their unwavering encouragement and belief in me have been the driving force behind my accomplishments.

I extend my heartfelt thanks to my co-author, Ms. Farha, whose dedication, insights, and collaborative spirit have greatly enriched this work. Her contributions are truly invaluable.

I am profoundly grateful to Professor Abduraheem K., for his pivotal role in shaping my intellectual growth. His firm dedication to sharing insight has consistently been a wellspring of inspiration. I am deeply appreciative of the knowledge and wisdom generously imparted by Professor Syed Asif A. Naqvi, which has significantly enhanced my comprehension of the field of intangible cultural and natural heritage.

I would also like to express my appreciation to my family members for their constant support and encouragement throughout this endeavor. Their belief in me has been a persistent source of motivation. Lastly, I am thankful to all my teachers, well-wishers and friends who have supported me along this journey. Their encouragement and faith in my work have been a source of strength.

Dr. Ameeza Zarrin

List of Tables

Introduction

India has gained a well-developed reputation as a country brimming with wonders and diversity, owing to its invaluable cultural and natural heritage. Within India, there are regional variations in languages, music, dance, architecture, food, religious beliefs, and customs. Numerous facets of India's rich cultural diversity have had a significant influence on people in every nation in the world. Indian culture is frequently described as a synthesis of various aspects of other cultures, including traditions, festivals, cuisines, languages, skills, music, etc, that date back millennia. All humankind's achievements while residing in social groups can be summed up as culture. Thus, culture is an environment that has been created by humans and contains all the tangible and intangible by-products of collective life that are handed down from one generation to the next. We observe people in our immediate surroundings who speak and practise a variety of languages, religions, and customs. Their dietary preferences and vogue for dressing are some examples of these differences. However, there is a fundamental commonality that serves as a unifying factor beneath all these differences. They take great pride in the unbroken continuity with which they are lived, safeguarded, and kept.

The emergence of culture is a historical process shaped by the wisdom passed down by our forebears. As time passes, we continuously add new ideas and perspectives to those that already exist, and we occasionally discard those that we no longer feel to be pertinent. These ideas are the culmination of several social and religious practices which might be observed in rituals, dance, music, habits, way of life, and patterns of behaviour and physical appearance. They are in a transitional stage between ancient, mediaeval, and contemporary times. All these customs and ancient ways of living are remnants of our illustrious past; what we acquired from our forebears is referred to as heritage. As a result, heritage includes a nation's history, cultural beliefs, historical buildings, and locations of significant historical events. The cultural heritage of India is not only among the ancient but also among the incredibly comprehensive and diverse. Throughout the course of history, numerous races and religions have visited this region, leaving their influence on the local culture. These folks either permanently emigrated to India or briefly entered its territory in order to establish a separate culture. This led to the fusion of numerous cultures as Indian Culture. Cultural heritage is deeply rooted in individuals and has evolved over an extensive period as a result of their creativity, imagination, intelligence, skills, aesthetic sensibilities, etc. As we delve into the chapters of the past, the vibrant history of India is brought to life by all the colour and scent that still permeate in the festivals, craftsmanship, dances, music, monuments, forts, palaces, and temples that can be found in every nook and cranny of this multifaceted nation. The magnificent architecture, intricately carved designs, and adorned facades of cultural monuments reveal the extraordinary ability of the artisans who have mesmerised the world for many years. It is a living legacy that is hidden but observable, which consists variety of components, such as ideas, traditions, ways of living, conventions, and beliefs. It is fascinating to remember that Indian civilization was referred to as *Ajaib-Ul-Hind* by Arabs in the 10th century. Ajaib-ul-Hind's literal translation is "Incredible India" (National Institute of Open Schooling, n.d.). This apt translation captures the essence of a nation that continues to inspire awe with its incredible cultural heritage. Cultural heritage encompasses the cultural elements and values that we receive from previous generations. These include aspects of culture that are passed down to us by our ancestors, cherished, protected, and upheld with uninterrupted continuity. Cultural heritage can be further classified as;

- **Tangible Cultural Heritage** is related to physical heritage such as buildings and historical places, monuments, books, documents, and artifacts that are considered worthy of preservation for the future and are significant to the archaeology, architecture, ethnography, anthropology, science, and technology of a specific culture.

- **Intangible Cultural Heritage** is related to cultural expressions and practices that form a body of knowledge and provide for continuity, dynamism, and meaning of social life to generations of people as individuals, social groups, and communities. Intangible Cultural Heritage allows for identity and a sense of belonging for people as well as an accumulation of intellectual capital for current and future generations in the context of mutual respect for human, social and cultural rights.

This book will provide an in-depth exploration of Intangible Cultural Heritage, which means the customs, depictions, manifestations, wisdom, capabilities, and cultural environments linked to communities or groups. They have been recognized in the following five domains by the United Nations Educational, Scientific and Cultural Organization (UNESCO)-

- Oral traditions and expressions, including language as a vehicle of intangible cultural heritage,
- Performing arts,
- Social practices, rituals, and festive events,
- Knowledge and practices concerning nature and the universe,
- Traditional craftsmanship

Venugopal (2011) discussed that Intangible heritage has predominantly revolved around culture. This is evident in the UNESCO instrument's title, "Convention for the Safeguarding of the Intangible Cultural Heritage 2003." While the document recognizes five domains of ICH, natural heritage is just one of them. Natural heritage is often given less attention in discussions of intangible heritage. However, all of the domains mentioned also encompass various aspects of Natural Heritage. Notably, the fourth domain, "Knowledge and Practice concerning Nature and the Universe," is exclusively dedicated to Intangible Natural Heritage (INH). To ensure that INH is rightfully acknowledged and given equal standing alongside ICH in all discussions regarding Intangible Heritage (IH). National Museum of Natural History, New Delhi, on 23-24 March 2012, organized a workshop on Intangible Natural Heritage in which it further delineates the domains of INH as follows:

- Oral traditions and Expressions on nature and the environment
- Performing Arts on themes related to nature and the environment
- Social practices, Rituals and Festive events on themes related to nature and the environment
- Knowledge and Practice concerning nature and environment
- Traditional Craftsmanship on themes related to nature and environment.

The ICH is recreated continuously by communities as a result of their surroundings by being transferred from one generation to the next, which gives them a feeling of continuity and identity through connections between the environment and history. This encourages appreciation for cultural diversity and the uniqueness of people. The UNESCO 2003 Convention describes intangible cultural heritage as-

> Practices, representations, expressions, knowledge, skills – as well as the instruments, objects, artefacts and cultural spaces associated therewith – that communities, groups and, in some cases, individuals recognize as part of their cultural heritage.

There is no conceivable order that might be used to differentiate one community's intangible legacy as being superior, more significant, or more fascinating than the heritage of any other community, which is another core precept of the Convention. Each component of an individual community or group's intangible heritage has a value that cannot be measured and cannot be compared to other components of the heritage of other communities; rather, each component is equally valuable to the communities, groups, or people who recognise it as a part of their heritage. As a living phenomenon, intangible heritage is always a part of the present and the future even though it often evokes the past. Folklore cannot exist without the folk, much as intangible cultural heritage cannot exist without the communities and people that act as its bearers, stewards, and guardians. Living heritage has recently attracted more attention from throughout the world and turned into a focal point of international cooperation, in large part due to the leadership of UNESCO. The Convention states that all communities, regardless of size, dominance, or lack thereof, deserve our respect for their intangible cultural legacy. Thus, the Convention is firmly focused on the viability and sustainability of intangible cultural heritage. With the introduction of its "Living Human Treasures Program in 1950", Japan became the first nation to recognise the importance of ICH. This programme permitted "living national treasures" or "holders of major intangible cultural properties" to be recognised, either singly or as a group, as a result of laws that safeguarded both tangible and intangible heritage. The Cultural Properties Protection Act of 1962 was established in reaction to the fact that rapid modernisation during the Korean War of 1950-1953 was causing a decline in interest in traditional crafts and skills (du Cros, 2012). In December 1964, the first Intangible Cultural Properties and Living Human Treasures were both recognised. Several nations, such as Thailand (1985), the Philippines (1988), France (1994), etc., have established their own formal initiatives to recognise intangible cultural values and the individuals who exemplify them (UNESCO Korean National Commission. 2002). As early as 1972, during the discussion that led to the acceptance of the World Heritage Convention, several state parties expressed an opinion that the Convention's scope was extremely restrictive and that the international community's participation in the sphere of cultural heritage should encompass intangible manifestations as well. This marked one of the initial occurrences of the concept that the extent of a convention should not be limited to only its tangible manifestations. The Colombian government proposed adding a protocol to the Universal Copyright Convention for safeguarding folklore. In a broader sense, countries in Africa, Asia, and Latin America pushed for the protection of ICH because their own ideas of culture centred on live traditions. "Intangible cultural heritage" is often seen as a "loose English translation" of the Japanese phrase '*mukei bunkazai*'. The Mexico City Declaration on Cultural Policies in 1982, gave culture a new, more complete meaning. It said that culture is "the whole complex of distinctive spiritual, material, intellectual, and emotional features that make up a society or social group." So, cultural heritage comprises "tangible and intangible works through which people's creativity finds expression: languages, rites, beliefs, historical places and monuments, literature, works of art, archives, and libraries" (Lenzerini, 2011). The UNESCO General Conference approved the Recommendation on the Safeguarding of Traditional Culture and Folklore document in 1989, but it did not result in limitations for Member States. About a decade later, certain nations, such as Brazil and Algeria, made significant advances at the national level by adopting progressive laws pertaining to this issue (Bedjaoui, 2004). This allowed different groups to declare their cultural identities and retain humanity's diversity, focusing the world's decision-makers on intangible heritage (du Cros, 2012). There were several efforts made in the 1990s within the framework of UNESCO to ensure the safeguarding of ICH. The UNESCO Living Human Treasures programme began in 1994 and is one example of such an effort. It encouraged member states to recognise highly skilled tradition bearers and craftspeople who can perform or create specific elements of the ICH and pass on their knowledge, know-how, and skills to younger generations. The UNESCO General Conference embraced a resolution in 1997 declaring spaces or forms of cultural expression to be part of the "oral heritage of humanity" to highlight the significance of the ICH to peoples and nations. In 1998, the Executive Board launched the Programme of the "Proclamation of Masterpieces of the Oral and Intangible Heritage of Humanity" (Lenzerini, 2011). In the context of this programme, the Director-General of UNESCO designated 19 cultural expressions or spaces as "Masterpieces of Oral and Intangible Heritage" in May 2001. Another group of 28 "masterpieces" received international recognition in November 2003 and 43 in 2005 (Bouchenaki, 2007). By the mid-1990s, people all around the world had begun talking publicly about the effects of globalisation. A series of regional conferences sponsored by UNESCO on local, national, and regional cultural survival led to a global conference held at the Smithsonian Institution in Washington, DC, in 1999. The conference and a subsequent book, Safeguarding Traditional Cultures, demanded a more active view of cultural traditions as 'living' and enacted by communities. A 1995–1999 UNESCO survey of national efforts to protect intangible cultural heritage exposed a dearth of institutions in the field and effective programmes (Kurin, 2004). In partnership with the Smithsonian Institution, the international conference titled "A Global Assessment of the 1989 Recommendation on the Safeguarding of Traditional Culture and Folklore: Local Empowerment and International Cooperation" took place in Washington, D.C., in 1999. The goal of this Conference was to look at the "Recommendation on the Safeguarding of Traditional Culture and Folklore" again ten years after it was adopted in 1989 (Seitel, (ed)

2001). The Istanbul Declaration, which was adopted at a Round Table of Ministers of Culture held by the Director-General of UNESCO in Istanbul in 2002, says that "an all-encompassing approach to cultural heritage should prevail, which takes into account the dynamic link between tangible and intangible heritage and their deep interdependence". During the 7th Asia Pacific Regional Assembly of the International Council of Museums in Shanghai in 2002, the Shanghai Charter was ratified that recommends "interdisciplinary and cross-sectorial approaches that bring together movable and immovable, tangible and intangible, natural and cultural heritage" and "develop documentation tools and standards in establishing holistic museum and heritage practises" (Bouchenaki, 2007). In 1999, during its thirty-first session, the General Conference approved the initiative to develop a standard-setting instrument. On January 22–24, 2002, UNESCO held an international meeting of professionals in Rio de Janeiro on "Intangible Cultural Heritage: Priority Domains for an International Convention." At this meeting, experts stressed how important and urgent it was to have an easy-to-find glossary for ICH. In order to determine the meanings of the most pertinent terms, it was determined to host a meeting of experts at the UNESCO headquarters in June 2002. In order to get ready for this meeting, the Netherlands National Commission for UNESCO asked a group of experts from the Netherlands to come up with draught definitions of terms related to ICH. It also looked at older definitions from UNESCO and groups of scholars, such as the work done at a meeting in Turin in March 2001 and two lists of definitions from Member States and intergovernmental organisations put together by the Secretariat of UNESCO. In 2002, a glossary came out (See Appendix I). The short definition of "Intangible Cultural Heritage" is partly based on what was mentioned at the Turin Round Table in March 2001. At UNESCO's Executive Board meeting in May 2002, it was noted that the 2001 Turin definition was scientifically valid but too abstract for practical application. In addition, it was considered that domains should be included in the definition of ICH in order to clarify its scope (Van Zanten, 2004). "The Convention for the Safeguarding of Intangible Cultural Heritage" replaced the 1989 Recommendation and UNESCO Masterpieces project. The UNESCO General Conference in Paris adopted it on October 17, 2003, and implemented it in 2006. Its goal was to safeguard ICH by supporting an integrated approach, heritage being defined as "traditional, contemporary and living at the same time," inclusive (so that people might feel part of the same or different communities), representative of cultural components globally, and community-based (du Cros, 2012).

The intangible cultural heritage found in developing nations is incredibly varied and valuable, encompassing customs, practices, and skills that define specific societies. Among the oldest cultures in existence is the Indian culture, which has managed to endure even as ancient civilizations like Egypt, Greece, and Rome have faded away. Despite the passage of time, Indian culture continues to thrive in the present day, preserving its rich traditions and customs. Its underlying ideas are the same as they were in the past. Village panchayats, systems of caste, traditional healing methods, and the practice of residing within joint family systems are all apparent. Throughout history, people have found wisdom and encouragement in the instructions of Buddha, Mahavira, and Lord Krishna. People in this country are still motivated by various beliefs, including spirituality, praying outside, believing in karma and reincarnation, nonviolence, truthfulness, purity, and an absence of acquisitiveness (Satpathy, n.d.). Srivastava (2015) stated that there is an Indian saying, "*Kos-Kospe badle pani, Kos-Kos pe badlebani*," which means that every kilometre or change of place changes the taste of the water and the language. India's cultural variety and unity in diversity are reflected in the ways in which people communicate. And this mix of cultures is at the heart of Indian culture and what makes it special. Kapur (2022) mentioned that Baudhayana, Aryabhatta, and Bhaskaracharya's work in mathematics, astronomy, and astrology, Varahmihir's work in physics, Nagarjuna's work in chemistry, Susruta and Charak's work in medicine, and Patanjali's work in yoga are all treasures of Indian culture. It has a sense of the universe as a whole, a sense of harmony, transparency, tolerance, continuity and stability, the ability to change, morals and ethics, hard work and responsibility, a focus on duty, and the joint family system.

In this country, a wide range of dialects and languages are spoken, which have encouraged the formation of a diverse body of literature. Numerous world religions, including Jainism, Buddhism, Sikhism, and of course Hinduism, have their origins in India. Due to the wide range of influences, Indian culture is now complex, rich, and beautiful all at once. Our music, dance, theatre, cuisines, dresses, and artistic expression all represent the multifaceted characteristics of our culture. This multilingual composition is also reflected in our literature and our political structures exhibit unity in diversity as well. Civilization means the use of materials, while the term "culture" describes the way of life, customs, and traditions. This explains why ancient civilizations perished whereas Indian culture has persisted to the present day because spirituality rather than materialism served as the foundation for growth. Indian culture is therefore considered to be an old culture whose past is still present today that is thriving in all its glory and splendour despite having experienced numerous ups and downs.

We should not simply assume that there is a single correct way of life or that any one way is universally valid, given the increasing global interconnectivity of our world, where we coexist on a more global level. Cultures and beliefs must coexist because coexistence is vital. The best thing we can do to avoid making such errors is to learn about other cultures while simultaneously learning about our own. How to identify, manage, and support in the safekeeping of intangible heritage practises without interfering with the fundamental relationship between that heritage form and the practising community—those who have the moral authority to speak as the moral "owners" of that heritage—is one of the biggest challenges facing by heritage practitioners. Heritage professionals must simultaneously make choices about heritage assets that safeguard both concrete and intangible heritage values. Thus, these discussions have an impact on both "the 2003 Convention for Safeguarding Intangible Cultural Heritage" and the "World Heritage Convention's" implementation. The Convention lays out a wide range of educational initiatives that each State should carry out for the community, especially the youth, both inside and outside of communities that have a rich legacy. The writing of this book is an approach to the identification and documentation of the Intangible Cultural Heritage of India, as it is the foremost step according to UNESCO 2003 Convention of Safeguarding ICH. It will introduce various traditions and practices of India to readers, which has its uniqueness in the world. It has been composed to highlight the living cultural heritage of India, as well as some traditions which have vanished or are on the verge of extinction according to the domains of ICH such as *dastangoi, marsiyakhwani*, different languages, rogan art, knowledge of herbal medicines, ventriloquism, kalbeliya etc. The objective of the 'UNESCO Convention on Safeguarding Intangible Cultural Heritage' is to promote and preserve cultural practices and traditions within communities, ensuring the protection of our heritage and showing respect to every community, regardless of its size, strength, or influence. Although some examples of ICH of India are included in the "Representative List of the Intangible Cultural Heritage of Humanity" managed by UNESCO such as Durga Puja (2021), Kalbelia (2010), Buddhist chanting of Ladakh (2012), Ramman (2009) etc. but some traditions of India are still struggling to be recognized, if we do not document them and do not create awareness they will disappear. Therefore, it is crucial to preserve and record such history in order to make it available to both current and future generations.

The importance of ICH in preserving cultural history and fostering cross-cultural understanding across communities cannot be overstated. As a result, it strengthens social value and expresses the community's cultural identity. This intangible cultural heritage gives individuals, communities, and organisations an aura of identity and continuity, assisting them in making sense of the world, giving their lives purpose, and sustaining their way of coexisting. Intangible heritage, which is practised and passed down from person to person and generation to generation, is a major source of cultural variation and an undeniable testament to humanity's capacity for creativity. It creates cultural understanding and fosters the well-being of the community, drives economic growth, and presents a strategic framework for cultural tourism. The growing cultural tourism sector supports the development of sustainable economic growth in developing nations like India. Traditional indigenous knowledge is given significant importance at this time. There are several ways to record tacit information in this digital age. If not preserved, this knowledge will eventually disappear without leaving a trace for subsequent generations. The UNESCO Convention (2003) provides a specific definition of this, stating that preserving intangible heritage is about the dissemination of information, skills, and meaning. When transmitting tradition, it also placed more value on communication than it did on production. The practise, usage, and interpretation of intangible legacy forms give meaning to all tangible heritage forms since "the tangible can only be explained through the intangible." However, intangible values can exist without a physical source. Any human who is still alive today must be familiar with their history, oral traditions, religious beliefs, native tongues, etc.

Museums and museums like institutions which are dedicated to cultural heritage, play a vital role in safeguarding and documenting intangible heritage, historical documents and makes them accessible to the public. In addition to documentation of objects, museums also greatly affect the tourist industry. People come from all over the world to visit them so they can learn about and interact with cultural heritage directly. In museums, libraries, and archives, recorded knowledge can be documented and kept for access in the present and the future. They may cooperate, disseminate recorded information to a large audience via the World Wide Web, and increase income for sustainable economic growth in developing nations with a wealth of intangible cultural assets. If intangible cultural heritage is to continue to foster long-term, sustainable economic growth, it must be preserved. It needs to be used continually in order to qualify as a living heritage, as living traditions can be transmitted from one generation to the following. However, if it is not constantly used, it might eventually fade away and vanish from the region. Therefore, it is critical to preserve the intangible cultural heritage, and this is easily accomplished with the help of modern multimedia tools. The gathered information can be stored for use by both current and future generations and made accessible through museum websites. The convention emphasises transmission as a crucial protective strategy and places a high value on educating the next generation. Indian oral history, traditions, and intangible cultural assets are rapidly disappearing. Sociocultural knowledge and memories will be lost as the old generation dies. There is an immediate and critical need to connect the memories of our societal legacy intertwined with digital advancements, specifically through the recording of cultural memories in a digital form.

Modern technology aids cultural institutions in documenting and preserving legacy. These digital technologies have the potential to assist communities and societies in the transmission of intangible cultural elements into tangible formats. It is essential to document and create digital archives of these memories before they become permanently lost. It is necessary to transform the ICH into a tangible form for protection, using techniques like audio-video recording, still photography, inventory, etc. This can be accomplished by using digital tools like tablets, smartphones, and digital cameras. The goal of putting the ICH into physical form is not to turn it into a set of static records but rather to provide a powerful platform from which future generations can learn about and contribute to the ICH. According to the Convention, preserving intangible cultural heritage entails ensuring its survival, particularly through strengthening the processes of innovation, transfer, and respect for one another that are essential to it. One of the primary aims of the Convention is to forward appreciation for intangible cultural assets and an understanding of their significance, and this public education and awareness-raising serves as both an aim and a means to achieve this goal.

Table 1: UNESCO's Representative List of the Indian Intangible Cultural Heritage of Humanity

S. No.	Elements of Intangible Cultural Heritage	Year
1.	Durga Puja	2021
2.	Kumbh Mela	2017
3.	Novruz, Nowrouz, Nowrouz, Nawrouz, Nauryz, Nooruz, Nowruz, Navruz, Nevruz, Nowruz, Navruz, Nawrouz,	2016
4.	Yoga	2016
5.	Traditional brass and copper craft of utensil making among the Thatheras of Jandiala Guru, Punjab, India	2014
6.	Sankirtana, ritual singing, drumming, and dancing of Manipur	2013
7.	Buddhist chanting of Ladakh	2012
8.	Chhau dance	2010
9.	Mudiyettu, ritual theatre and dance drama of Kerala	2010
10.	Kalbelia folk songs and dances of Rajasthan	2010
11.	Ramman, religious festival and ritual theatre of the Garhwal Himalayas, India	2009
12.	Kutiyattam, Sanskrit theatre	2008
13.	Ramlila, the traditional performance of the Ramayana	2008
14.	Tradition of Vedic chanting	2008

This book comprised six chapters, which will provide an overview of all five domains of intangible cultural heritage and their important parts with descriptions of the key issues of negligence to follow these traditions and their safeguarding measures. In chapter-1 "Oral Traditions & Expressions" some famous oral traditions of India have been discussed, such as- Marsiyakhwani, Buddhist Chanting of Ladakh etc. Chapter-2 "Performing Arts" discusses various performing arts of India such as dance, music, theatre of different states of India. Various festivals, social and religious practices have been discussed in Chapter-3 "Social Practices, Rituals & Festive Events". Chapter-4 "Knowledge, and Practices Concerning Nature and Universe" talks about Indian traditional knowledge system including ayurveda, Yoga, Unani etc. Chapter-5 "Traditional Craftsmanship" includes various crafts and arts of different states such as Madhubani Paintings, Bones Craft, Rogan Art etc. Chapter-6 explores the functions of UNESCO's 2003 Convention, as well as the involvement of various Indian cultural centers, academies, university departments, and the role and potential of museums in the safeguarding of ICH.

References

1. Abeita, A. P. (2001). *Safeguarding traditional cultures: a global assessment.* P. Seitel (Ed.). Washington, DC: Center for Folklife and Cultural Heritage, Smithsonian Institution. https://folklife.si.edu/resources/Unesco/index.htm
2. Bala, S. (2012). Digital inventories on cultural memories and intangible cultural heritage: case study of Yadav community of Haryana, India. *Incl. bibl, 1*, 11-19.
3. Beazley, O., & Deacon, H. (2007). The Safeguarding of Intangible Heritage values under the World Heritage Convention: Auschwitz, Hiroshima and Robben Island. *Safeguarding Intangible Cultural Heritage-Challenges and Approaches-. Institute of Art and Law: Builth Wells*, 93-107.
4. Bedjaoui, M. (2004). The Convention for the Safeguarding of the Intangible Cultural Heritage: the legal framework and universally recognized principles. *Museum International, 56*(1-2), 150-155.
5. du Cros, H. (2012). Intangible Cultural Heritage, Education and Museums. 10.13140/RG.2.1.3217.5522.
6. Bouchenaki, M. (2007). A major advance towards a holistic approach to heritage conservation: the 2003 Intangible Heritage Convention. *International Journal of Intangible Heritage, 2*(1), 105-109.
7. Munjeri, D. (2004). Tangible and intangible heritage: From difference to convergence. *Museum International, 56*(1-2), 12-20.
8. Kapur, R. (2022). Understanding Indian Culture and Heritage.
9. Kurin, R. (2004). Safeguarding Intangible Cultural Heritage in the 2003

UNESCO Convention: a critical appraisal. *Museum International, 56*(1-2), 66-77.

10. Lenzerini, F. (2011). Intangible cultural heritage: The living culture of peoples. *European Journal of International Law, 22*(1), 101-120.
11. National Institute of Open Schooling. (n.d.). *MODULE – 1. Understanding Culture. Culture: An Introduction.* Retrieved from https://www.nios.ac.in/media/documents/SecICHCour/English/CH.01.pdf
12. National Institute of Open Schooling. (n.d.). *MODULE – 2. Cultural Dimension of Tourism. Understanding Indian Culture and Heritage.* Retrieved from https://nios.ac.in/media/documents/tourism_337_courseE/337_Tourism_Eng/337_Tourism_Eng_L6.pdf
13. Perera, K., & Chandra, D. (2014). Documenting the Intangible Cultural Heritage for Sustainable Economic Growth in Developing Countries. *CIDOC 2014.*
14. Satpathy, D. B.B. (n.d.). Indian Culture and Heritage. Retrieved from https://ddceutkal.ac.in/Syllabus/MA_history/paper-8-N.pdf
15. Srivastava, S. (2015). A Study of Awareness of Cultural Heritage among the Teachers at University Level. *Universal Journal of Educational Research, 3*(5), 336-344.
16. *UNESCO - India.* (n.d.). Retrieved from https://ich.unesco.org/en/state
17. UNESCO Korean National Commission. (2002*). Guidelines for the establishment of living human treasures systems.* https://unesdoc.unesco.org/ark:/48223/pf0000129520
18. Van Zanten, W. (2004). Constructing new terminology for intangible cultural heritage. *Museum international, 56*(1-2), 36-44.
19. Venugopal, B. (2011). "Project INH": A Case Study of the Role of Museums in the Interpretation of Intangible Natural Heritage. In Intangible Natural Heritage (pp. 88-104). Routledge.
20. Zanten, W.V. (2002). Glossary Intangible Cultural Heritage. *Hague: Netherlands National Commission for UNESCO.* Retrieve from https://ich.unesco.org/doc/src/00265.pdf

Chapter - 1

Oral Traditions and Expressions, including Language as a Vehicle of Intangible Cultural Heritage

Oral tradition is a part of the evolution of human civilization which has own characteristics. In the absence of script, it is a complex process of transmitting information about the culture of people from generation to generation orally through stories. Oral literature is any type of verbal art that is shared orally or by word of mouth such as jokes, proverbs, legends, fairy tales, folk tales, personal experience narratives, myths, *bhajans and kirtans*, believes, customs, poetry, *qawwali* etc. Oral tradition, in general, refers to the transmission of cultural and social values, and collective memories by word of mouth and it has long been practised by rural folk as folklore. Two words make up the term "folklore" **Folk+Lore.** Any group of individuals from a similar socioeconomic, religious, generational, or racial background who are interested in the same things are referred to as "Folk." The word "Lore" usually refers to the expertise and creativity of a community expressed via tales, humour, artwork, architecture, music, dance, tradition, belief, ritual, and celebration. Folklore is an oral tradition that is passed down orally. It is the information, customs, and beliefs of a culture that frequently has no written language. Like written literature, they contain both prose and narrative along with myths, plays, rituals, and many more. The expression of a particular population's traditions, specifically oral traditions, through stories, popular beliefs, music, dance, proverbs, legends, oral histories, jokes, customs, and other means is referred to as folklore. Oral tradition is a practice that is rooted in our culture and customs and helps us remember and carry on information through spoken means. It is a way for communities to share their history, social structure, literary works, and a variety of knowledge. All of these are transmitted from one generation to the next without the use of a writing system. Oral tradition may be described as **recording, preserving, and interpreting historical knowledge, or the narration of events based on personal experiences, or it can be characterised as oral singing, chanting, or the telling of a narrative belonging to a certain community**. Without a system of written notes, the oral tradition remains a unique reference to the human brain's ability to acquire, recall, and replicate structures of extraordinary complexity and sophistication. It might include **rituals, prayers, legends, riddles, epic poems, proverbs, songs, stories, dramatic performances, tongue twisters, chants, nursery rhymes, myths, lullabies, etc.,** that have been passed down orally over multiple generations. Songs, chants, and stories were recited and retold story time has always been a joy for the children as many questions were asked, and compelling answers were offered. This intangible cultural legacy is expressed through language and oral expressions need language to be effective. Language itself contains many elements that express the history and cultural identity of a community. They are essential to the survival of cultures and are differ from written information in some manner. For communities, languages are more than just mechanisms for transmitting ideas. They are subtle coverings that envelop their spirits and give all of their symbolic expression a predetermined structure. Similar to how a sculptor uses materials like clay, bronze, or marble as their medium, language serves as oral traditions.

For more than a thousand years in India, oral tradition has dominated. The four Vedas, *Ramayana,* and *Mahabharata* were all told orally before the script or writing existed. The entire scriptures were recorded in personal memories. For example, the ***Mahabharata*** is believed to have existed and passed orally for over a millennium before being recorded in writing form we all know it today. Vedic civilization's scriptures, known as the ***Vedas*** **(knowledge),** are claimed to be among the earliest written texts, written around 1500 BCE (Raghavendra, 2019). There is a prevailing belief that every oral tradition aspires to literacy, but in India the *Brahmins* derived their ability to recite the sacred *Vedas* with the right intonation. The *Vedas* and their related teachings, the *Upanishads* were passed orally through the generations before being written down, creating the core of the Indian oral tradition. It was reinforced further by the *guru-shishya parampara*, the practice of a lineage of mentors transmitting knowledge verbally and handing down the teachings to their pupils, and the *gurukula* system, where disciples live with their *gurus* to orally assimilate knowledge from them. Knowledge imparted orally is only possible to those chosen by the teacher (the *gurukula* system) and this is perhaps how the *Brahmins* kept their position; *Vedic* knowledge can only belong to them.

People of India speaks different languages, and sometimes they speak multiple languages at once - think of the rhythmic transitions between Persian, Arabic and Brajbhasha in the verses of *Amir Khusro*, the Sufi poet of medieval Delhi. In all early civilizations, the oral tradition existed and grew. Storytelling was a popular form of entertainment prior to the Industrial Revolution. Grandparents act as effective tools of oral teaching, transferring knowledge and information about a people's past and customs in each culture. They served as a link between the present and the past, and played vital role in social integration. A number of extensive oral traditions are shared across the country, creating glorious local versions; and some extremely specific sections, such as; herbal medicine recipes or the preparation of cuisines which include knowledge regarding medicinal plants and their therapeutic applications. Transmission of ancestral methods of preparation, including spice mixes that retains traditional flavours and recipes of special foods and sweets are passed down through the generations with the words of mouth. This wealth of traditional knowledge can now be captured and shared through books, magazines, and online platforms. In India, myths and superstitions have been around for a very long time and have changed and adapted over the years. There are some ancient traditions that gave rise to superstitions, and these traditions are transferred from one generation to another. People take part in a variety of activities as a means of protecting themselves against danger. It is in the nature of humans to share their thoughts and their worldviews with others around them. Therefore, it is no surprise that such communal life has resulted in the development of such beliefs and practises. They were a very important part of Indian society, including how they were venerated, how they knew if they were going to have good or bad luck, how they healed, and how they kept disease and accidents from happening. Examples of myth or superstition may include one should not sweep the floor after sunset, eat some curd before you leave, lemon and chillies can keep bad things away, a black cat crossing one's path is bad luck, to avoid harming the baby, pregnant women should avoid funerals and graves, do not cut your nails after dusk, the evil eye is warded off by black are transmitted orally generation to generation without any written records. India's population believes numbers (numerology) affect their lives and they often do things like break a coconut before starting an important job or tie a thread around a tree to make a wish come true etc. In India there is a specific song for every occasion whether it is related to child birth or festivals. The wide variety of cultural traditions that may be found in India has played an significant role in the evolution of folk music. Folk practises are generally characterised by distinct forms of music, instruments, languages, and subject matter. The majority of Indian folk songs focus on describing the surroundings of the household as well as the domestic rituals that are tied to the festivities, and other specific occasions such as- religious ceremonies, social issues, harvesting seasons, historical events, etc. In addition, these melodies are sung by women while they are engaged in domestic activities such as grinding grains, fishing, churning curd, cooking, weaving, farming, at *dhobhighaat* by *dhobhi or dhobhan* (washerman or washerwoman) etc. Songs that describe a pregnant woman or are related to the birth of a child are referred to as *sohar*. These songs are often sung at various rituals that take place after the birth of a child, including those that take place on the sixth day (*chata*), the tenth day (*dastaun*), or the twelfth day (*barahan or barahin*). *Vivah ke geet* is the collective name for all the songs performed at weddings. India celebrates every season with a song that includes songs like *baramasa, kajari, and savan*. Both *kajari and savan* usually talk about things that happen during the rain, like the dark skies, the slight drizzle of the raindrops, the thunder, the croaking of frogs etc. The *thumri* style of singing is quite famous in India. *Thumri* is a song of love and the singer has to match the sensitivity of the words with his or her voice. All light tunes fall under *thumri* for instance; *Kajri, Chaiti, Sawan, Jhoola, Baramsa, Bhäjans,* or mild devotional songs. Some patriotic songs are also passed by words of mouth by generation to generation to recite them during school assembly or on national festivals. Classical music and dance have mostly been taught by word of mouth. The teacher teaches the *shishya* about the *raga* and how it is put together, as well as the minute details of the *tala*, or rhythm, and how to put the *raga* and *tala* together into a composition. The same holds true for Indian classical dance, wherein a teacher's proficiency determines the quality of a student's footwork, movement, *abhinaya,* usage of hand gestures, and dancing for compositions. It is not possible to find them in written form. Orally, it is passed down from the *guru* to the *shishya* from generation to generation. Poems or rhymes are also transferred to children through their elders by recited them. According to Encyclopaedia Britannica "poetry is a literature that evokes a concentrated imaginative awareness of experience or a specific emotional response through language chosen and arranged for its meaning, sound, and rhythm." Indian poetry covers a wide range of topics, from ancient history to contemporary life to praise of deities. Poems about Indian ethics, practises, cultures, customs, and religious roots are written in many Indian languages. The best Indian poets include Kabir Das, Kali Das, Mirza Ghalib, Tulsidas, Amir Khusro, Mirabai, Amrita Pritam, Mir Taqi Mir, Mir Baber Ali Anis, Rabindranath Tagore and many more. People who are interested in music seem to be drawn to the *ghazals* of the Urdu language. *Ghazals* are poems or song lyrics in Arabic, the word *ghazal* means sweet words said to someone you love. A *ghazal* is a kind of poetry that is characterised by its use of rhyming couplets known as *shers* and their pleasant and persuasive remarks capture the listener's attention. If we look around us, we will see many examples of the different ways that oral tradition operates throughout India. Without the written word, it is the only tool for conveying culture, skills, values, and a sense of identity one such example is *qawwali.* The term "*qawwali*" refers to a culture that combines aspects of music, poetry, and Sufism into one tradition. These oral traditions hold greater significance than being mere performances for an audience; they may also play vital functions in culture and society, such as singing of songs during agricultural work or lullabies to help babies sleep in a more comfortable atmosphere. It is challenging to make broad generalisations about the folklore of the Indian subcontinent because of the diversity of ethnic, linguistic, and religious groups that inhabit it. Kutty (2002) categorised the following essential attributes of folklore based on the characteristics;

1. **Folk arts or artistic folklore;** Folk gestures, folk theatre, and folk dance are all forms of performing arts. Folklore also includes non-performing arts such as sculpture, painting, embroidery, carpet making, costume design, weaving, and archery.
2. **Folk Practices;** Folk literature and folk art are not the same as folk behaviors. Folk practices are those that are ingrained in a community's culture and are used in everyday life, such as superstitions, rites and rituals, festivals, and beliefs. The folk's life is represented by folk games, folk sports, animal sports, etc.
3. **Folk Literature;** Folk tales are a crucial and well-liked element of folk literature. These include fairy tales, anecdotes, short stories, myths, and legends. Additionally, folk literature includes a variety of other things including proverbs, ballads, riddles, songs, folk titles, rhymes, metaphors, poetry, chain letters, etc. The majority of these components of folk literature were developed and disseminated orally. Some of them were fundamentally oral literature that has recently been preserved in the script, and others have historically been maintained in written form.
4. **Folk Science and Technology;** Folk science includes techniques for traditional medicine, dairy product processing, fertilizer use, agricultural practices, and seed technology. Folk building, tool and ornament making, ceramics, and other typical forms are examples of folk technology.

Folklore develops as a means of communication as a result of human interaction. The majority of Indian folklore has a religious undertone and may be connected to holy rituals or celebrations. The Hindu caste system and social stratification have an impact on Indian folklore as well. Religious writings predominate in Indian cultural literature. The reason why is that most of what is taught in these works is believed to be true by the public. All those values are included in the Sanskrit literary tradition but are not readily available to everyone. As a result, people created several forms of folklore that included the key components of Indian tradition but, in layman's terms, made heritage more accessible and intriguing. People produce and enjoy folklore to uphold their values and enlighten themselves. Folklore and society have a symbiotic relationship; folklore influences social change, and social change influences folklore change. The experts state that because folklore is a product of society instead of the other way around, society has a considerably greater influence on it than folklore does on society (Dixit et al., 2017). Religion affects every part of a lifestyle and culture and ideas, and it is at the heart of every culture. Hindu priests must memorise a full book of instructions on how to perform religious rites and recite them to the host, who follows the instructions. Even though these books are printed, priests recite them by memory. These books are called *Pothis.* Songs that praise female Gods are called *devi ke geet. Mantra* chanting and singing *bhajans* are mainly acts of *smarana* (to remember or to recall.) They are done to reach the most significant or noble part of one's existence, which is the basic idea that Hinduism, Sikhism, and other religions try to teach. *Bhajans,* which are brief songs of devotion, are a significant component of devotional music in India. They can be sung in small or large groups, by close family members and friends or by a bigger group of community members. Before the invention of writing all these traditions have been pass through words of mouth, although now we are technologically more advanced some of these traditions are still passed to lineages through words of mouth without any written records. The most effective method of transferring knowledge of a people's culture in the pre-literate period was through stories presented as a part of the oral tradition. It is generally accepted that storytelling has been an essential component of each and every human society, even since the earliest times. For thousands of years, stories were the main way that culture and ideas were passed down from one generation to the next. Stories amuse and educate, and as a result, they have been crucial in ensuring that traditional ways of living are transmitted from one generation to the next such as The *Mahabharata,* The *Ramayana, Jataka Tales, Shabad Kirtan, Gurubani, Bhajans* and *Kirtans, Krishna Leela* etc. The saint has also been the subject of countless tales and legends, the majority of which have been passed down to us through storytelling. These tales are told verbally, most frequently during storytelling sessions, meetings, or religious rites, by more experienced community members and scholars who have studied the tradition. The oral transmission of stories is encouraged by holding cultural events and festivals tied to Sufi saints and their shrines. Through attentive listening and engaged participation, younger members of the community are able to understand and assimilate the community's narratives. Practising and devoting oneself spiritually in accordance with the teachings of Sufism sometimes involves paying a visit to the shrines of the various Sufi saints.

In India, proverbs play an important role in oral traditions. Wisdom, cultural standards, and moral ideals are communicated effectively through these concise statements that are also very insightful. They are frequently employed in regular conversations. Some of the common proverbs which are used in daily life are as follows-

- *aap bhala to jag bhala* - Good mind, good find.
- *apni dafli apna raag*- Many men, many minds.
- *bad accha badnaam bura*- A bad name is worse than bad deeds.
- *ek phool se mala nahi banti* - One flower makes no garland.
- *laalach buri bala*- No vice like avarice.
- *behti ganga me haath dhona*- Make hay while the sun shines.
- *jesa raja wesi praja* - As the king, so are the subject.
- *andho main kaanaa raja*- A figure among ciphers.
- *oonth ke muh main zeera*- A drop in the ocean.
- *ant bhala to sab bhala* - All is Well that ends well.
- *aam ke aam guthli ke daam*- Earth's joys and heaven's combined.

Since ancient times, folklore and folktales have been an integral component of every civilization. India's folklore and folktales reflect our diversified society and are crucial for conveying age-old timeless knowledge as well as social etiquette which attracts a large number of tourists to India for cultural study. Folklore fulfils two crucial purposes: first, it amuses, and second, it teaches social lessons. Children can be entertained while learning moral lessons or religious principles from Indian folktales. There have been several written collections of Indian folktales for over a thousand years. The folktales of various cultures share many of the same themes, either as a result of cross-cultural influences or because such themes are so universal that they appear everywhere people dwell in a group. Indian folk tales were used to preserve history, significant individuals, and locations, as well as the religious rites and festivals of diverse Indian areas. India, a nation with many different religions, languages, and traditions, offers a wide variety of folktales and short stories. Numerous mythological traditions and stories that come from all areas of life are found in Indian folklore. The extraordinary *'Panchatantra'* to *'Hitopadesha,'* from *'Jataka'* to *'Akbar-Birbal,'* are just a few of the intriguing tales. The classic Indian epics like '*Ramayana,*' '*Mahabharata,*' and '*Bhagavad Gita*' are also loaded with instructive tales drawn from the lives of great individuals. These old tales have been passed down from one generation to the next, fusing traditional values with the modern age. Folklores have been transformed into a variety of performing arts, including folk dances, folk paintings, and murals, in order to maintain this oral history. More than the privileged elite, the ordinary people had then reinforced and nurtured the emerging storytelling traditions. As a result, oral tradition enabled prehistoric communities and religions to maintain their communal, cyclic, and egalitarian nature for instance Buddhist chanting of Ladakh, *dastangoi, kavad* storytelling, *marsiyakhwani* etc. Oral tradition was as sacred in the Indian culture as the transmission of texts and writing was in the West. The oral form of literature has a distinct advantage over the written form in India. Oral tradition has existed since ancient times and will continue to evolve in the future, although it may take on various forms depending on the socio-cultural setting. Folklorists (folklore specialists), sociologists, historians, and journalists are among those who are well-versed in oral traditions. They encounter a variety of oral traditions from diverse areas throughout their study and field activities. The substance of these traditions may be applied to everyday life, society, and the belief systems of ordinary people in a given community. Previously, these were documented and written about in books and newspapers however, now they are acknowledged as a vital academic field. Scholars and traditional practitioners are collaborating to document, revitalise, and restore these practises. In cultures whose oral tradition is vital to their existence, there is a high level of awareness. However, India's rural society remains vast, with a major portion of the people living in villages. So, the oral tradition is still alive. One of the finest sources of folktales in the world is still India. Oral traditions, such as proverbs, sayings, stories, rumours, songs, and impromptu street performances, capture and reflect the distinctive culture and values of the people who live in various locations. These expressions have been passed down orally for decades, preserving each region's tradition. Additionally, they have assisted in connecting the wildly distinct social conventions and customs of even a single site. Indian literature has made a significant contribution to the invisible fusion of countless stories, songs, and dramas that are sprinkled with local proverbs and aphorisms. There is no way to overstate the significance of Indian literature in preserving and promoting cultural identity and togetherness in such a vast country as India. More than any other literature in the world, Indian literature contributed significantly to the preservation and spread of oral traditions and folklore. Due to the rise of industrialization and globalisation, traditional forms of artistic expression have been disappearing in many regions of the world. Indian traditional literature, however, provides a potent reminder and caution against this trend. It demonstrates how literature and folk art serve as more than just vehicles for culture or philosophy; they also symbolise introspection at a deep level and the profound realisations that result from it. It is also true that these folk literatures, which are often restricted to a narrower space and only reach out to smaller groups and communities, attain mass appeal when they are written down and distributed in printed form. Traditional folktales are typically restricted to "grandparents narrating, stories to their grandchildren" as they are unable to compete with the different digital channels that deliver stories. These folktales are losing favour with younger generations despite being adapted for several films and translated into many different languages. These folklores, which have their roots mostly in regional tongues, have been translated into hundreds of other different languages as they became widely known and appreciated by the early twenty-first century. However, the oral folklore tradition has suffered a significant blow since the beginning of the digital era, particularly in the last few years. Ancient folktales/folklores have served a much larger purpose than simply amusing people, whether it is to preserve history or provide moral lessons. Here are some well-known and intriguing tales that have educated Indians for many centuries:

- Jataka Tales
- The Wedding of the Mouse
- Tenali Rama's Dream
- Akbar and Birbal
- Panchatantra
- Betal Pachisi
- Between Two Wives
- Hitopdesha Tales

Numerous threats to the long-term viability of oral traditions can be posed by tourism as it involves a level of intensive cultural exchange. In the face of concerns about revitalization and documentation of endangered languages, UNESCO endeavoured to address this matter through its 2003 Intangible Cultural Heritage framework, aiming to foster projects at both national and centered around communities. Certain kinds of oral expression are widespread and may be practised by entire communities, whereas others are restricted to specific social strata, such as males, females, or the elderly. In many cultures, expert performers of oral traditions are held with the most reverence as custodians of cultural heritage. You can find these kinds of performances in regions all across the globe such as- *Qawwals* are invited to perform *qawwalis*, *pandits* to recite *bhajans, mantras, moulanas* for *Qurankhawani* on special occasions according to communities need. Oral traditions and phrases differ widely in their telling since they are passed down through word of mouth. Stories are a mixture of replication, improvisation, and creativity that varies from performer to performer, genre to genre and context to context. In addition to being a lively and brilliant mode of expression, this combination also makes them susceptible because their existence depends on a long legacy of performers handing traditions down from one generation to the following.

Although language is at the heart of many communities' intangible heritage, the 2003 Convention does not include the safeguarding and preservation of specific languages, even though they are mentioned in Article 2 name of the article as a way of conveying intangible cultural heritage. Article 2 (2) of the Convention states that language is crucial as the best channel for communication and cooperation between performers and other tradition keepers, as well as between them and other community members. This is one of the key domains of ICH. Almost all expressions, activities, and representations fall into this category such as; music, gesture, facial expressions, etc. In the traditional methods of passing down the ICH from generation to generation, language and gesture are equally essential tools. Languages are a complete and intricate expression of a country's culture in addition to being a part of its cultural legacy. Different languages determine how songs, poems, and stories are conveyed and influence their content. When a language dies, oral traditions and expressions are lost with it forever. Thus, losing a language also means losing a cultural legacy. However, rather than grammars, dictionaries, and databases, these oral expressions and their use in public are the best ways to safeguard a language. That is why language is called as a "vehicle of the intangible cultural heritage." Riddles and rhymes, stories and songs keep languages alive, therefore safeguarding of language and the transfer of oral traditions and expressions are inextricably connected.

Many countries have lost the ability to remember and transmit as cities and economies have grown. As a result, many traditional customs, songs, and stories have vanished and they do not appear to be alive. Oral traditions, like other types of intangible cultural heritage, are endangered by growing urbanisation, industrialization, massive immigration, and environmental change. Oral traditions and expressions can be particularly damaged by books, magazines and newspapers, television, radio, and the Internet. Forms of oral traditions and expression may be considerably altered or replaced by modern mass media. Traditional courtship songs that were sung prior wedding may be replaced by CDs or digital audio clips, and epic poetry that formerly took several days to recite in full may be shortened to just a few hours (UNESCO, 2003). The Industrial Revolution left a vast portion of the world untouched for a long time, composed largely of what are now known as developing societies. The oral tradition remained alive in these societies, and it played a significant role in spreading knowledge of its customs through folklore. However, as the technological revolution progresses, even these societies' oral traditions are becoming less secure and new modes of information sharing is progressively overtaking them. Forms that have remained the same over many generations are decaying as a result of the fact that we no longer need to memorize them in order to pass them on to others, that they can be constantly replicated in a variety of media, and that they were formed with an outdated cyclical self-destruct routine. Our notions of stability and certainty have been destroyed; indeed, language, speech, the foundation of our existence, may disappear without a trace, as it has in many places, especially in our tribal areas and territories. The global communication revolution has also influenced the way traditions are passed. Since the advent of the printing press, this trend has evolved and influenced the tradition of assigning certain members of the community with the task of oral storytelling to future generations. Additionally, it is quite challenging to convey and interpret oral traditions to tourists in a way that will increase their appreciation and comprehension of the host community's culture. The advancement of new printing technologies, such as moveable type and now automated desk-top printing devices, has contributed to the widespread and quick dissemination of written text in the form of books. Another element is the rise of electronic mass media, such as radio, television, and social media. Their extensive networks are now reaching out to far-flung locations. These advancements are also having a negative influence on the oral tradition. Another troubling issue affecting oral tradition is that its primary tool, languages, is in the midst of a "global extinction catastrophe." Language Vitality and Endangerment, published by UNESCO in 2003, identifies six levels of endangerment that may be distinguished in relation to intergenerational transmission:

Safe (5): All generations speak the language. The intergenerational transmission of the language is unbroken, and there is no indication that it is under threat from any other languages.

Stable yet threatened (5-): Although the language has been passed down uninterruptedly through generations in most circumstances, multilingualism in the local language and one or more dominant languages has displaced several crucial communication contexts. It should be noted that multilingualism alone does not always threaten languages.

Unsafe/Vulnerable (4): The majority of children and families in a particular community do speak their language as their first language, but this may be limited to particular social domains (such as at home, when youngsters communicate with their parents and grandparents).

Definitively endangered (3): Children in the family are no longer learning the language as their mother tongue. Therefore, the youngest speakers belong to the parent generation.

Severely endangered (2): The language is only spoken by grandparents and other members of older generations; while members of the parent generation may still be able to understand the language, they normally do not use it while speaking to their children.

Critically endangered (1): The language is not utilised in daily interactions, and the youngest speakers are in the great-grandparental generation. These elderly folks frequently just remember a portion of the language but do not speak it because they do not have anyone to converse with.

Extinct (0): There is not a single person alive who is able to speak the language, nor does anyone remember it.

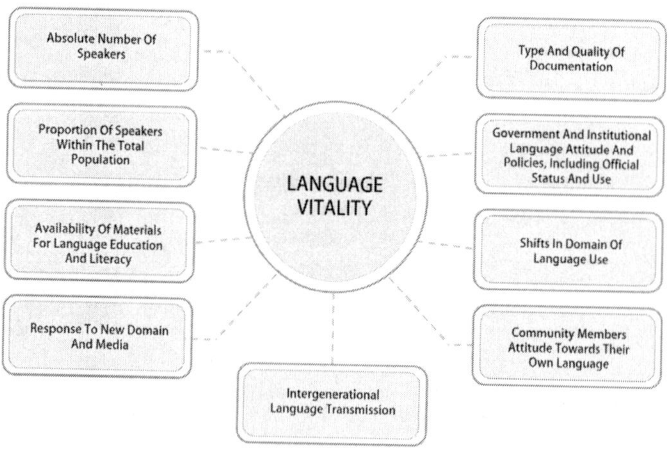

© UNESCO Atlas of the World's Languages in Danger

The UNESCO Atlas of the World's Languages in Danger (2011) states that - "no single factor is sufficient to assess the state of a community's language. However, taken together, these nine factors can determine the viability of a language, its function in society and the type of measures required for its maintenance or revitalization."

Lindell Bromham stated that world's 7,000 recognised languages, around half were currently endangered. More than 2,000 are in dire risk. When a language dies, it leaves behind priceless information about historical traditions as well as the current state of the natural world. According to Census of India (2011) languages are classified into two parts which are given below-

Scheduled Languages- languages which are mentioned in the Eighth Schedule to the Constitution of India are called Scheduled languages, it includes 22 languages.

Non-Scheduled Languages- languages which are not mentioned in the Eighth Schedule to the Constitution of India are called Non-Scheduled Languages, it includes 99 languages as well as the section "Total of other languages" comprising all other languages and mother tongues which returned less than 10,000 speakers each at the all-India level or were not identifiable on the basis of the linguistic information available.

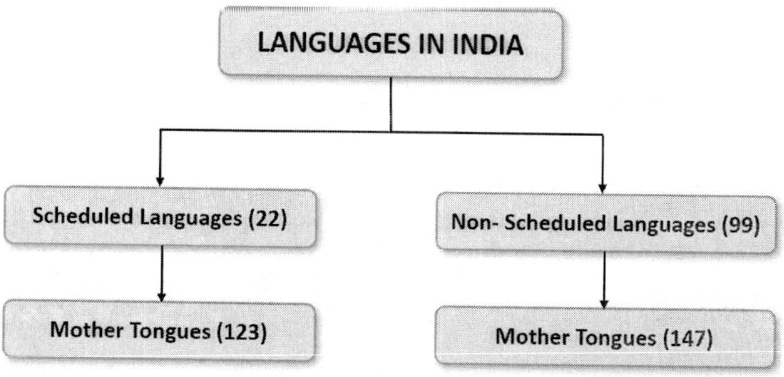

There is a total of "121 languages" and a total of "270 recognised mother tongues" in India, each of which has at least 10,000 speakers at the all-India level. Of these, 123 mother tongues are classified as Scheduled Languages (Part A), while the remaining 147 mother tongues are classified as Non-Scheduled Languages (Part B). Mother tongues assigned to a given language and provided less than 10,000 speakers each are listed under that language's "Others" category (See Appendix - II). "India is a major linguistically diverse country, with more than 1,500 "mother tongues" spoken, but it is also the home to most of the endangered languages in the world". "According to the UNESCO Interactive Atlas of the World's Languages in Danger, India is the most threatened country (197 languages), followed by USA (191), China (144), and Indonesia (143). Among the 197 endangered languages in India, 81 are "vulnerable" followed by "definitely endangered" (63), "severely endangered" (6), "critically endangered" (42) and "already extinct" (5). The cause of concern is that 96% of the Indian languages are under the threat of extinction" (Dash, 2020). "Nine languages – Ahom, Aimol, Andro, Chairel, Kolhreng, Rangkas, Sengmai, Tarao and Tolcha – have become extinct in India from the 1950s" (Sengupta, 2009). A language's extinction eventually results in the loss of numerous forms of intangible cultural heritage, including the irreplaceable group's spoken traditions and forms of expression (poems, jokes, sayings, and stories) that have been passed down over time, performing arts, social customs, religious festivals, traditional craftsmanship etc. The extinction of indigenous languages is pretty terrible for biodiversity because they preserve time-tested methods for managing ecosystems and using natural resources sustainably, which are now more important due to the serious new problems brought by climate change. These include conventional knowledge of the natural world and the universe, religious convictions, and cultural values expressed in indigenous languages. With the extinction of languages, the human knowledge base is eroding, and the rich reservoir of oral tradition is being lost. It is crucial to document the language in order to preserve it for future discoveries that will use in religious practices, culinary arts industrial know-how with traditional herbal treatments etc. Therefore, continuing proficiency in the indigenous language would seem to be necessary for the development of the ICH. In developing countries like India, oral tradition still remains the top in rural regions, where the majority of the population lives. Traditional and, folk songs, folk theatre, folk dance forms and puppet performances, all of which have the inherent ability to restore oral tradition, are still popular among India's rural population. However, the threat posed by the significant degree of radio, television and internet networks into rural areas must be countered with creativity so that they might become transmitters of oral tradition. Electronic media, such as radio and television, are a two-edged sword as they appear to represent a serious threat to oral tradition that must be addressed however; they can be helpful in its revival. In terms of families, clans, and tribes, the focus of its efforts should be to encourage oral traditions and popularise what is integrative to the exclusion of everything that is divisive. Furthermore, it would be required to describe oral tradition not just as our societies' cultural basis, but also as the acquisitions and inventions that may be adapted to fit new requirements in new times. To prevent oral tradition from being extinct, a global effort is required. Storytelling has to be revived, particularly among children with poor literacy levels and for those who are socially, physically, and financially deprived. It will require a deliberate effort to reach children all across the world, to connect them with the magic of storytelling, and to bring smiles to their cheeks. The abundance of stories contained in great epics from all cultures should be documented, adapted into animated films and theatrical versions, and taught to children; particularly those who are still deprived their fundamental cultural right to education. The oral tradition retains its potential to resurrect traditional values, and that potential should be nurtured and used for the greater welfare of children all around the world. In this way, they will be able to pass on their knowledge to the next generation. The most crucial aspect of preserving word of mouth ensuring that they continue to play a part in society and that the opportunities for knowledge to be transmitted from generation to generation are maintained. One example of this would be creating settings in which seniors have the opportunity to interact with younger generations and share stories, such as in homes and schools. At all costs, the culture of folktales needs to be revived. Many generations have been entertained, engaged, and taught moral principles by it. Folktale culture serves as a link between older and younger generations, making its preservation crucial. According to the 2003 convention, UNESCO designated folklore as an oral history category of Intangible Cultural Heritage. In modern, democratic India, folk literature is studied both within and outside academia, unlike in most other cultures. This collective effort to conserve and propagate Indian folk literature includes the work of *Sahitya Akademi* and other organizations of a similar nature. *Sahitya Akademi,* India's preeminent literary institution, is devoted to preserving and promoting Indian literature in all 24 languages for which it is recognized. The focus of the *Akademi*'s activity is the translation between different Indian languages, including minor languages and dialects, intending to foster cultural unification in India and foster regional cooperation in such a linguistically and culturally diverse nation. The *Sahitya Akademi* additionally encourages Indian folk literature in every way possible, including by holding conventions and awarding prizes for writing in minor languages, languages without writing systems, and tribal dialects, publishing folk tales in its journals as part of the second tradition, publishing folk literature books, and operating centers to protect and advance India's oral traditions (Ministry of Culture, 2023). More such efforts are required by different institutions and organizations to safeguard our cultural heritage through the preservation of folklore.

Oral tradition is frequently an essential aspect of various cultural celebrations, and it might be essential to advertise these events and create diverse contexts, for instance; storytelling festivals, should be fostered to give conventional creativity freedom to explore new forms of expression. Information technology may also be used by communities, scholars, and institutions to protect the complete breadth and depth of oral traditions, including textual variants and varied performance styles. It is now possible to record audio or video of distinctive expressive aspects like pitch and a far wider range of varied styles, in addition to interactions between performers and audiences, including nonverbal story aspects like gestures and imitation. Through the dissemination of recorded performances to both their communities of origin and a broader audience, broadcasting and communication technologies have the potential to both maintain and even improve oral traditions and expressions. The degree to which the preservation of ICH elements necessitates action in the area of language planning can vary substantially; in other cases, no action at all may be required in the case of people or communities that speak a national language or another official language, or simply a language that is not endangered at all. However, even in these situations, action may be required. It may be important to gather the specific lexicon that practitioners employ, particularly in the fields of traditional knowledge and handicrafts, in effort to preserve the knowledge concerned facilitate its transmission. Additional methods of transmission are being investigated because conventional, intergenerational methods are becoming less popular globally. The amount of work necessary to record the specialised layers of the lexicon of non-written languages will be evidently different from the amount of work required when the language is fully documented and has a widely used writing system. Certain linguistic registers may need to be protected in various circumstances. There may be a need for documentation in order to transmit the aforementioned phrases. The Ministry of Education (Government of India) developed the "Scheme for Protection and Preservation of Endangered Languages" (SPPEL) in 2013 as a solution to the devastating situation of the country's lesser-known languages. The sole purpose of the Scheme is to document and archive the country's languages that are currently endangered or are on the verge of extinction. The programme is maintained by the Central Institute of Indian Languages (CIIL) in Mysuru, Karnataka. The CIIL has collaborated with several universities and organisations across India to achieve this goal. In its current stage, the SPPEL has 117 languages on its list to be documented. Social customs and rituals frequently have their own records as well. The type of language planning action that must be devised when a group's language is in danger depends on more than just the immaterial cultural legacy that needs to be preserved. The persons involved must also decide whether the components that need to be protected are meant to be enjoyed by broader groups of people or should only be targeted at a select few. In the second scenario, much planning may be required for the preservation and transfer of proficiency in the traditional language, either only verbally or both orally and in writing. Translations will undoubtedly be used to share a group's intangible cultural legacy with the outside world and to pass down to forthcoming cohorts of a community facing the decline of its indigenous language. Texts must be written down in the original language, and audio-visual recordings must be made for documentation, which is one of the methods meant to ensure the survival of the ICH, as defined by the term "safeguarding" in Article 2(3) of the Convention.

The United Nations General Assembly (Resolution A/RES/74/135) proclaimed the period between 2022 and 2032 as the "International Decade of Indigenous Languages" (IDIL 2022-2032), to attract global attention to the plight of numerous indigenous languages and to activate stakeholders and resources for their safeguarding, revitalization, and propagation. The International Decade aims to protect the right of indigenous people to maintain, revive, and promote their languages, as well as to integrate multilingualism and linguistic diversity into efforts for sustainable development (UNESCO, 2021).

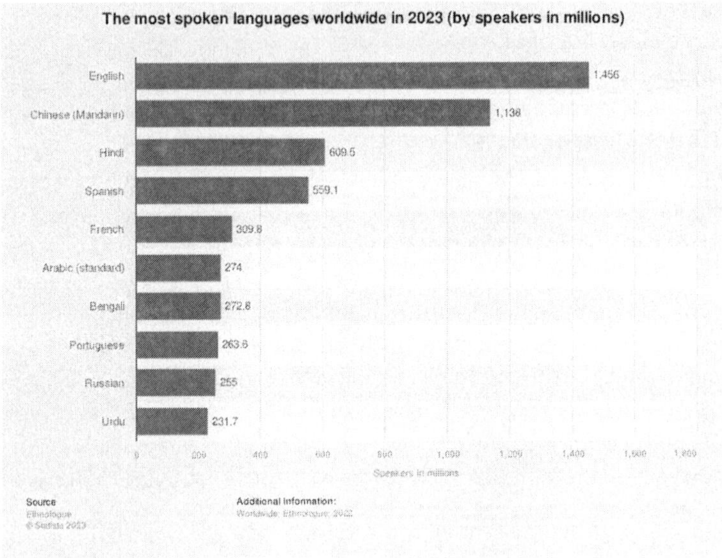

Source: https://www.statista.com/statistics/266808/the-most-spoken-languages-worldwide/

SOME IMPORTANT ORAL TRADITIONS OF INDIA

Pattachitra

Storytelling has always been a part of Indian culture. Stories and legends about deities and spirits, kings and villains have been retold in various literary and theatrical traditions for countless years. In various regions of India, *pat or phad* (Rajasthan) or *Pattachitra* (Orissa) refers to a piece of fabric depicting various mythological tales with vivid colours and a variety of patterns. They may tell stories of local heroes, monarchs, and warriors that come to life during the narrative, as well as religious stories about a god commonly hanging in temples during festivities.

The Bengali art form called *Pattachitra* is renowned for its bright hues, lines, and strokes. *Pattachitra* is the collective term for traditional cloth-based scroll painting found in eastern Indian states. The word *"Patta"* literally translates to "cloth" in Sanskrit, and the word *"Chitra"* means "picture" in Sanskrit. The system "*Patachitra*" has been used to introduce several communication techniques, such as pictorial messages, oral traditions, and music. These techniques combine, involve, and show mythology, nature, society, and culture while coexisting in musical lyrics. Bengal's *Pattachitra* performative art follows an oral tradition of ICH transmitted from one generation to the next. The states of West Bengal, Odisha, Jharkhand, and Bihar are all located in close proximity to one another, and each of these areas has a history of *Pattachitra* painting.

Pattachitra is a rural Bengali folk-art form practised for centuries and is renowned for its vibrant use of colour. It is considered the world's first endeavour to create motion pictures. Although their exact beginning as a profession is unknown, it can be reasonably estimated from various oral traditions and folklore that they started in Bengal during the 10th and 11th century AD. The narratives and social messages in these paintings are inspired by Hindu mythology and tribal tradition, as well as current events and contemporary society. There are two varieties of *Pattachitra*: square *Pattachitra* (*Choukopata*) and rolling *Pattachitra* (*Jarhanopata*). All the colors utilized in the artwork are derived from seeds, flowers, leaves, trees etc. There are many sizes for the *Pattachitra* scrolls. Depending on the story, it ranges in size from one to one and a half feet wide and three to 25 feet long.

Generally speaking, all *Pattachitra* varities contain some form of storytelling. Religious minstrels called *Patuas* (refers to the community of painters) use these paintings to spread their religion. It was a crucial tool for telling the stories of oral as well as written epics. These traditional *patuas or chitrakaars* travel from village to village, providing entertainment and information to the villagers in exchange for rice, vegetables, and coins for their hard labour. On specific evenings, the entire community congregates, and the narrator hangs the painting (in a big format) at a location that is easily accessible and visible to all of them. This serves as a backdrop for his tale. He emphasises the pertinent areas (captures) of the painting as he tells the story. Each hand-painted scroll would be unfolded by a *patua or chitrakaar,* who would then sing *pater gaan,* or narrative songs that they had written frame by frame. The *patuas,* professional artists who visited rich people's homes, would present the scrolls and recite the deities' stories in exchange for grains, food, and garments. On certain occasions, like pujas or religious festivals, they were invited to the homes of the powerful and opulent to tell the stories of the deity being worshipped and rewarded. The listeners treated this performance as sacred, sitting quietly in silence and paying attention to the *patua's* narration as if they were worshipping a deity.

Although the *Patua* community has made an expedient contribution to the rural economy of India, it has not received the appropriate assistance from the relevant government agencies, financial organizations, banks, credit societies, or corporations. Since *patuas* work primarily in the traditional or unorganized sector, their development and advancement are crucial for the growth of the rural economy in order to achieve an equitable distribution of income and wealth and economic independence. It is incumbent upon the government to undertake the necessary strategies to provide financial assistance with the fewest formalities possible, create a platform to assist *patuas* in developing high-quality skills in the fields they need and organize a marketing campaign to increase the products' viability. These *patuas,* who historically served as the foundation of Indian society, are now seen as the most important figures in advancing society and culture.

Buddhist Chanting of Ladakh

Ladakh Buddhist chanting is the invocation of ancient sacred Buddhist texts in Jammu and Kashmir's trans-Himalayan Ladakh region. These texts are chanted by the monks (Lamas) every day in different monasteries throughout the Ladakh area to represent the spirit, philosophy, and teachings of Buddha. In general, the chanting is also done to maintain peace and prosperity of the world.

Buddhism in Ladakh has two important schools- Vajrayana and Mahayana. There are four major Buddhism sects in Ladakh namely *Nyngma, Kagyud, Shakya and Geluk* and they have their own different forms of chanting. Each monastery can have its own style of chanting, even though they belong to the same sect. In some sects, chanting is accompanied with dance (cham) in the courtyard of the monastery.

Chanting is conducted by each sect on special days such as-lifecycle rites, agrarian, annual festivals, for general well-being of the people and to attain Buddhahood by purifying the mind, to repel evil spirits and to summon the Buddhist deities for blessings. Some musical instruments like hand drums, bells, flutes, etc. are used as complements to bring in rhythm and musicality during chanting.

The tradition is practiced every day by the monks in a group as a prayer to God for the practitioner's personal development and world peace. It is an aid to meditation, and the purpose of chanting is to attain enlightenment and to get liberation from the sufferings of the world. On various special occasions, monks are invited by the people to their homes for the chanting of mantras. To represent Buddha, monks don specialized garments and make specific *mudras* (hand gestures) while chanting.

The Buddhist chanting of Ladakh is a living heritage transmitted from one generation to the next as an oral practice of monks. Under the painstaking and strict control of head monks, young monks are trained. These texts are recited by young monks until they are memorized, which makes Chanting an oral tradition knowledge that is passed on from one generation to another. In 2012 Chanting was included in the "UNESCO Representative List of Humanity's Intangible Cultural Heritage." The monasteries are the repository of knowledge and tradition of Buddhist scriptures which serve for the continuation and preservation of chanting. Chanting is a part of Ladakh's daily life and cultural heritage which reflects the community's lifestyle and its spiritual and cultural heritage.

Many people think that Ladakh's culture was more diverse in the past than it is now. Currently, Buddhist of Ladakh is striving to reinterpret the entire structure of their Buddhist culture, which developed during Ladakh's 2000-year history of Buddhism (*Buddhist chanting of Ladakh,* 2014). Ladakh is a distant region of India, and due to its harsh climate, it is cut off from the outside world for a considerable proportion of the year. The majority of people are unaware of the customs and traditions that are unique to this area. Ladakh's forward-thinking leadership had predicted the current cultural apathy. Several actions were taken to protect this distinctive cultural identity about 50 years ago. In 1959, the Central Institute of Buddhist Studies in Leh was founded under the direction of the late Kushok Bakula Rinpoche.

Monasteries have served as Ladakh's primary archives of Buddhist literature, philosophy, metaphysics, and oral tradition. Every Lama is a skilled practitioner of Buddhist chanting. At this time, it appears that Ladakh's youth feels monastic life to be somewhat archaic and choose to pursue modern careers instead. The protection of Ladakhi culture and its spiritual heritage depends on the continuation of monastic practices, especially chanting. To increase public awareness of the necessity to preserve these traditions and the significance of chanting in Ladakhi culture, campaigns should be run throughout the entire region of Ladakh. To involve younger people, conferences, seminars, and debates should be arranged. Financial support is necessary for the realization of all these initiatives, and both national and local groups ought to step forward to support and promote this great but vanishing legacy. The community and monks must thus lead any endeavor to protect this intangible heritage. The efforts to maintain this heritage will not be successful without the community's active participation and senior monks' in-depth knowledge of the monastic tradition and related aesthetic, arts, and crafts activities. Efforts have been made in order to safeguard cultural heritage by the Indian government to generally and monastic chanting specifically. The endeavor is demonstrated by the installation of CIBS (Central Institute of Buddhist Studies) and its feeder monastic "*gonpa*" schools. Along with regular workshops, efforts are being made to conserve, preserve, and record the chanting heritage of the monastic lifestyle and other related arts and crafts. Cultural organizations and NGOs are actively supporting these efforts. The Government's Ministry of Culture administers a number of financing programs to protect Buddhist cultural heritage for instance, "Scheme of Financial Assistance for the Development of Buddhist/Tibetan Culture and Art." This program gives funds to Buddhist/Tibetan organizations, like Monasteries, that are working to spread and develop Buddhist/Tibetan culture, tradition, and research in related fields.

Kavad Storytelling

Storytelling is a rich tradition in India, which includes employing the use of only speech and gesture, painted scrolls and boxes, written content, dance, and music, performances, or any mix of these. It establishes our identity and culture. Stories can be memories or bridging pieces that convey the goals of a society by bringing the two worlds together. The first known human communication method is probably storytelling. It has a way of tricking the audience into silence and inspiring the storytellers to articulate, either overtly or covertly, the innermost aspirations and fears of their society. In various parts of the nation, stories—whether mythological or historical, were recounted using the visual and performing arts, which are now a part of India's cultural history, even though some of them are in danger of becoming extinct.

The art of Indian storytelling is believed to have existed practically everywhere on the subcontinent as early as the second century B.C.E. In the absence of written books, knowledge and information were passed down orally from one generation to the following in ancient India through the art of storytelling. Writing became more prevalent as civilization advanced. The Ramayana and the Mahabharata, or the five major epics of Tamil and Sangam literature, have their roots in oral tradition and are among the oldest surviving epic poems and sources of narrative throughout the Indian subcontinent. The Panchatantra was among the earliest writings in this nation to be used for storytelling.

In Rajasthan, the oral storytelling tradition known as "*Kavad Banchana*," which includes tales from the Puranas, caste genealogy, and the epics Mahabharata and Ramayana, dates back at least 400 years, but like many other oral traditions in India, its origins are either rooted in mythology or ascribed to an unknown force. Some religious books include historical evidence of moveable shrines, but there are no outright mentions of the Kavad. The Tarikh-I-Firoz-Shahi of Afif, which refers to the *Kavad* as a "*Muhrik*" (a wooden tablet covered in paintings from the inside and the outside), makes an indirect reference to it (Sabnani, 2009).

The audio-visual experience is enhanced by the "Kavad shrine," which enables the narration to be accompanied by a visual trip for the listener. The Hindi term *kivaad*, which means a wooden door, is said to be the source of the word *kavad*. Kavad is a wooden box or cabinet with numerous folding doors, each of which is brightly painted with images of gods, narratives from myths and legends, and stories from the epics. It is frequently referred to as a portable shrine that tells mythical and folktales visually. The shrine is not merely a place of prayer; it is also a beautiful collage of pictures that the storyteller, or "*Kavadiya*," has put together into stories. The most well-known tales conveyed through *kavad*, among many others, are those of Lord Ram and Krishna. Instead of the devotees traveling to the temple, this mobile shrine comes to them. Periodically, the *Kavadiya Bhat* carries the shrine to the residence of his patron to sing liturgical traditions to his ancestors and narrate his lineage.

Traditional storytellers in Rajasthan have been telling religious tales and folklore in people's homes for ages using the *kavad*. A wooden cabinet called a *kavad* has ten to twenty painted panels that each depicts a different story. *Kavadia* begins unfolding the outer panels as he recounts the story and works his way gradually within. When the story comes to a finish, he opens the last panel, giving his audience a *darshan*—or glimpse—of the god depicted there. The brightly painted face of either the Sun God or a local king or patron, which is larger than the other images painted on the *kavad*, is typically seen on top of this temple-like building. In the context of storytelling, it evokes the concept of a sacred space that gives a sense of identity to everyone participating in its formation, narration, and reception.

The tradition is practised by three major communities. Firstly, The Suthar community creates these vibrant wooden boxes, called *kavads*. The second is the *Kavadiya Bhat*, who tells stories with it. The third group consists of the *Jajman*, or patrons, who both commission and listen to these stories. The *kavad* is regarded as a sacred shrine by the *Kavadiyas* (storytellers) and their *jajmans* (hereditary patrons), who demand that rituals be performed as well as listening to genealogies and epic tales and giving donations. The practice of listening to stories is thought to cleanse the soul and secure a devotee's position in heaven.

The custom of telling stories has existed in India continuously up until recently. The use of visual aids to accompany discourses started to decline with the development of the media, technological advancement, and fast urbanization. In Indian communities, the practise of sharing stories eventually disappeared. Researchers have discovered that the ritual is being reintroduced in a different way, though. While the basic plot of the narrative has not changed, the way it is told today has been impacted by modern tools and technology, which has altered the flavour of the tale. The maker, the storyteller, and his patron work together in harmony, which has preserved the tradition. Since no one else creates *kavad* outside of the village of Bassi, the Suthar community takes great pride in having preserved the craft for generations. The Suthar community in the Rajasthani village of Basi is the sole provider of this craft. The *Suthars* are skilled painters and carpenters who create these exquisite structures.

Dastangoi

Dastangoi is made up of two Persian words- *dastan* (a tale) and *goi* (to tell a tale) which has been taken from 13th century Urdu-Persian art of storytelling. A dastan is an elaborative tale of various interlinked stories of magic, romance, new worlds including both prose and poetry. There are four vital elements of this oral tradition- ***razm* (battle), *bazm* (soirees), *sahiri* (magic), and *ayyari* (trickery).** The main motive of this art is to narrate various fascinating stories and hold the attention and curiosity of the audience for a long period

Dastangoi is known for its unique style of story narration by the *dastangos* (the story-teller) through their voices and gestures. The success of this oral tradition depends on the *dastango,* whose voice is the primary artistic element in verbally recreating the story by holding the listeners captive, with merely the intonations and modulations of his voice without any visual aids. To recreate Mughal Court (Darbar) environment the Dastango wears classical milky-white Mughal *Angrakha* (a long-sleeved outer garment worn by South Asian men) while performing. The material of Dastangoi traditionally consists of magical tales that are taken from Amir Hamza's story, popularly known as Dastan-e-Amir Hamza. A well-known chapter of Dastan-e-Amir Hamza, Tilism-e-Hoshruba, is another source from which Dastangoi's content is taken. These two texts serve as a major definition of the traditional Dastans' content, which is subsequently picked up and reinterpreted by the performers. These Dastans' narrative structure and distinguishing characteristics give them a sense of uniqueness when compared to other stories. Dastan-e Amir Hamza is an invaluable source for learning about ourselves in the pre-colonial era because there we can find descriptions of our literary, performative, and fictional history. Its neglect extends beyond just Dastans and include a number of other performances and creations that are now completely lost to us.

Under the rule of the Mughal dynasty during the 16th century, Dastangoi emerged in India when Babur was the Mughal emperor in Delhi. During Akbar's rule, dastangoi gained more popularity who was dyslexic ordered a massive artwork of Hamza-Nama (The Story of Hamza), which was presented to him in a creative way. According to some scholars that the great scale of the panels' points to its use as a kind of audio-visual storytelling, where the speakers would stand behind the panels, and describe the story from the text, changing the panels as the story preceded, imagining it as a form of proto-television. In 1857, when many people migrated to Lucknow from Delhi, Dastangoi reached its zenith in India. To preserve this oral tradition, a number of people felt that the stories would work well in printed form. At the beginning of the nineteenth century, Fort William College, Culcutta, published the first Urdu version of the story of Amir Hamza in Urdu. However, the tradition remained largely oral for many years after that. In the 1880s, Munshi Naval Kishore founded the famous Lucknow Press and published Tilism-e-Hoshruba for the first time in its written form, which consisted of a vast 46-volume set. Due to the mesmerizing performances of Mir Baqar Ali, a famous storyteller of the 19th century, this art form flourished. However soon this tradition of story narration was lost with his death in 1928. But in the last ten years or so, a group of artists in Delhi revived Dastangoi by reorganising it as a performative art wrapped in oral traditions, with some changes in its content, performer, and audience. In 2005, Dastangoi resurfaced as an art-form when its first performance was showcased at the popular India Habitat Centre (IHC). Thereafter India Habitat Centre has remained its epicentre. Along with magic and fantasy, *"aiyyari"* (the art of deceit) also started to take centre stage in Indian storytelling. Mahmood Farooqui and his groups perform dastangoi in the modern era. New youth are drawn to this culture of storytelling as well. As a result, storytelling is continuing to spread throughout Indian cities.

The meticulous scholarly effort of S R. Farooqui, the only person in possession of the full 46 book collection, meticulously built up during his research, has undertaken a substantial role in the resurrection of Dastangoi. Jawaid Danish a playwright is also reviving this art form as he established Rang Manch a not-for-profit theatrical group in Canada to promote dastangoi and Indian theatre.

In the late 19th and early 20th centuries, a single individual typically performed this oral tradition in crowded bazaars (market place). But now it is performed in an auditorium atmosphere with two *dastangos* on stage. Nowadays, Dastangoi has been developed as a performance act in the modern environment, considering audiences' reception capacities in a society where the visual has taken over. The simplicity of the form is that it can be performed anywhere, i.e., at a street-side corner or in an auditorium with equal ecstasy, and it makes audience active participants rather than passive, by setting up constant dialogue with them and by resorting to direct addresses to them. Dastangoi can be created on any subject. It can be used to perform traditional as well as contemporary stories. Dastangoi is a valuable tool for education, and schools can use it to develop students' storytelling, literary composition, narration, and performance skills. Because the Dastan-e Amir Hamza has a large number of couplets and quatrains in the languages of Hindi, Braj, Awadhi, and Magahi as well as the speech patterns of various social groups, examples of the text must be included in the curricula of Urdu and Hindi.

The Dastan-e Amir Hamza has completely disappeared from the public's perception as a result of the genre's long-term neglect. Few Urdu students have read them, and the entire 46-volume set is currently only available in one collection in the entire world. Few reviewers have taken it seriously. While it is unacceptable that they have been neglected as writers, they have also been completely erased from the canon of the performing arts. After knowing the history of oversight of this art form, as there has been no known Dastango in the last seventy years, it is crucial to revive this tradition that has now been lost to us (*Dastangoi Revival: The Story so Far*, 2018).

Recently the International Museum Expo held in Delhi from 18th to 20th May 2023, organized by the Ministry of Culture, a special Dastangoi performance titled "Dastaan-e-Ajaib" on the theme of museums took place to commemorate International Museum Day. Such kind of initiatives should be taken by the government as well as private sector for revival of this art form.

The practise currently requires newer audiences more than it needs new Dastangos. Although it has already been shown beyond a doubt that it can enchant individuals in a theatre setting, regular theatre-going audiences, it still has the power to draw in even people who are not accustomed to seeing performances in a theatre. Its main topics are accounts of conflict, love, social gatherings, and extraordinary magic that would make ordinary magicians' shudder. As the oral performances of *mushairas* continue to be a great draw for audiences knowledgeable with Urdu in the majority of the nation, despite the language's overall decrease. Dastangoi also has the power to reach an untouched yet thriving audience because it is filled with Urdu poetry and phrases and has some of the best Urdu prose ever written. That would need it to leave the proscenia of large cities and head to smaller cities and newer spaces. Dastangoi's distinctiveness rested in bridging the gap between elite and common culture, and as the varied reactions to our performance demonstrate, it continues to be able to do so (Farooqui, 2010).

Marsiyakhwani

Marsiya is a seventh-century C.E., Urdu-Persian poetry derived from the Arabic word *risa*, which means grieving the loss of a dear one. Marsiya deals with the real scenes of Karbala which narrates the battlefield, pain, valor, and chivalry rather than just pleasant narration. A general cut made to meet the description, where each scenario of Karbala presented is articulated through special and delicate phrasing of the Marsiya, is used when a scene of Karbala is versified in the style of the Marsiya. Marsiya has Persian and Arabic literary influences especially *shia* community among muslims. At Shia mourning gatherings conducted during the month of *Mohharum* (the Islamic Calendar's first month, the tragedy of Karbala took place in the same month), they are customarily either recited by *Marsiya-Khwans* or sung by a *Marsiya-Soz*. People wear black attire as it signifies grief during mourning gatherings.

It was first recited in Iran to commemorate and lament the martyrdom of Imam Husain A.S., the grandson of the Prophet Mohammad (PBUH), and his family members at the Battle of Karbala. According to Pawar (2016), After the death of Caliph Muawiyah I in 680 AD, Hussain, the son of Ali Ibn Abi Talib, who was both the cousin and son-in-law of the Prophet Mohammed, launched a rebellion against Yazid I, who succeeded his father as the new Caliph. Hussain and his family left Mecca in expectation of being joined by people of the Kufa region but instead found that they had broken their commitment. On October 10, 680AD, Yazid I's troops halted their convoy. Hussain's family and friends, even his six-month-old child Ali Asghar, were tortured, slaughtered, and beheaded with him. Sayyeda Zainab, the Prophet's granddaughter Ali's daughter was among the women and children who were taken captive. She sobbed and mourned the loss of her brother in the presence of congregations. Because of this, Yazid I decided to set her free.

There are two types of marasiya. One of them is Shaksi marsiya, which is a Marsiya written on a person's death by a follower, admirer, or loved one, and the riwayati marsiya, which is written to remember the martyrdom of Imam Hussain and his family and friends in the battle of Karbala, which was fought on the 10th of October 680 AD. A marsiya written by Mirza Ghalib (a famous Urdu Poet) following the passing of his older brother and a marsiya written by Jan Nisar Akhtar (Urdu Poet) following the passing of his wife, Safiya, are both examples of shaksi marasiya (Sani, 2020).

NOHA and *SOZ*, which respectively signify mourning and burning of the (heart), are the sub-parts of MARSIYA. *Soz-khwani* (soulful chanting), which is usually the first part of mourning assemblies or majlis, is followed by the full recital of the marsiya. The shorter marsiya known as noha is recited by mourners, who finish with *maatam* (lamentation). Usually marsiya includes six-line units, which has been recited on various occasions chiefly in the month of Muharram.

The Marsiya tradition originated in Delhi and the Deccan, but it achieved its pinnacle under the support of the Nawabs of Lucknow, who promoted the art form in the 18th and 19th centuries, at a period when Mughal power was steadily declining. The nawabs were admirers of literature and art, but their Shia faith greatly influenced the construction of ***imambaras*** (congregational buildings used mostly to commemorate the events of Karbala) known as *azadari*.

The first Marsiyas in Urdu were composed in the 'Shiite' kingdoms of Goloconda and Bijapur, which were more closely associated with Iranian culture. It originated in the Deccan as a type of folk poetry, first with local roots and then later independent of Persian tradition (Qamar, n.d.). The Urdu Marsiya is significantly influenced by Arabic and Persian terminology, but it also has a distinct Indian subcontinental taste. Mir Baber Ali Anis and Mirza Salamat Ali Dabir are well-known Marsiya authors in Urdu.

In the Revolt of 1857 and subsequently throughout the Khilafat and Non-Cooperation Movements, Marsiya was used to inspire the mutineers, which led Mahatma Gandhi to invite many marsiyagos to prayer meetings (Pawar, 2016). Even though it was a significant genre with a significant impact on the cultural, social, and literary landscape, Marsiya did not have the same longevity as other forms of Urdu poetry like Ghazal and Rubai. There are many Marsiya manuscripts available written by many famous poets and writers in Arabic, Kashmiri, Persian, and Punjabi during different times. These Marsiya manuscripts are intended for recitation at various events, particularly during the month of Muharram. Due to the need for preservation and conservation, several of these Marsiya manuscripts are currently facing the imminent threat of extinction (Nazir, 2014). According to Qamar, *Marsiya* is practically the pinnacle of religious ritual as of right now because it only exists to be read in *Majlis*. Exploiting available opportunities in the context of the present is crucial for the survival of any literary heritage. Some of the significant advancements in the discipline during the 20th century that took the shape of *nazm* have been utterly disregarded. Urdu marsiya writers are sometimes criticized for being repetitious since they did not alter their plot and kept the battle of Karbala as their focus. This genre calls for innovation, and it can only happen if freshly created traditions are welcomed into Urdu Marsiya.

References

1. Adnan, A. (2016). *Dastangos: Nazrul Hassan, Fawad Khan & Syed Meesam Naqvi.* Newsline. Retrieved from https://www.academia.edu/26333318/Dastangos_Nazrul_Hassan_Fawad_Khan_and_Syed_Meesam_Naqvi

2. Bajpai, L. M. (2015). Myths and folktales in the Patachitra art of Bengal: Tradition and modernity. *Chitrolekha international magazine on art and design*. *5*(1).

3. Banik, S., & Kundu, U. (2018). Patachitra-A Micro Scale Industry: Overview and Challenges. *IOSR Journal of Business and Management (IOSR-JBM) e-ISSN*, 24-29.

4. Basu, T., & Das, B. (2017). The Folk Canvas of Pata-chitra: Transferring Continuity from Tradition to Modernity. *Organising Committee.*

5. Biswas, S. (2021). *Patachitra of West-Bengal.* Design Research. Retrieved from https://spaindustrialdesign.wordpress.com/2020/12/22/patachitra-of-west-bengal/

6. Bromham, L., Dinnage, R., Skirgård, H. *et* al. (2021). Global predictors of language endangerment and the future of linguistic diversity. *Nature Ecology & Evolution*, *6*(2), 163–173 (2022). https://doi.org/10.1038/s41559-021-01604-y

7. *Buddhist chanting of Ladakh: recitation of sacred Buddhist texts in the trans-Himalayan Ladakh region, Jammu and Kashmir, India*. (2014). ichLinks. Retrieved from https://www.ichlinks.com/archive/elements/elementsV.do?nation=undefined&page=1&elementsUid=13829896117982900102&mode=grid

8. Bullet, I. (2006). *Dastan in An Attic*. blogspot.com. Retrieved from http://dastangoi.blogspot.com/2006/12/dastan-in-attic.html

9. Chandra, S. (2019). Storytellers and the Tradition of Storytelling in India: A Look into the Past and Present. *Studies in Humanities and Social Sciences*, *26*(2), 28-48.

10. Chitrasri. (2020). *Ghazal & Qawwali*. Chitra Srikrishna. Retrieved from https://chitrasrikrishna.com/2020/11/28/ghazal-qawwali/

11. *Convention for the Safeguarding of the Intangible Cultural Heritage: Intergovernmental Committee for the Safeguarding of the Intangible Cultural Heritage.* (2012). Seventh session, Paris. https://ich.unesco.org/doc/src/16292-EN.doc

12. Dash, R. K. (2020). Revitalizing Endangered Languages in India: Can Public-Private Partnership (PPP) Work. In *2nd International Conference on Social Sciences in the 21st Century, Seminar Paper.*

13. Dastango, F. (2020). '*It is surreal to perform dastangoi on Zoom, where viewers are muted and all cameras are off.*' Scroll.in. Retrieved from https://scroll.in/article/980283/it-is-surreal-to-perform-dastangoi-on-zoom-where-viewers-are-muted-and-all-cameras-are-off

14. *Dastangoi Revival:The Story so Far.* (2018). Dastangoi. Retrieved from http://www.dastangoi.in/dastangoi-revival.php

15. Dixit, V., Kaur, G., & Shanwal, V. K. (2017). Emotional Intelligence in Indian Folklore. *Integrated Journal of Social Sciences*, *4*(1), 1-8.

16. Drude, S., & Intangible Cultural Heritage Unit's Ad Hoc Expert Group. (2003). *Language vitality and endangerment.* Retrieved from https://ich.unesco.org/doc/src/00120-EN.pdf

17. Farooqui, M. (2010). *What is Dastangoi?* blogspot.com. Retrieved from http://dastangoi.blogspot.com/2010/02/what-is-dastangoi.html

18. *Folklore of India.* (n.d.). In New World Encyclopedia. Retrieved from https://www.newworldencyclopedia.org/entry/Folklore_of_India

19. Gargi College. (n.d.). *Discovering India- The meaning of oral tradition.* Retrieved from https://gargicollege.in/wp-content/uploads/2020/03/ORAL-TRADITION.docx#:~:text=What%20does%20'oral%20tradition'%20mean,their%20children%2C%20and%20so%20on.

20. Gosain, S., Kant, D., & Das, A. K. (2016). *Dastan-e-Dastangoi: The Tale of a Revival.* Centre for Development Economics. Retrieved from http://cdedse.org/wp-content/uploads/2018/06/5Dastan-e-Dastangoi-The-Tale-of-a-Revival.pdf

21. Goyal, A. (2023). *Kavad – Colorful Storytelling Box of Rajasthan.* Inditales. Retrieved from https://www.inditales.com/kavad-storytelling-box-of-rajasthan/

22. Hajra, V. (2015). Role of Indian Folk Culture in Promotion of Tourism in the Country. *Paripex - Indian Journal of Research.* 4(2), 231–235. ISSN - 2250-1991

23. Indian Culture. (n.d.). *Buddhist Chanting of Ladakh: Recitation of Sacred Texts in the Trans-Himalayan Ladakh Region, Jammu and Kashmir.* Retrieved from https://indianculture.gov.in/unesco/intangible-cultural-heritage/buddhist-chanting-ladakh-recitation-sacred-texts-trans#:~:text=The%20Buddhist%20chanting%20of%20Ladakh,Heritage%20of%20Humanity%20in%202012

24. *Indian Fairy Tales, Folk Tales and Fables.* (n.d.). FairyTalez. Retrieved from https://fairytalez.com/region/indian/

25. *Indian Folktales.* (n.d.). Cultural India. Retrieved from https://www.culturalindia.net/indian-folktales/

26. Jahan, I. (2016). Dastangoi: A Diasporic Culture of Storytelling. *Pune Research an International Journal of English, 2*(2). ISSN: 2454-3454

27. Jalathota, A. (2022). *Origin of Indian Poetry.* LaFictioner. Retrieved from https://lafictioner.com/origin-of-indian-poetry/

28. Junik-Łuniewska, K. (2019). Towards the Visual. New Genres and Forms of Storytelling in India. *Politeja-Pismo Wydziału Studiów Międzynarodowych i Politycznych Uniwersytetu Jagiellońskiego, 16*(59), 149-160.

29. *Kavad/Kavad.* (n.d.). Gaatha. Retrieved from https://shop.gaatha.com/buy-indian-crafts/kavad?_route_=buy-indian-crafts%2FKavad&bfilter=f21:131;

30. Kajiru, I., & Nyimbi, I. (2020). The impact of myths, superstition and harmful cultural beliefs against albinism in Tanzania: A human rights perspective. *Potchefstroom Electronic Law Journal/Potchefstroomse Elektroniese Regsblad, 23*(1).

31. Kaushal, M. (n.d.). *IGNCA Inventory on the Intangible Cultural Heritage: Buddhist Chanting of Ladakh: Recitation of Sacred Buddhist Texts in the Trans Himalayan Ladakh Region, Jammu and Kashmir, India.* IGNCA. Retrieved from https://ignca.gov.in/ICH/ich_detail/ich00001.pdf

32. Khan, N. A. S. R. A., & Mohyuddin, A. N. W. A. A. R. (2014). Socio-economic impacts of superstitions among Pakhtoon women. *Eur J Acad Res, 8*(1), 10696-10713.

33. Kharbanda, S. (2021). *The Dastaan of Dastangoi: Resurrection of the Urdu art of storytelling.* CitySpidey. Retrieved from https://www.cityspidey.com/news/12993/the-dastaan-of-dastangoi-resurrection-of-the-urdu-art-of-storytelling

34. Krishnan, N. (2012). *Dastan-e-Dastangoi.* Fountainink. Retrieved from https://fountainink.in/qna/dastan-e-dastangoi

35. Kutty, M. P. V. G. (2007). National Experiences with the Protection of Expressions of Folklore/Traditional Cultural Expressions. *Geneva: World Intellectual Property Organization, 912.*

36. Marathe, O. (2019). *Explained: The tradition of Marsiya poetry in India.* The Indian Express. Retrieved from https://indianexpress.com/article/explained/urdu-marsiya-poetry-in-india-hamid-ansari-6018644/lite/

37. Ministry of Culture. (2022). *'Scheme of Financial Assistance for the Preservation and Development of Cultural Heritage of the Himalayas' protects and preserves the cultural heritage of Himalayan region.* Retrieved from https://pib.gov.in/PressReleaseIframePage.aspx?PRID=1810604

38. Ministry of Culture. (2023). *Literature & Folklore.* Retrieved from https://indiaculture.gov.in/literature-folklore

39. Mondal, A. (2015). *Patachitra, a storytelling tradition – photo essay by Arunima Mondal.* Private. Retrieved from https://www.privatephotoreview.com/2015/09/patachitra-a-storytelling-tradition-photo-essay-by-arunima-mondal/

40. Moseley, C. (Ed.). (2010). *Atlas of the World's Languages in Danger.* UNESCO. Retrieved from https://unesdoc.unesco.org/ark:/48223/pf0000187026/PDF/187026eng.pdf.multi

41. Nandgopal, C. (2018). *Unit-1 Oral Traditions.* IGNOU. Retrieved from https://egyankosh.ac.in/handle/123456789/47251

42. Nazir, T. (2014). Kashmiri Marsiya (Elegy) Manuscripts: The Valuable Sources for the Dissemination, Reconstruction and Safeguarding the History and Culture-II. *Library Philosophy and Practice,* 0_1.

43. Nemerov, H. (2023). *Poetry*. In Encyclopedia Britannica. Retrieved from https://www.britannica.com/art/poetry

44. Nigam, R. (2020). *Revisiting Indian folklores*. Media India Group. Retrieved from https://mediaindia.eu/culture/revisiting-indian-folklores/

45. Office of the Registrar General & Census Commissioner, India (ORGI). (2018). LANGUAGE (PAPER 1 OF 2018)-CENSUS OF INDIA 2011. Retrieved from https://censusindia.gov.in/nada/index.php/catalog/42458/download/46089/C-16_25062018.pdf

46. Oral Traditions, Myths & Legends of India. (2017). *The Indian Trust for Rural Heritage and Development (ITRHD), 2*. Retrieved from https://www.itrhd.com/magazine/oral-tradition.pdf

47. Pawar, Y. (2016). *From elegy to devotional art.* Dna. Retrieved from https://www.dnaindia.com/lifestyle/report-from-elegy-to-devotional-art-2262529/amp

48. Perera, K., Chandra, D. (n.d.). *Documenting the Intangible Cultural Heritage for Sustainable Economic Growth in Developing Countries.* International Committee for Documentation. Retrieved from https://cidoc.mini.icom.museum/wp-content/uploads/sites/6/2018/12/H-2_Perera_Chandra_paper.pdf

49. Qamar, A. (n.d.). Tracing the Rise and Fall of Marsiya.

50. Raghavendra, M. K. (2019). *Examining oral tradition in India and its impact on society, from Vedic literature to larger-than-life actors, politicians-India News.* Firstpost. Retrieved from https://www.firstpost.com/india/examining-oral-tradition-in-india-and-its-impact-on-society-from-vedic-literature-to-larger-than-life-actors-politicians-5828411.html

51. Rai, M. (2018). *7 Fascinating Indian Folk Tales*. Culture Trip. Retrieved from https://theculturetrip.com/asia/india/articles/7-fascinating-indian-folk-tales/

52. Rajvanshi, N. (2021). *Kavad: From Portable Shrines to Social Platforms.* PeepulTree. Retrieved from https://www.livehistoryindia.com/story/living-culture/kavad-art

53. Ratanjankar, S. N. (1952). Folk songs and music. *The Journal of the Ceylon Branch of the Royal Asiatic Society of Great Britain & Ireland, 2*(2), 103-122.

54. Sabnani, N. (2009). The Kavad Storytelling Tradition in Rajasthan. *Design Thoughts*, 28-33.

55. Safvi, R. (2016). *The Art of Marsiya Writing and Reciting*. Rana Safvi. Retrieved from https://ranasafvi.com/the-art-of-marsiya-writing-and-reciting/amp/

56. Sani, S. (2020). *Urdu poetry and the tradition of Marsiya Goi.* Swati's Blog. Retrieved from https://swatisani.net/blog/2020/08/30/urdu-poetry-and-tradition-of-marsia-goi/

57. Sengupta, P. (2009). Endangered languages: Some concerns. *Economic and political weekly*, 44(32), 17-19.
58. Singh, K., Sigroha, S., Singh, D., & Shokeen, B. (2017). Religious and spiritual messages in folk songs: a study of women from rural India. *Mental Health, Religion & Culture, 20*(5), 464-477.
59. Smeets, R. (2004). Language as a vehicle of the intangible cultural heritage. *Museum International*, *56*(1□2), 156-165.
60. SPPEL - Scheme for Protection and Preservation of Endangered Languages. (n.d.). *About SPPEL*. Retrieved from https://www.sppel.org/
61. Srivastava, I. (1991). Woman as portrayed in women's folk songs of North India. *Asian Folklore Studies*, 50(2), 269-310. https://doi.org/10.2307/1178387
62. *Storytelling*. (n.d.). Britannica Kids. Retrieved from https://kids.britannica.com/students/article/storytelling/277912
63. *The most spoken languages worldwide 2023*. (2023). Statista. Retrieved from https://www.statista.com/statistics/266808/the-most-spoken-languages-worldwide/
64. UNESCO. (2003). *Intangible Cultural Heritage Domains*. Retrieved from https://ich.unesco.org/doc/src/01857-EN.pdf
65. UNESCO. (2011). *UNESCO "Atlas of the World's Languages in Danger"*. Retrieved from https://unesdoc.unesco.org/ark:/48223/pf0000192416/PDF/192416eng.pdf.multi
66. UNESCO. (2021). *Indigenous Languages Decade (2022-2032)*. Retrieved from https://www.unesco.org/en/decades/indigenous-languages
67. World Tourism Organization. (2012). *Tourism and Intangible Cultural Heritage*. UNWTO, Madrid.

Chapter - 2

Performing Arts

India is a country with diverse culture and history, thus any type of performing arts may be instantly recognised with these aspects. Dance, music, and theatre have been a part of human culture since the origin of civilisation. People from India have communicated their pleasures and grief via singing and dancing through diverse art forms throughout history, beginning with the dancing figure discovered in the Indus valley civilisation and continuing to the present. The idea of performing arts in India is completely regional. Each region has its own language, history, and culture, and each has a strong regional theatre and dance tradition. This type of art has been used to communicate feelings. The manifestation, expression, or reaffirmation of one's cultural values and beliefs can be seen in the performance of traditions, rituals, dances, and practices. Long-standing customs dictate when, where, and who is allowed to execute the craft, practice, or expression.

Performing arts are one of the five domains of ICH defined by UNESCO 2003 Convention which include art performances in festivals or other communal ritual activities like dance, music, theatre and so on. As a result, performing arts are inextricably related to other domains, resulting the most distinctive, remarkable, and representative expressions of a culture. Originally, these creative forms were meant to spread religion and social changes, with music and dance being added to promote appeal. Dances and songs portray the diverse stages of our existence throughout history. They used to reflect rural people's socio-religious customs and practises, but they are now a form of contemporary urban culture as well. They have been linked for generations, and potentially began with fertility ceremonies to bring prosperity to the agricultural society, such as productiveness of land and livestock, but also fertility and longevity of children. Performance is frequently intertwined with social, ceremonial, and spiritual rituals. Instrumental and Vocal music, theatre, and dance, along with pantomime, melodic verses, and further types of art performances, are all entailed in the performing arts. The performing arts are quite diverse in India. In the context of the Convention, the term "intangible cultural heritage" refers to the instruments, artefacts, items, and spaces that are connected to cultural manifestations and practises. The Convention considers areas intimately connected to a performance to be cultural spaces because these locations are typically the sites where the performing arts are performed.

India has many of the religious instructors and *gurus* who guided people down the road of devotion and higher cognition. Artistic representations, such as communal singing, dance, and devotional music, were used to make their teachings more approachable. These artistic pursuits and lifestyles were a far healthier alternative to destructive and immoral lifestyles. Community singing, such as *bhajans, kirtans, and hari kathas*, had a lot of promise for bringing people closer together, regardless of class, creed, or colour. *Snake charmer, Bahurupi Kala, Terahtal, Kathpulti,* Nat acrobatics, Dummy horse dancing, and other folk entertainments were so prevalent that they were performed in every Indian home, whether they lived in the city or the countryside, ideally once a year. Dances and music were a part of every Indian ceremony, marriage, and celebration. As a tool of spiritual growth and knowledge of complicated human nature, all religious and communal centres were linked to some form of creative expression. These art forms were used in conjunction with life in order to accomplish *Artha, Dharma, Kama*, and *Mokshah* – or the development of a whole human being. They assisted us in loving one other and living in peace and harmony with others. These enjoyable activities also facilitated the development of a calm mental attitude, which is essential for a healthy body and mind.

The performing arts remained a significant source of mass education from the Vedic era until the mediaeval period. The Vedas established strict guidelines for reciting Vedic hymns. The pitch and emphasis of several hymns have been specified as well. They were more remarkable in their presentation than in their education or social changes. People across the world now enjoy these creative forms as a kind of entertainment. Every aspect of the human intellect is reflected attractively through art. These characteristics are known as *"RAS,"* and they encompass a variety of human emotions. '*Ras*' literally means sweet drink in Hindi. It represents '*aanand's* i.e., ultimate satisfaction. Human emotions are reflected in art, and people spontaneously express themselves via many forms of art. As a result, the intellectual mind and the creative streak combine, giving birth to art. Singing, dancing, sketching, painting, acting, and sculpture are all examples of how people express themselves. Some are represented through live performances, while others are expressed through the visual arts. Participating in the arts and culture fosters innovative problem-solving and promotes excellent interpersonal communication and expression. These abilities enhance mental health and wellness in both adults and children, facilitating greater achievement in regular tasks. When these individual-level advantages are added up, they reflect enhancements to the workforce's efficiency and adaptability, which have a beneficial influence on production.

The performing arts contain a wide range of commendable traits. They are appealing, vibrant, and easy to grasp, and full of emotion. Thus, most tourist programmes make an effort to include as much indigenous performing arts as possible. The creative arts can encourage visitors to spend more money. Some people travel to a nation particularly to enjoy the cultural attractions and the arts, whereas some participate in these activities while travelling for other reasons, thus lengthening their vacations, and leading to more expenditure. They are frequently used in cultural marketing aimed at attracting visitors and are frequently included in tour operators' itineraries. While this might result in higher numbers of visitors, greater revenues, and a window into a country's or community's culture, it may also result in the birth of new ways to present the performing arts that have been modified for the tourist market. In the name of amusement, traditional art forms are frequently converted into commodities, resulting in the loss of key means of communal expression. While tourism may help in revival of traditional performing arts and provide ICH a "commercial value," additionally, it could have a distorting effect, since shows are frequently shortened to display modified highlights to fulfil tourist expectations. As a result, traditional arts are mistreated and undermined, the community has become cold to them, and traditions have shifted in a negative direction. These are issues that have arisen as a result of tourism development.

Indian tradition and culture have always placed a high value on the performing arts. In the past, these acts were formerly carried out according to local ethics and customs in every region of India. However, as time passes, our traditions, and practises change. These essential components of Indian heritage are changing and, to a certain degree, disappearing as a result of our rapid shift toward western civilization. As time has passed, a steady decline in these public performances has been seen. Everything is changing so quickly in the age of smartphones and the internet. In every facet of human existence, there is now a constant demand for advancement. Many forms of performing arts are at risk nowadays. Many old traditions are being faded out as cultural practises become more standardised. Even when they increase in reputation, only some expressions may prosper while others fall. Music is possibly one of the finest illustrations of this, with the current growth in popularity of 'Music World'. Though it facilitates cultural interaction and fosters innovation that improves the worldwide art scene, the phenomena may also be problematic. Many different types of music can be homogenised in order to produce a uniform result. There is little scope for some forms of music vital for the tradition and performance processes in some countries.

Asia–Pacific communities' performing arts, which are deeply ingrained with identity, have a lot of potential, but they also have a lot of challenges. One of the biggest obstacles in the performing arts business is encouraging artists to set aside their differences and work together because of the linguistic, class, caste, and ideological divisions that exist within this industry. Second, due to their relative poverty, performing artists will struggle to maintain forums and networks by paying membership dues. Therefore, fostering collaborations and alliances among performing artists is a responsibility of grant makers and governments. Even though the India's performing arts industry receives assistance from businesses, the government, charitable trusts, and bilateral agencies, the amount of financing available is insufficient to satisfy the demands and problems in this field. In India, the financial environment for the performing arts is dismal. The Ministry of Culture, which continues to be the largest funder, does not spend the full amount of its allotted budget each year; this is not because there are fewer worthy projects; rather, it is because it is unwilling to alter its programming and operational procedures in order to keep up with the evolving demands and aspirations of the arts community. International institutions like the Ford Foundation, which once had a robust arts and culture programme in India, have scaled back their funding for the arts and culture, preserving only those aspects of their work that directly and tangibly improves socioeconomic conditions. Additionally, due to a lack of funding, theatre and dance performing organisations are unable to properly publicise their performances, which results in a lack of awareness and poor attendance.

The foundation of Indian art and culture has always been the performing arts. However, performance has suffered recently as a result of the development of alternative types of entertainment. The expansion has been hampered by a lack of resources and inadequate infrastructure. Regardless, the creative arts have been flourishing at a satisfactory pace and provide both the government and artists a wide range of options. As mentioned above performing arts sector is supported by a number of institutions, including grants and donations from the state and central governments, businesses, foundations, trusts, and charitable organisations. The Indian industry's situation is still dire as compared to other countries across the world. Opportunities for the industry to prosper are being created by growing national and worldwide exposure for the theatre, dance, and music; the advancement of new technologies and settings; growing global demand; and the creation of diverse performances that are being tested as sources for performance. The sector may take advantage of extra opportunities that will arise from the development of creative clusters in smart cities. The industry's biggest obstacles are finding funding and sponsorship, a lack of infrastructural venues for performing dance and theatre, and a preference for alternative creative arts platforms. Given that it provides a significant portion of the population with a means of living, the government must take some steps to improve the industry's current situation.

Traditional performing arts safeguarding methods should place a strong emphasis on the imparting of skills, the passing down of knowledge, the use and building of instruments, and the development of the master-apprentice relationship. A song's intricacies, a dance's moves, and dramatic interpretations should all be emphasised. Research, documentation, inventory, and archiving of performances are also possible. Many of the world's sound archives contain thousands of recordings from over a century ago. If they are not digitised, these older recordings could degrade to the point that they are lost forever. The digitization process makes it possible to correctly identify and inventory documents. In order to be recorded or for educational purposes, many musical traditions have been modified to match Western standards of notation, although this process can be disastrous. Cultural media, different institutions, and enterprises may also be vital in ensuring the continuation of traditional performing arts forms by expanding their audiences and raising public awareness. Educating audiences about various aspects of a particular form of expression can expand its reach and popularity. This can also cultivate a deeper appreciation for the art, stimulating interest in its regional variations and potentially motivating individuals to actively participate in the performances. Training and infrastructural advancements may also be necessary to properly train individuals and people to safeguard the complete spectrum of performing arts. Protecting the performing arts does not mean "freezing" traditions in a specific period, but rather keeping them alive. "Living" signifies that the legacy continues to exist and is passed down from generation to generation through a variety of ways and situations. As a result, "living heritage" is a concept that must be thoroughly conceptualised and implemented in order to ensure the feasibility of cultural safeguarding in modern life. Values, lifestyles, decision-making processes, social structures, indigenous people's lives, customs, religion, and a feeling of community are all intangible aspects of our history that provide both distinct opportunities and challenges. Indians have grown increasingly interested in promoting their feeling of national identity and cultural unity since independence. As a result, indigenous traditional arts have revived, particularly in the fields of song and dance. It is now the responsibility of our educational and cultural institutions to make sure that the next generation continues to carry the torch of spiritual and cultural renaissance for the rest of the world to see and emulate, rather than succumbing to Western society's materialistic ideology, where man has accomplished incredible success in uncovering the secrets of nature but feels isolated and disconnected from his own community and society. We must be certain that modern India never forgets its rich cultural history, which is an inheritance of our ancient seers, scholars, and saints. The Ministry of Culture oversees the performing arts sector and offers financing for infrastructure development, travel, prizes, scholarships, and fellowships. The promotion of all kinds of art and culture, both physical and non-physical, as well as the preservation and protection of the country's cultural legacy, is within the purview of the Ministry of Culture. It is also accountable for fostering cultural awareness at all levels, from local to global. Additionally, independent organisations have been established to support the nation's performing arts sector:

- The Sangeet Natak Akademi offers performing arts organizations funds for salaries and production costs as well as scholarships, travel, and research awards for performers. To help playwrights who write in regional languages and to showcase emerging talent, it arranges regional and national festivals and performances.
- The Indian Council for Cultural Relations (ICCR) provides financial assistance to both Indian and foreign performers at several international events. For international students seeking to pursue studies in the performing arts in India, ICC also provides fellowships and awards.
- To encourage the performing arts in their respective zones, the Central Government also provides funding for seven zonal cultural centers. The state does, however, provide ineffective support for the performing arts. The state infrastructure receives the lion's share of the public financing that has been established to support the arts. Additionally, the application and distribution processes are both exceedingly time-consuming and difficult.

Music

Music has been India's primary art form for centuries. The

continuity of Indian music's development is noteworthy. Among the performing arts, music is the most ubiquitous, and it may be found in every community, most frequently as an essential part of other performing arts and ICH areas, deeply ingrained within them such as oral traditions, joyful events, and rituals etc. It may be found in diverse settings, including holy and profane, classical, and popular, and labour and leisure. Music may also have an economic or political element: it can narrate the past of a community, praise a notable individual and play a significant role in employability. It is performed at a broad-spectrum of events, including **weddings, ceremonies and initiations, festivals, funerals, diverse entertainment, and an array of social gatherings.**

The Vedas play a pivotal role in the development of musical system that ruled India for centuries. The Indian musical system depicts the extent to which human creativity could explore in search of fresh ways to express himself musically. The Sama Veda, which contains the slokas that were set to music, is where Indian music got its start. Hindustani and Carnatic music are the two major schools of classical music. Both are based on the traditional themes of *Bharata's Natyashastra* and *Sarangdeva's Sangeet Ratnakara*. The phrases Carnatic and Hindustani first appear in Haripala's "*Sangeeta Sudhakara*" from the 14th century A.D. Since the emergence of Muslims, especially in the time of Delhi's Mughal Emperors, the two unique forms of Hindustani and Carnatic music became popular. Both musical systems derived their nourishment from the same primary source. The music of the Persian and Arabic artists who delighted the courts of the Mughal kings of Delhi was incorporated into some aspects of Northern Indian music, while the music of the South continued to evolve along its own unique lines. However, the core components of the North and South's respective systems have remained the same. It is said that, South Indian music as we know it today originated in the Middle Ages in *Deogiri,* the capital city of the *Yadavas*. Following the Muslim invasion and looting of the city, the entire cultural life of the city is said to have sought refuge in the Carnatic Empire of Vijayanagar during the rule of Krishnadevaraya. There is around 250 *Ragas* that are regularly used in both the North and the South. *Bahar, Sindhu Bhairavi, Bhairavi, Darbari, Bhim Palasi, Jai Jayanti, Desh, Todi, Megha Malhar, Yaman, Shyam Kalyan, Pilu,Khambaj and Hamsadhwani* are the most often used *ragas*. *Bharata's Natyashashtra* (written between second century BC and second century AD), which comprises six chapters on music, is the first work dealing completely with performing arts. The Hindustani music styles include *Dhrupad, Dhamar, Thumri, Khayal, and Tappa, Flutes, drums, veena,* and *cymbals* have all been mentioned in ancient literature. Hindustani classical music performers are frequently linked to a *gharana,* or musical school. *Gharanas* are hereditary associations between musicians that serve as the essence of the genre and set them apart from one another. The *gharanas* work in *gurushishya parampara*, meaning that students studying under a certain *guru* and passing down his musical knowledge and style would be a member of the same *gharana.* **Gwalior, Kirana**, and **Jaipur *gharanas*** are a few well-known *gharanas.*

Music was appreciated by several monarchs, including Samudragupta, King Bhoja of Dhara, and King Someshavra of Kalyana. Samudra Gupta, the Gupta ruler, was an accomplished musician. He is portrayed playing the Veena on several of his coins. In temples, music was also involved with the worship of Gods and Goddesses. Jayadeva of Orissa authored the most magnificent raga kavya, the *Gita Govinda*, in the twelfth century, with each song set in a raga and constructed on the topic of Radha and Krishna's love. The *Abhinavabharati* of *Abhinavagupta* (993-1055) contains significant knowledge regarding music. Similarly, Sufi and Bhakti saints promoted music during the mediaeval period. In Sufi khanqahs, *qawwalis* were sung, and devotional music such as *kirtan* and *bhajan* became popular among Bhakti saints. Religious music is intimately linked with the names Kabir, Mirabai, Surdasa, Chandidasa, Tulsidasa, and Vidyapati. Amir Khusrau, a great scholar, contributed equally to the growth of music. The origins of Hindustani classical music may be attributed to Amir Khusrau (AD 1253–1325), who promoted the practise of musical performance using specific instruments, during the Delhi Sultanate era. He is known for inventing the *sitar,* the *tabla,* and with introducing new ragas. *Kitabe Navras* is a collection of songs penned by Ibrahim Adil Shah II in the seventeenth century in honour of Hindu deities as well as Muslim saints. The majority of Hindustani musicians may trace their lineage back to Tansen. Tansen was Akbar's most renowned musician, and no one could equal him, despite the fact that there were many other types of vocalists. Tansen's music was believed to have a magical impact. He had the power to stop the Yamuna's rising waves and to make it rain by using the might of his "*Megh Rag*." In fact, his melodic tunes are being performed throughout India today with a lot of enthusiasm. *Baiju Bawra, Surdas*, and other musicians were paid well by some of Akbar's courtiers. The ancient and mediaeval kings' encouragement of these artists was crucial in keeping the traditions alive.

Apart from classical music, India has a long tradition of **folk music**. The feeling of the masses is represented by this music. All of life's significant events are remembered by these uncomplicated songs. A few examples of memorable occasions include weddings, the start of a new season, festivals, and the birth of a child. Songs for these occasions are plenty. A lot of songs are dedicated to planting and harvesting. The people regularly sing about their hopes, anxieties, and aspirations during these events. Bengali *Bhatiali* and other Rajasthani traditional tunes like *Mand* are well-known throughout India. Around Muharram, Muslims sing *Sozkhwani,* or mourning melodies, while during Christmas, carols and choral music are sung in gatherings on special occasions. Folk music contain unique messages or meanings. They frequently refer to historical events and significant rites. The teaching of tribal and folk music differs from the teaching of Indian classical music. The economics of rural life do not allow for a structured apprenticeship period during which the learner can dedicate their entire life to mastering the art of music. In the villages, music is ingrained from an early age. Countless community events give the residents the chance to practise and improve their abilities. Instruments used in music are frequently distinct from those used in classical music. Although it is occasionally possible to find instruments like the *tabla,* it is more common that simpler drums like the *daf, dholak, or nal* are employed. Folk music lacks the *sitar* and *sarod* that are so prevalent in the classical genre. Instruments like the *ektar, dotar, rabab*, and *santur* are frequently found in folk music. They are frequently not referred to by these names but rather by names from their native tongue. There are also instruments that are only used in specific regional folk music. There are countless of these instruments. The instruments used in classical music are made by artisans whose sole profession is making musical instruments. The musicians themselves often make the folk instruments, in contrast. It is fairly typical to come across folk instruments made from materials that are easily accessible. Making musical instruments can be done with a variety of readily available materials, including skin, bamboo, coconut shells, pots etc.

Beyond its ability to amuse, music was prized and practised for its capacity to elevate humanity to a higher realm and grant the soul access to eternal happiness. Indian music can be compared to any other sophisticated musical system in the world due to its flawless tonal system and comprehensive *raga and tala* systems. Indian music has had an influence on Western music. The influence of Western music is spreading across music in the twenty-first century, frequently leading many magnificent indigenous traditions to become nothing more than archival relics or the subject of scientific dissertations. Changes in wedding music, such as the preference for Western music over traditional folk music, can be understood as a reflection of the increasing influence of Western culture leading to decline of folk music. Great Maestros such as Pandit Ravi Shankar, Zakir Hussain, and others have contributed significantly to popularising and promoting Indian music in other countries. All of them reflect the people's innate joy, abandon, and rhythm. Religious ceremonies still include the recitation of *Vedic* hymns with set pitch and emphasis. Indian artists are asked to play and participate in numerous festivals and occasions all around the world. Music departments can be found at schools and institutions. The Indira Kala Vishwa Vidyalaya in Khairagarh is a music school, whereas Gandharva Maha- Vidyalaya, Kathak Kendra, and many more institutions in the south also support music in different ways. Music is being spread throughout India through conferences, *baithaks,* speeches, and plays. A new dimension has been brought to the performing arts by radio and television. They have a remarkably wide reach within the common person's home, and cable TV and CD-ROM have extended it even further. While FM has expanded the possibilities of radio, audiotapes and videocassettes have allowed practically any well-known musician to perform in the seclusion of one's living room. Indian pop music has gained international exposure because channels like MTV and the numerous satellite channels that have made it possible for everyone to enjoy. Arts and their expressions in post-Independence India have been an endemic occurrence, encouraging the artists to create new works, in contrast to the classical artists of the middle centuries who mostly performed for the amusement of temple priests, royal patrons, and wealthy houses. However, it will be up to future generations to judge whether fame and mass media, which have culminated in video CD and DVD, will improve the grade rather than the quantity of our arts. Folk music, in addition to this, demonstrates a very rich cultural legacy. Western music became popular during British control. To meet the needs of Indian music, Indians adopted several of their instruments, including the violin and clarinet. On-stage orchestration of music is a recent innovation. Making musical instruments has declined in recent years. The prevalence of Western musical instruments has resulted in a move away from traditional acoustic instruments, which has further contributed to the declining demand for instrument makers. Additionally, the younger generation's shifting interests and job requirements may not match the traditional trade of instrument making, reducing the number of people entering this field. The oral transmission of songs and ragas was superseded using cassettes. Thousands of music enthusiasts around the nation may now see performances that were previously only accessible to a select group of people. The master-disciple system is no longer necessary to transmit music instruction; instead, institutions that teach music can do it. Folk music in India is passed down orally. Due to a lack of thorough recording and preservation efforts, many customs are in danger of being lost forever. To secure the survival of various musical genres, recording and preserving them is crucial. Despite efforts made by the Indian government to promote and protect traditional music, but still, there is frequently a lack of continuous and significant assistance. Promoting and maintaining various artistic expressions are facing constant challenges due to limited financing, administrative roadblocks, and insufficient policies.

Table 2: State Wise List of Indian Music

S. NO	State	Music
1.	Andhra Pradesh	Oggu Katha, Carnatic Music, Suvvi Paatalu, Madiga Dappu etc.
2.	Uttar Pradesh	Rasiya Geet, Alha, Hori, Sohar, Kajri, Fag, Chaita, Qawwali, Purvi, Birha, etc.
3.	Uttarakhand	Shakunakhar-Mangalgeet, Thadya, Barhamasa, Basanti/ Basant Geet, Ghasiyari Geet, Chapeli, Jhoda etc.

4.	Arunachal Pradesh	Ja-jin-ja, Nyioga, Baryi etc.
5.	Assam	Bihu songs, Tikir etc.
6.	Chattisgarh	Pandavani etc.
7.	Jammu & Kashmir	Chhakri, Bhakha, Henzae, Sufiana Kalam, Wanawan, Surma, ladishah, Hafiz Nagma etc.
8.	Himachal Pradesh	Jhoori, Laman, Ainchaliyan etc.
9.	Punjab	Tappa, Jugni, Dhadi, Bhangra etc.
10.	Maharashtra	Powada, Lavani, Ovi etc.
11.	Chhattisgarh	Pandavani etc.
12.	Goa	Banvarh, Mando, Fughri, Ovi, Dekhni etc.
13.	Rajasthan	Pankhida, Pabuji Ki Phach, Lotia, Teej Songs, Panihari, Maand etc.
14.	Odisha	Daskathia etc.
15.	Manipur	Sana Lamok, Khongjom Parva, Khubakeshei etc.
16.	Mizoram	Saikuti Zai (songs of Saikuti), Chai hia (songs of the Chai Dance) etc.
17.	Tamil Nadu	Villu Pattu, Bow Song, Ammanaivari etc.
18.	Karnataka	Bhavageethe , Jaanapade Geethe etc.
19.	Madhya Pradesh	Alha, Pai etc.
20.	Kerala	Bhuta, Sopana Sangeetham, Mappila Pattu, Pulluvan Pattu, Panchavadyam etc.
21.	Bihar	Sukar ke Biah, Sohar, Katnigeet, Sumangali etc.
22.	West Bengal	Baul, Bhatiali, Baromasya, Kabigaan, Nazrul Geeti, Shyama Sangeet etc.
23.	Nagaland	Hekaileu, Heliamleu, Neuleu, Hereileu etc.
24.	Gujarat	Garba, Bhavai, Bhajan, Dandiya etc.
25.	Sikkim	Lu Khangthamo, Gha To Kito etc.
26.	Jharkhand	Jhumar, Domkch etc.

Dance

For immeasurable years, India has been a genuine treasure trove of dance traditions, with its huge range of races and situations. This has given rise to a diverse array of dance styles, with each one being shaped by the time and place of its origin. Dance seems to have evolved prior to the advent of speech or visual art, as it has been an integral part of human existence across the spectrum from the most primitive to the most civilized societies. In the early stages of human history, primitive people danced to bridge the gap between reality and the divine, whereas in more civilized societies, dance became a means of enjoyment and artistic self-expression.

Dance may be simply characterised as organised body motions, usually done to music, despite its complexity. Aside from its physical element, dance's rhythmic motions, steps, and gestures sometimes communicate a feeling or mood, or depict a specific event or everyday conduct, such as religious dances and dances depicting hunting, combat, or sexual activity. The notion of rasa is very important in dance. The rasa is transmitted in dance through Bhava or emotions through using skill *Abhinaya*. Dances on earth and in heaven are frequently mentioned in the Epics. Indian dance and music have a long and glorious history. It has a lot of expressive and emotional force while presenting a narrative. Classical dance traditions like *Kathakali, Kathak, Bharatnatyam, Kuchipudi, Manipuri,* and *Odishi,* are an essential component of our cultural legacy.

It is impossible to pinpoint when dance began, but it is certain that it was born out of a need to convey pleasure. Dance and its different *angas* (limbs) have been extensively explored in India. *Nritta* (pada sanchalan), *nritya* (anga sanchalan), and *natya* (natya sanchalan) are three categories that have been used to classify facial expressions, physical gestures, *hasta mudras*, and footsteps (*abhinay*). The art of dance in India may be traced back to the Harappan civilization. The finding of a bronze figure of a dancing girl indicates that some Harappan women danced. Dance served as a symbolic manifestation of religious ideas in ancient Indian culture. The cosmic cycle's creation and destruction are symbolised by Lord *Shiva* as *Nataraja*. The traditional representation of *Shiva* as *Nataraja* elegantly conveys the appeal of dance among Indians. In the southern portion of the nation, there is not a single temple that does not have statues of dancers in various poses. The laws of dancing, which were derived from old Sanskrit literature, were particularly strict in the mediaeval period in the south. As dancing schools initially entered in the southern region, it became a centre for study. The south Indian classical dance stream has the most dance genres in the current era. Dance piqued the curiosity of both men and women. People have begun to consider women artists in high regard as a result of the efforts of great music philosophers and numerous religious and social reform organisations. The Muslim monarchs popularised Kathak dancing throughout the medieval period. Temples, courts, and other areas of the structure offered an essential platform for all dancers in the south. The legendary tales of *Rama, Krishna, Ganesh*, and *Durga* were all portrayed via dance during *Navaras*. Some northern rulers, like Wajid Ali Shah, were big supporters of music and dance, and it was here that the Lucknow gharana, or 'school of dance,' was born.

Dances were eventually divided into two categories: folk and classical. The classical style of dancing was practised in both royal courts and temples. In temples, dance served a sacred purpose, but in courts, it was solely for pleasure. The Hindu temples are said to be the birthplace of classical dance. The temples were where they were initially created and nourished. Although dances were performed at royal courts on special occassions, the impetus for their creation was religious. In India, there are three main classical dance traditions: ***Kathakali, Baratnatyam,* and *Manipuri***. Some other well-known dances are Andhra Pradesh's *Kuchupudi*, Kerala's *Mohiniattam* and Orissa's *Odissi*. *Bharatanatyam* and *Mohiniattam* became major aspects of temple rites in southern India. *Yakshagana,* a form of *Kathakali* with origins in Kerala, depicts tales from the *Mahabharata,* and *Ramayana* whereas *Manipuri* and *Kathak* focus mostly on *Krishna* and his *leela* (exploits). The worship of Lord *Jagannath* is linked to *Odissi* performance. Despite the fact that *Kathak's* topic was the *Krishna leela* and stories about Lord *Shiva*, it became popular in royal courts during the Medieval Era. This is reflected in *Thumri* and *Ghazal's* romantic gestures, which were also performed with kings' accompanists. *Manipuri* dancing was also used in religious ceremonies.

Folk dancing evolved alongside classical dance forms. Indian state folk dances are mainly group dances that are quite popular among people of all social groups. They originated from ordinary people's lives, either as a sort of ritual or as a form of pleasure and were performed in harmony. Ethnic dance, street dance, traditional dance, and vernacular dance are all terms used to describe folk dance. The dancers dress up in their traditional clothes and accessories for the performances. Each type of dance has its own rhythm, costumes, and expressions, all of which are accompanied by energy, experience, and celebration. Dancers and musicians complement each other's performances, and the dancers are fascinated by the local or traditional music. The dancers sing most of the time, joined by musicians playing musical instruments, emphasising the bonding force. Dancers' ability and creativity have a significant impact on their performance. Some dances are performed by men and women separately, while others are performed by both. In Assam, *Bihu* is used to mark the bulk of the harvesting season. In India, some folk dances have become prominent including *Santhal* dance, *Manipuri* dance, *chhau, ras, gidda, bhangra,* and *garba*. They are performed in groups as part of local rites and customs in villages and isolated areas of the countryside. During religious, social, cultural, and seasonal festivals, such dances are performed.

They are equally well-liked and possess exceptional intelligence and creativity. Almost every region of our country has evolved its own distinct folk-dance culture. The country's diverse terrain and geography have given rise to a wide range of folk dances. Indian traditional dance is a rich source of symbolic language that contributes to modern art. Folk Dances of Indian States are an exciting platform that includes a creative extravaganza from various Indian states. They have a high aesthetic value due to its profundity of thought and directness of presentation. When folk dances are performed on various occasions, they tend to reveal that culture. Indian state folk dances are an important aspect of popular culture. The idea of expressing emotion via folk dance is both natural and unique. Much of what comprises the Indian folk, tribal, and ceremonial dance traditions have close ties to everyday life activities. It has the ability to revive and rejuvenate itself eternally while stay committed to antiquity and tradition. Many indigenous cultures use it to commemorate every possible occasion.

Many folk dances have little or no economic value; thus, this dance genre is not regarded seriously for professional stage performances. Folk dance is also uncontrollable since it lacks a regulatory or promotional organisation. It is acquired through past traditions, and newer dancers generally learn to dance by copying the moves of more experienced dancers. Folk dance is accorded considerable priority by governments since it depicts the traditional life of a country's people and is showcased at events such as Independence Day celebrations, film festivals, and so on. These dance forms are still alive and well in today's commercially driven world as a result of special treatment by governments and cultural organizations. Folk dance is enjoyable to learn since it is based on our natural dancing feelings and body motions. Many people nowadays believe that dancing is just something that can be done on stage and that it must be learned at a dance studio. And they are enthralled by dance competitions on television. The most common type of social dancing that makes it to the big screen is a well-choreographed performance by well-trained dancers. Real folk dancing, which is done on the ground of a village, is nothing like this TV art form. Indian classical dance has also been fading over time. People no longer relate to them and are unwilling to put up the time and effort necessary to do so. On the other hand, several new and western dance styles are gaining popularity and may be observed in Indian cinema as well. They are particularly popular among the younger generation. There has been a modification of cultural values and tastes as a result of the massive urbanisation and globalisation that has taken place in India. Folk dance frequently struggle to keep up with contemporary forms of entertainment, which often leads to a reduction in public interest and support for these folk-dance forms. Folk dance styles are frequently overtaken by more well-known and financially lucrative dance forms, which results in fewer opportunities for performances, inadequate financial support, and a lack of space to display their talent. The younger generations may be less interested in learning and performing traditional dances, resulting in decreased transmission. Folk dancers have a tough time finding continuous work and earning an income that can support them because there is a low demand for folk dance performances. A number of factors, including rapid urbanisation, globalisation, and shifting cultural preferences, have contributed to the fall in the popularity and significance of folk dancing. There is a possibility that the next generation will abandon traditional folk dances in favour of Western dance traditions or contemporary styles. This makes it difficult for folk dancers to safeguard and promote their art. Chaam dance, Nati from Himachal Pradesh, Bamboo dance from Mizoram, Sattriya dance, Chhau dance, Wangala dance from Meghalaya, Gotipua from Odisha, Chakyar Koothu from Kerala, Chaiti Ghoda from Odisha etc. are some of the endangered dance forms of India (*World Dance Day 2021,* 2021).

The position of dance and its performers has shifted in recent decades. In order to enhance their personal attributes, young people have started learning to dance. Many schools, colleges, and universities have established separate departments for dance instruction. Workshops on folk dances are the best options for tourists to immerse themselves in culture that are organised nowadays by certain state tourism boards (for example, the Chhau Dance workshop organised in the Victoria Memorial grounds by the West Bengal Tourism Development Corporation on World Tourism Day 2014). A visit to a theme village like Chowki Dhani in Jaipur, Rajasthan, or a home stay experience in India are all incomplete without a folk-dance performance. The Kalbelia dance and the fire dance, accompanied by music by native Manganiyar musicians, are the primary attractions of Rajasthan's desert safaris.

Table 3: State Wise List of Indian Dance

S. No.	State	Dance
1.	Andhra Pradesh	Vilasini Natyam, Kolttam, Kuchipudi, Kolattam, Andhra Natyam, Veeranatyam, Dappu, Lambadi, Gobbi, Butta Bommalu, Kolannalu etc.
2.	Arunachal Pradesh	Pasi Kongki, Ponung, Bardo Chham, Buiya, Chalo; Popir; Wancho etc.
3.	Bihar	Kajri, Jhumar, Jata Jatin; Natua, Purbi; Bidesia, Karma etc.
4.	Chhattisgarh	Saila, Gendi, Pandwani, Panthi, Gaur, Maria, Raut Nacha, Chandaini Gonda, Tertali, Karma, Panthi, Gendi, Suwa, Kaksar etc.
5.	Goa	Dhangar, Koli, Samayi Nrutya, Fugdi, Ghode-Modni, Dhalo, Tonnya Mell, Dekhni; Tarangamel, Talgadi, Goff, Kunbi, Dasarawadan etc.
6.	Gujarat	Padhar, Dandiya, Tippani, Bhavai, Garba, Raalila etc.
7.	Himachal Pradesh	Dhaman, Chham, Nati, Chhanak Chham, Jhora, Jhali, Giddha Parhaun; Dangi, Hikat etc.
8.	Lakshadweep	Lava, Kolkali, Parichakali etc.
9.	Haryana	Jhumar, Loor, Dhamyal, Gangor, Khoria, Gugga dance, Daph, Sang; Ghoomar etc.
10.	Jammu and Kashmir	Kud, Hikat, Dhumal, Rouf, Mandjas, Hafiza, Dhamali, Jagrana etc.

11.	Jharkhand	Hunta, Alkap, Domkach, Mundari, Paika, Santhali, Sarhul, Karma, Phagua, Mardana Jhumar, Janani Jhumar, Danga, Jhitka, Barao, Ghora Naach, Bheja etc.
12.	Karnataka	Karaga, Huttari, Simha Nutrya, Lambi, Dollu Kunitha, Bayalata, Kunitha, Veeragase, Kai Silambu Attam etc.
13.	Kerala	Dappu Kali, Kaikottikali, Mudiyettu, Kummi, Kathakali, Mohiniattam, Thirvathirakali, Kaikotti Kalai, Koodiyattam, Krishnavattam, Ottam Thulal, Theyyam, Bhootham Thullal, Kolam Thullal, Padayani, Kaliyattam, Kalaripayattu, Padayani, Mayil Attam, Chakyar Koothu etc.
14.	Madhya Pradesh	Phulpati, Lota, Selabhadoni, Grida, Aada, Bhagoria, Maach, Tertali, Khada Nach, Charkula, Jawara, Matki dance etc.
15.	Mizoram	Chailam, Sarlamkai, Cheraw (Bamboo Dance), Tlanglam, Parlam, Sawlakin, Zangtalam, Khuallam etc.
16.	Meghalaya	Wangala, Ka Shad Suk Mynsiem, Behdiengkhlam, Nongkram, Lahoo, Dorsegata, Do Dru Sua etc.
17.	Manipur	Pung Cholom, Lhou Sha, Thangta, Nupa, Lai Haraoba, Dhol cholom; Manipuri, Khamba Thoibi etc.
18.	Sikkim	Sikmari, Tashi Yangku, Denzong Gnenha, Yak Chaam; Maruni; Rechungma, Singhi Chaam, Chu Faat Dance, Bhutia, Khukuri Naach etc.
19.	Maharashtra	Nakata, Tamasha; Dhangari Gaja, Pavri Nach, Gafa, Dahi Kala, Koli, Lavani, Lezim, Povadas, Dindi etc.
20.	Nagaland	Gethinglim, Hetateulee, Zeliang, Rangma, Changsang, Nsuirolians, Temangnetin, Chang Lo etc.
21.	Punjab	Bhangra, Giddha, Daff, Dhaman, Malwai, Bhand, Naqual, Sammi, Dandass, Ludi, Jindua, Jaago etc.
22.	Odisha	Odissi, Savari, Chhau, Ghumura, Munari, Chaiti Ghoda, Paika, Gotipua, Sambalpur, Pala, Ruk Mar Nacha, Dalkhai etc.
23.	Rajasthan	Ghumar, Chakri, Gangaur, Kalbelia, Terah Taali, Jhulan Leela, Suisini, Ghapal, Kachhi Ghodi, Dandiya, Gair, Chari, Chang, Bhavai etc.
24.	Tamil Nadu	Kolattam, Bharatnatyam, Kummi, Karakattam, Puliyaattam, Oyilattam, Karagram, Parai Attam, Kaliyattam, Kavadiyattam, Paampu Attam, Mayilattam, Karagattam, Poikal Kudirai Attam etc.

25.	Telangana	Mayuri, Perini Thandavam, Gusadi, Dappu, Lambadi etc.
26.	Tripura	Bijhu, Hojagiri, Goria, Lebang Boomani, Dhamail, Gajan etc.
27.	Uttarakhand	Chappeli, Chholiya, Barada Nat, Jhora, Jhainta, Jagar, Thali-Jadda, Langvir, Hurka baul etc.
28.	Uttar Pradesh	Jhora, Raslila, Kajri, Mayur Nritya, Chhapeli, Jaita, Nautanki, Charkula etc.
29.	West Bengal	Jatra, Chau, Keertan, Kathi, Gambhira, Baul, Dhunuchi Naach, Kalikapatadi, Raibenese, Ranpa, Brita, Domni etc.
30.	Assam	Bihu, Ojapali, Bagurumba, Jhumar, Kaligopal, Naga dance, Deodhani, Bhortal, Sattriya etc.

Theatre

Drama is a kind of performance art that has been practiced since the dawn of time. The child enacts, imitates, and caricatures, which is certainly the start of drama. A theatre is a form of collaborative creative art that uses live actors to present insight into an authentic or fictional occasion in front of an actual audience in a particular location. **Acting, singing, dancing, and music, as well as speech, narration or recitation, versification, religion, and festival celebrations** are common elements of traditional theatrical performances, which may also incorporate **puppets or pantomime**. Along with offering popular entertainment, they have long served Indian society as traditional means of inter-village communication, culture transfer, and improved understanding.

In India, theatre has a long and distinguished history. The origins of Indian theatre may be traced back to the *Vedas*, according to both indigenous tradition and contemporary study. Ancient writings such as the *Atharvaveda*, *Rigveda,* and the epics *Ramayana* and *Mahabharata* provided inspiration for playwrights in early Indian theatre. Later on, a fifth Veda dealing with a religiously proper style of theatre was introduced, and it was called *'Bharata's Natyashastra.'* This work, which was originally written in Sanskrit, is notable for its precise instructions on how to execute theatre. Drama is an art form with a long history in India, but Bharata gave an analytical evaluation and grammatical analysis of it in *Natyashastr*a. Music and dance have been recognised as important elements of theatre in this literature. *Patanjali's Mahabhasya*, written in the second century B.C., addresses to numerous components of play, including the actors, music, stage, and *rasa* in *Kamsavadha* and *Balibandha* performances. Drama was used to communicate the ideas of their respective religions during the Buddha's and Mahavira's times. To preach and educate the public, short skits and lengthy plays were performed. The popularity of drama was also boosted by music and dance. Dramas developed to reflect tragedies, comedies, and the complexities of urban life. Alongside it, folk theatre forms like *jatra, nautanki, khyal*, and *naach* emerged. Up to the tenth century, Sanskrit was the language of learning in the ancient world. As a result, plays were usually performed in this language. Characters from the lower classes and women, on the other hand, were forced to speak Prakrit. *Vatsyayan's Kamasutra, Kautilya's Arthashastra,* and *Kalidasa's Abhijnan Shakuntalam* were all important plays at the period and were written in Sanskrit. *Bhasa,* who penned thirteen plays, was another well-known dramatist. Women's theatrical troupes are mentioned in the Ramayana, while musicians, dancers, and dramatic acts are mentioned in *Kautilya's Arthshastra*. By the ninth century AD, Prakrit plays had become popular. The writing of *Jayadeva's Gita-Govinda* in the 13th century was the most significant literary event, influencing not just dance and theatre but also painting. It had a huge effect on dance and theatrical forms all throughout India, spanning Manipur and Assam in the east to Gujarat in the west, to Tamil Nadu and Kerala in the South and from Mathura to Vrindavan in the north. There are many manuscripts that deal with the *Gita-Govinda* as a source of dance or theatre content, and this literature has served as the foundational literary text for many regional dramatic traditions. During this time, the growth of *Vaisnavism* accelerated the development of many types of dances, drama, and music. The *Ramayana, Mahabharata, and Kalidasa's, Bana Bhatta's,* and *Bhasa's* plays are evidence of combining all three art forms: music, dance, and theatre. *Kalidas, Bhavabuti,* and *Bhrata* were among India's bards. Shakuntala by *Kalidasa,* translated by Sir William Jones, was the first famous play for Europeans. The play, as a product of the people and as a result of an unconscious evolutionary process driven by the creative force of the people, depicted various social movements in their real colours.

Although the mediaeval period was rich in music and dancing, theatre did not receive much attention. Wajid Ali Shah, a major patron of the arts, was also a major supporter of theatre who encouraged and supported artists to participate in theatre. Folk theatre using local dialects was more prevalent in the southern region. The arrival of the British in the nation altered the social landscape. In the eighteenth century, an Englishman established a theatre in Calcutta. Horasim Lebedev, a Russian, built a Bengali theatre in India, which marked the birth of modern Indian theatre. Indian drama was influenced by English play, particularly Shakespeare's. Indians with higher education-built stages that were different from the conventional open-air theatre. Rolling curtains and scene changes were now available on the stages. A Bombay-based Parsi enterprise demonstrated that theatre might be utilised for commercial goals. The adaptation of traditional forms to classical ones was another factor that affected the performing arts.

In the context of Indian drama, two types developed- the **classic drama,** which had complexity of theme and delicate nuances of dramatic features and **folk theatre**, which was spontaneous in nature. The classical theatre has a more than 2000-year history. The majority of classical theatre was performed on high platforms in temples, courtyards, and palaces. The subjects were mostly drawn from folk tales, epics, and religious sources. It was a multi-faceted production that included dance, acting, and music. **Folk theatre** utilised local dialect, and as a result, many different styles of folk theatre arose in different regions. A folk drama's existence is defined by its informal presenting style, simplicity, and lack of technicality dullness. Some of the props utilised in folk theatre included the *dhol, kartal, manjira, and khanjira*. The audience should have a sense of oneness with the artist and be aware of his feelings and objectives. If these elements are lost, the entire drama will be lost. In India, traditional folk play has deep roots in society due to its strong adherence to tradition. The vibrant array of Indian folk culture is best expressed via its distinctive art form of folk theatre, which reaches out to a wide range of audiences. The following characteristics define Indian folk-art theatre:

- A *Vidushak* (comedian), a *Sutradhar* (narrator), and an introductory prayer song are all included.
- Music, dancing, and make-up, as well as colorful masks and temporary stages.

- An understanding of the local accent, attire, humor, and attitude.
- The topics might be mythical or socio-political in nature.

Folk theatre has been deployed to communicate dramatic messages about social, political, and cultural concerns to raise public awareness. In India, several types of folk theatre are significant because they represent a long-established method of communicating ideas for the country's overall economic, social, and cultural development. Traditional theatrical performances occasionally incorporate pantomime or puppetry, which often feature singing, acting, dancing, and music along with narration, conversation, or recitation. But these arts may also play significant cultural and societal functions, such as songs sung while doing agricultural work or music used in rituals. They are capable of more than only "performances" for an audience. Puppetry is a popular kind of folk theatre in India, especially in the states of Andhra Pradesh, Rajasthan, Orissa, Karnataka and Kerala. Tourists may watch daily puppet plays at the Bharat Kala Museum in Udaipur, Rajasthan. Drama and the arts, which are collectively or often referred as the performing arts, also have another component. People prefer folk dramas because of their communicability and the rapport between the audience and the performer, not merely because of their production qualities. *Jatra* from West Bengal, which originated from *Sri Chaitanya's Bhakti* Movement, *Naqal* from Punjab, *Ramleela* from all over Northern India during the *Dussehra* festival, *Kalaripayattu* – a martial dance-drama and *Theyyam* from Kerala, *Terukkuttu* – a Tamil Street theatre, *Yakshagana* from Karnataka, *Bhavai* and *Akhyana* from Gujarat, *Bhand Pather* from Kashmir are popular kind of folk theatre in India.

Since India's independence, the theatre has seen a number of changes. English and a number of tribal languages are among the 24 major languages used today for theatrical performances. Even if Indian theatre is still relatively specialised, it has endless variations infused with unique qualities, which continues to draw audiences despite the enormous popularity of its competitors (*Creative arts in India,* 2016). In recent years, emerging nations like India have begun to appreciate this. The theatre and arts play a crucial part in the educational process by encouraging creativity, intelligent learning, critical thinking, and logical reasoning in learners. Students find it simple to recall and comprehend when asked to recreate a historical incident in a controlled environment rather than having to memorise several names and dates from History. To encourage effective learning, drama and the arts have been incorporated into the curricula at numerous institutions across the world. Students may learn public speaking, interpersonal communication, and group dynamics through puppetry or role-playing, and this technique also encourages their natural curiosity. In the educational process, institutions may employ varying degrees of drama depending on the methods they choose and the specific objectives they aim to fulfill. It should be mandated for all relevant departments at universities all over the nation to include performances in rural regions in their course curricula. A "Role Play" is a popular type of drama used in the process of delivering education. In a role play, a group of students act out a historical event, a scene from a play, or a scene from a movie. The pupils are assigned the parts of the event's characters. They gain knowledge of behavioural psychology, which they use to form critical opinions, in addition to understanding the characters' mentalities. The utilisation of costumes and settings allows the pupils to get fully immersed in the scenario and grasp its meaning. This practise helps children become better thinkers and storytellers and gives them the self-assurance they need to interact with others in healthy ways. This endeavour ends up serving as the foundation of the careers of aspiring filmmakers and playwrights. In addition to role play, there are co-curricular activities available to keep students interested and improve their learning opportunities.

Theatre may appear to have lost its position in people's thoughts with the advent of all modern kinds of entertainment, such as the Internet, particularly social media, and online gaming, yet the genre has been continuously developing and evolving all these years, if perhaps less obviously. In India, puppetry has long served as both a source of amusement and a way to spread religious and cultural ideas. Numerous puppetry traditions were in danger of extinction during the post-colonial period due to India's rapid modernization wave. Several public and private initiatives helped rescue these traditions, but many are still battling to exist in the digital age. The local organisations and the government are required to support the artists and promote this form of expression. The idea of street theatre has been demonstrated to be quite successful.

Indian folk theatre is a rich cultural legacy and a traditional mode of communication. It is one of the most potent representations of modern India and the rest of the globe and a possible channel for disseminating information on economic, social, and cultural development, all of which contribute to total national development. From this point on, it is the responsibility of policy makers, communication researchers, the participants, and the government, the People to uphold the traditions of folk theatre. The value of theatre has increased among the general public as a result of the rise in the number of prestigious theatrical awards and festivals in recent years. This is crucial, especially in light of the decreasing amount of significant artistic coverage in the media. Some production firms have also taken the responsibility of making theatre profitable and economically sustainable. Organizing workshops, seminars, fairs, and festivals, many socio-cultural organisations are now playing a significant role in the revival, spread, and appreciation of Indian folk drama, thereby boosting India's cultural legacy and tourist possibilities on the world map. Currently, there are several experiments being performed in the theatre world Musical theatre, Stage theatre, radio theatre, short skits, *Nukkar* or street plays, one-act plays, Mono drama (one man show), and other sorts of dramas are now developing. The content and thematic elements of dance and theatre must be examined in creative writing. Street theatre performances that educate the rural populace about social problems should be encouraged and promoted as part of the National Service Scheme (NSS) at all institutions. It is obvious that the theatre is under a serious threat from a variety of different media. In the current environment, new creative programmes that make use of both theatrical and new media applications must be developed. The puppetry programme and Panchatantra that is broadcast on ETV is a good demonstration of such a derivative. The merging of folk theatre forms with mass media for faster information transmission was proposed at several national and international conferences on the role of folk theatre and development because it inspired the rural audience. Numerous suggestions are offered for this aim. For example, folk artists and craftsmen should receive more awards to show their appreciation and support in maintaining their original forms. Padma Shri, Padma Bhushan, Kalidas Samman, Lalit Kala Academy Award, etc. are some of the awards for appreciation of artists. The establishment of national-level organisations for the use of folk media in communication programmes should be supported with resources. Women's organizations, youth, rural cooperatives, and other village-level organisations should receive special assistance through the development of special assistance programs.

Table 4: State Wise List of Indian Theatre

S. No.	State	Theatre
1.	Andhra Pradesh	Veedhi Natakam, Burrakatha/Harikatha, Bham kalapam, Yakshagaana, Pagati Veshaalu etc.
2.	Arunachal Pradesh	Ka Fifai etc.
3.	Assam	Ankia Naat (Bhaona), Oja-Pali etc.
4.	Bihar	Bideshia etc.
5.	Chattisgarh	Nachya, Sonha Bihan, Lorik Chandas, Kari, Hareli, Gammatiha, Rahas etc.
6.	Goa	Dashavatar, Tiatr, Zagor etc.
7.	Gujarat	Bhavai, Akhyana etc.
8.	Haryana	Swang etc.
9.	Himachal Pradesh,	Kariyala, Banthra, Bhagtu, Jhanki, Chandroli etc.
10.	Karnataka	Yakshagaana, Burrakatha/Harikatha, Krishna Parijatha, Kamsale, Viragase etc.
11.	Kerala	Mudiyettu, Koodiyaatam, Krishnattam, Theyyam, Porattu Natakam, Chavittunatakam, Sanghakali etc.
12.	Madhya Pradesh	Maach, Ramleela, Chahur, Kathi, Nautanki, Karmas, Rai Swang etc.
13.	Maharashtra	Tamasha, Kalsutri Bahulya, Lalit etc.
14.	Manipur	Shumang Leela etc.
15.	Rajasthan	Khyal, Nautanki, Bhavai, Swang, Dhola Maru, Tamasha, Gavari etc.
16.	Uttarakhand	Ramman etc.
17.	Jammu & Kashmir	Bhand Pather etc.
18.	Uttar Pradesh	Rasleela, Nautanki, Swang, Ramlila etc.
19.	Punjab	Nautanki, Naqal etc.
20.	West Bengal	Jatra, Gambhira etc.
21.	Tamilnadu	Therukoothu, Kuruvanji, Burrakatha/Harikatha etc.
22.	Orissa	Suanga, Dhanu Yatra, Chadheya Nata, Prahlad Natak, Kundhei Nata, Bharat Lila etc.

SOME IMPORTANT PERFORMING ARTS OF INDIA

Qawwali

For millennia, qawwali and Sufi music have been woven into the fabric of Asian culture. It is a collection of compositions written by Sufi saints and it is part of a tradition that is associated with Islamic mysticism. Sufism promotes global unity via music and love (poetry). It consists of a lead male singer reciting philosophical writings in various languages and a small chorus of background singers, accompanied by handclapping and musical instruments.

The music known as qawwali can be dated back to the eighth century during what is currently referred to as Iran and Afghanistan. The traditional form of qawwali begins with an invocation spoken in *Farsi,* then moves on to Punjabi or Urdu, and then moves further eastwards by singing in Hindi and/or *Purbi*. For an audience that does not understand the qawwali's lyrics, rhythm is the underlying framework through which the voice's variation and pitch create a spiritual experience (Bhattacharjee & Alam, 2012). In South Asia, qawwalis are usually carried out by 11 people; historically, this number was odd, although it has changed over time. The singers are accompanied by a variety of musical instruments, including the harmonium, *sarangi, sitar, tabla, and dholak*. The song begins with *Hamd* (praise of Allah), moves on to *Qual* (the Prophet's sayings), *Naat* (praise of the Prophet), *manqabat* (praise of the Saints), and concludes with *Rang* (praise of the Chishti lineage). Hand clapping (*tali*) and percussion instruments, such as a pair of drums (table) or two-sided drums (*dholak and pakhwaz*), have always been the conventional accompaniments of folk music throughout the Indian subcontinent. When performing qawwali a drum with cymbals, and small hand cymbals (*kanjira*) are frequently utilised as well. The lead singer often plays a *harmonium* in the qawwali.

The traditional location for a qawwali is a saint's shrine or a Sufi order's gathering venue. Thursday is the typical day for performances to take place at a shrine. The yearly festival *Urs* (the transfer of a spiritual leader from their limited body to eternity) of a shrine is typically where the most important performances occur. A number of qawwals perform or sing in praise of the pir whom *Urs* is being honoured. It is typically a sincere religious performance devoid of any technical assistance or theatrics. Even if the crowd is big, no microphones are utilised, and the *qawwal's* loud voice carries throughout the courtyard. According to tradition, the *mohri*, a master singer, sits in the middle, directly facing the *dargah*, as if speaking to the *pir.* The chorus normally forms two rows on either side of the *mohri*, with the best singers in the front. The *mohri* is accompanied by two vocalists on either side, who use harmoniums, *daflis, and manjiras* (*avazia*). Another good singer often sits to the left of the avazia. This singer assists the lead singer and is proficient in musical theory. There are many Qawwalis that only speak about love on a spiritual level encompasses a variety of poetic forms, such as *naat, hamd, manqabat, Darood pak, and qasida.* Additionally, lyrics from or for songs are used in modern Qawwali.

The tradition has been maintained by oral transmission of knowledge and singing technique from generation to generation. The poetry and rhythm combine to create a dynamic performance. It is a reflection of the community's aesthetic and creative objectives and integrates the religious, mythical, and celebratory parts of the community into one whole. The context of qawwali has shifted to the point where contemporary fusion music is being experimented with. For instance, one can see this musical blending of qawwali and Western styles in Coke Studio Pakistan's productions. Qawwals like Farid Ayaz, Abida Parveen, and Rahat Fateh Ali Khan have provided soulful performances portraying qawwali in an entirely new avatar while keeping the *majaz* of qawwali (Singha, 2018).

The clapping is one distinctive aspect of a qawwali performance. The qawwals believe that the human body is another instrument through which the rhythm can be conveyed. Qawwali's soothing sounds can assist those with mental health issues get better and put their minds at ease. According to the study, many people frequently go to shrines in honour of the saints they admire because they feel closely connected to them. Thursdays and Fridays typically see a higher-than-average number of visitors. Qawwali serves as a diversion from monotonous, laborious, and routine tasks. Many listeners believe that enjoying Qawwali gives them satisfaction. The listener is emotionally and psychologically affected by qawwali (Alam & Khalid, 2021).

Kathakali

Kathakali is the name of the most well-known dance theatre from Kerala in southern India. Literally, "Kathakali" means "Story-Play." In contrast to the earlier forms of dance theatre to which it is related, it is now often performed in theatres and at special events as entertainment and is no longer limited to temples, palaces, and religious festivals. According to Philip Zarrilly, "Kathakali is a vigorous, masculine, dynamic dance-drama constantly evolving, changing and adapting in complex and fascinating ways as the world around it changes." It is a synthesis of ritual/folk, classical, and martial traditions, with the support of the leading landowners and rulers of Kerala. The best way to define Kathakali performances of the dramatized stories is as dance-dramas, which combine dance, acting, and music into one cohesive whole. It could be categorized as a type of complete theatre, like many other Indian and Asian performing arts genres. A unique confluence of performance genres—all Kerala adaptations of the classical, folk, and ceremonial performance traditions—and historical events led to the development of the Kathakali dance-drama in the 17th century. But the addition of another element—the martial art tradition of Kerala, *Kalarippayatt* had a greater impact on Kathakali's shape, spirit, and skills in its early years. The adaption of Kutiyattam's intricate gestural code (*mudras*) used to perform Kathakali texts and the focus placed on facial and eye motion to convey the proper sentiments (rasa) to the audience are both examples of Kathakali's classical influence. Additionally, a lot of the basic makeup and parts of the costumes used in Kathakali are adaptations of Kutiyattam types and styles. The ancient martial art of Kerala known as Kalarippayatt is a second significant source of Kathakli technique, substance, and aesthetics.

In Kathakali the dancer-actor portrays mythical figures, mostly from the Mahabharata, an ancient Indian epic. These tales were transformed into scripts for performance, or *attakathas*, in the Kathakali language. The text used for this is typically a Sanskritized version of Malayalam. Two singers recite the story *shlokas/dandakas* and then sing the dialogue ***padams*** while being accompanied by two percussionists, a *chenda* player, and a *maddalam* player. Specific melody scores or appropriate ragas are chosen to promote the bhava, or "emotional state," that is suited for each discourse or *padam*. These *padams* are performed by the dancer-actors employing hand gestures. In this way the play's entire storyline is revealed. Proper Kathakali is seen as combining five components of fine art:

- *Natyam* (Acting), the art of expressing emotion through facial expressions.
- *Nrithyam,* the art of expressing meaning and emotion using hand gestures, or "mudras."
- *Nritham* (dance), which incorporates rhythmic hand, leg, and body motions.
- *Sangeetham* (Music): a song with vocal *(Geetha)* and musical accompaniment *(Vadyam).*
- *Chutti*: Makeup or painting.

A Kathakali performance is a significant social gathering. They typically begin at sunset and last all night. It starts with the *kelikottu,* which summons the audience to attention, and is followed by the *todayam.* It is a devotional song in which one or two characters ask the gods for their favours. When cymbals and drums are played for a while in the courtyard during the evening performance, it is called a *kelikottu.* The next piece is a pure *nritta* composition called the *purappadu.* Then, the drummers and musicians hold the stage while entertaining the audience with demonstrations of their *melappada* talents. All characters other than the *pacha or minukku* (females), make their stage debuts in *Tiranokku* (peering over the curtain). Kerala's traditional sopana sangeet is included into kathakali music. Each actor delivers the lines of dialogue for his or her role using his or her hands, having been taught over time by becoming an expert in a sophisticated vocabulary of more than 500 hand gestures (mudras). According to its medium or method, the Hindu theorists have identified four elements or parts of Abhinayam as linked to;

(1) *Angikam* (body)—proper use of creative gestures, actor bearing, stride, and movement of features and limbs.

(2) *Vacikam* (speech) - Proper theatrical delivery of the text with appropriate pronunciation, voice modulation, accent, and rhythm (prose, poetry, and songs).

(3) *Satvikam* (mind) Representation of some of the fundamental psychiatric states through immobility, sweating, voice changes, etc.

(4) *Aharyam* (external): Stage decorations, costumes, and props. Both dance and music should be considered as part of Angikam in its broadest definition.

The main style of Kathakali dance is interpretive. No other dance form utilizes the body as totally as Kathakali does. Every bodily part is covered in the technical details, including the facial muscles, fingers, eyes, hands, and wrists. The muscles of the face are crucial. The motions of the brows, eyes, and lower eyelids as described in the *Natya Shastra* are not as extensively used in other dance genres.

Extensive makeup and opulent clothes are characteristic of Kathakali. The elaborate costumes worn in Kathakali are the most recognisable representation of Kerala. There are many different styles of costumes. There are four characters: *Thatti, Kathi* (the villain), *Minukku* (females), and *Sathwika* (the protagonist). These fundamental divisions are further split in a manner that Malayali (Keralite) audiences are well familiar with. The artist's face has been painted over to give the impression that a mask is being worn. It is done to make the eyebrows, eyelashes, and lips stand out. Many characters—including a god or a demon, a lady or a Brahman—are portrayed using about 60 distinct types of cosmetics and attire. The distinctive makeup and attire of each character make them readily recognizable. The makeup is quite complex, it is so elaborate that it appears more like a mask than traditional makeup. The majority of the characters' facial makeup requires 3-5 hours. All the makeup components are readily available in the region. Vermilion (a red earth such as cinnabar) is employed to create the red color, whereas rice flour is utilized to produce the white. Soot is used to make the black. The colours serve as more than just decoration; they can also be used to depict characters. For example, the colour red on the feet is utilized to represent evil character and evil intent. The "*chutty*" (white paper mask) used as border on the face gives the features new shapes. Similar to how Greek tragedians traditionally wore thick-soled shoes, it is placed to the cheeks to enlarge the face and give the character more presence. It is made of paper and rice paste mixed with lime. According to the character being depicted, the *chutty* will take a different shape.

Although there are some similarities between Kathakali music and the greater body of South Indian classical music (Carnatic sangeet), the instrumentation is noticeably different. The *Maddalam, Chenda, Ilathalam, Chengila, Idakka,* and *Shankhu* typically make up the orchestra, which is also employed in various traditional performing arts of Kerala. *Ilakiattam* is the section of the performance where the characters can showcase their skill in *abhinaya*. A full percussion orchestra that includes three different types of drums, two different kinds of cymbals, and the conch shell is used to accompany the vocalist and dancers. The dancers spend the majority of the performance behaving strictly in accordance with the words *(chodiattam)* of the *padams* sung by the accompanying musicians.

There is not much to the kathakali stage. Since the actors are able to convey every detail using facial expressions and mudras, no scenery is necessary. A big bell-metal lamp with two cotton wicks floating in coconut oil is set up in front of the stage, which is typically an open area of ground or the forecourt of a Hindu temple. It casts a mellow and captivating light. This is ideal, however nowadays performances are frequently held in venues with footlights, microphones, and other modern stage impediments. However, because of the lamp's religious significance, which is always in front of the stage, all actions are directed toward it.

Kerala's traditional dance, kathakali, requires extensive years of training. Attakkatha is the name of the language used in Kathakali songs. Like the majority of other Indian traditional dance styles, Kathakali draws inspiration from Sage Bharata's Natya Shastra, a lengthy treatise on dance. However, Hasthalakshana Deepika, another classical literature, serves as the basis for Kathakali's hand movements.

At the start of the 20th century, Kathakali was endangered and close to going extinct. At Cheruthuruthy in Thrissur, the eminent poet Vallaththol Narayana Menon and Manakkulam Mukunda Raja took the initiative to build Kerala Kalamandalam, a centre of excellence for ancient art forms. Since then, Kerala Kalamandalam has worked to bring this magnificent art form back. Hindu mythology and Indian epics are frequent sources of inspiration for Kathakali stories. Some of the important authors who contributed to Attakkatha, the text for Kathakali, include Kottayaththu Thampuraan, Unnayi Warrier, Irayimman Thampi, Vayskara Moos, etc. Almost all overseas tourists to Kerala desire to attend a Kathakali performance. Additionally, there has been an increase in interest in Kathakali among Western dancers and actors as well as Western academics studying cultural performance, not simply among casual tourists. The national Kathakali training centre, Kerala Kalamandalam, and other institutes teach makeup and costume crafts for kathakalis, but artisan families pass down their own ancient carving techniques.

Kuchipudi

Kuchipudi is one of the eight Indian classical dance forms. When compared to the other classical dance forms, it incorporates singing. The Kuchipudi dance style has evolved over the course of the 20th century from its rural, temple-centered, dance-drama origins in Andhra Pradesh to one of the most popular and significant classical dance styles in India. The village Kuchipudi, where the male Brahmin Kuchipudi practitioners lived, is where Kuchipudi got its name. It was only practiced in the Andhra region (Kuchipudi) before the 1920s and was a dance-drama genre. It had become a systematized form throughout the years, with a manner of presentation that was structured and a method that was based on the dance treatises *Natyasastra* and *Abhinaya Darpanam*.

Dance-drama has a very long history in Andhra Pradesh and was well known by the term *Yakshagaana*. Siddhendra Yogi, a gifted poet, and visionary who belonged to the Vaishnava sect and had the ability to give some of his visions solid form created the Kuchipudi style of Yakshagaana in the 17th century. Siddhendra Yogi is said to have had a dream in which Lord Krishna ordered him to compose a dance drama based on the myth of the delivery of the *paarijaata* (night-jasmine) flower to Sathyabhaama, Krishna's most adored queen. As a result, he is said to have set out on a mission to find dancers, and in Kuchipudi village, every Brahmin family was required to train one of their sons in dance-drama that featured both male and female roles. In 1675 A.D., the then Nawab of Golconda, Abdul Hasan Tana shah, granted the village Kuchipudi as an Agrahaarama to Brahmin families who practised this profession (Centre for Cultural Resources and Training, 2020). It evolved as a form of religious expression associated with spirituality and temples. Every Kuchipudi boy born in the village is supposed to be introduced to dancing along with his *upanayana* in his fifth year and dance at least once in front of Lord Ramalingeswara and Goddess Bala Tripura Sundari. The Kuchipudi youth are thought to have learned this art form as a result of guru Siddendra yogi's tireless efforts and dedication. From that point on, this particular art form developed into a family profession and a source of income for their daily needs.

The first historical evidence regarding Kuchipudi comes from Mackenzie's "Machupalli Kaifiyat" according to which Kuchipudi Bhagavathulu were permitted to perform a *"Keertana*" in the royal court of King Vira Narasimha Rayalu (1505-1509). Thus, the earliest mention of Kuchipudi Bhagavathulu dates back to 1505, to the reign of Vira Narasimha Rayalu; by that time, they are said to be well-known artists they must be practicing their art for at least fifty years, which puts the date of the origin of Kuchipudi art to 1450 A.D.12. The second available mention of the existence and popularity of the Bhagavathulu was when the Golkonda Sultan, Abul Hasan Tana Shah (1672-1685), had seen a performance of the Bhagavathulu around 1678 and was so pleased with it that they gifted the village, which is now the prominent Kuchipudi (Basa & Bijina, 2021).

The Kuchipudi dance dramas are all-night outdoor performances. The audience is seated on the ground with a makeshift stage set up. In the past, it was traditional to perform in a little street next to the Ramalingeshwara Temple. However, performances are increasingly held in larger venues. Before the dance-drama proper starts, several rites and rituals are performed. There is a recitation of a prayer to the goddess Amba. Incense is burned before the dance performance and holy water is sprinkled. After that, to drive away bad powers, the Indra flagstaff is brought into the stage, carried around it, and placed up there. As with various other classical dance forms a Kuchipudi presentation starts with an evocative song. Prior to this, only *Ganesha Vandana* was invoked. Now, other deities are also praised. *Nritta,* or non-narrative and abstract dancing, follows it. The next song is a story named

"*Shabdam.*" A *natyanumber* called *Kalaapam* follows the *Shabdam*. The classic dance drama *Bhaamaakalaapam's* arrival of *Satyabhama* is often performed by Kuchipudi dancers. A pure *nritya abhinaya* number based on literary-cum musical forms like *shlokam, padam, jaavli,* etc. follows in the sequence. Each word uttered in this song is defined in space by dancing *drishya-kavita* (visual poetry). Usually, *tarangam* is used to end a Kuchipudi recital. With this song, portions of *Krishna-leela-tarangini* are sung. The dancer in this often stands on a brass plate while locking their feet in the *shakatavadanam paada* position and moves the plate rhythmically and elegantly. The dance is accompanied by a wonderfully rhythmic piece of music that belongs to the classical school of Carnatic music. In addition to the vocalist, the ensemble also includes an *mridangam* player for percussion music, a violinist or veena player, or both, for melodic instrumental accompaniment, and a cymbal player who typically leads the orchestra and chants the *sollukattus* (mnemonic rhythm syllable). The most frequent raga in Kuchipudi dance-dramas is *Mohana*, and the music is traditional Carnatic. The harmonium, violin, flute, *tutti, mridangam*, and other musical instruments are employed as accompaniment.

To make ornaments with a gold-colored coating, a certain light wood is needed. For princely figures, chest and shoulder jewels are worn. The attire is regal, including a long coat, scarves, a dhoti, and other accessories. The women dress in *Kanjivaram* sarees and accessorize with ankle bells, and jewelry for the waist, nose, hands, and head. The *Sutradhara* is dressed with a *pugree and rudraksha* bead necklaces. Since mythology serves as the source for the majority of the stories, care has been made to create clothes that are fitting for both heavenly and human figures.

It is interesting that, in accordance with the social norm of the time, ladies from elite castes were not permitted to participate in the dances; as a result, men played the roles of women. Kuchipudi underwent a number of changes over time. It began as a male tradition, then included female customs, and is now performed by both genders. By the middle of the 20th century, Kuchipudi had fully developed into its own distinct classical solo dance form. Due to this, Kuchipudi now comes in two variations: the classic musical dance-drama and the solo dance. A presenting sequence for the solo recital has been largely established since the latter half of the fourth decade of this century. Kuchipudi gained popularity as one of India's classical dance styles in the late 1950s, and the solo format developed. Legendary Kuchipudi performer Lakshminarayan Shastry (1886–1956) was responsible for numerous innovations, such as solo dancing and the instruction of female dancers in this dance form. Practises such as dancing on the rim of a metal plate and while carrying a pitcher filled with water on the head emerged to demonstrate the dancers' proficiency in their feet as well as their control and balance over their bodies.

Many Kuchipudi artists who were born and raised in Kuchipudi village with a strong cultural background immigrated to other cities and nations, giving the art a larger audience. In turn, their learners are developing more performers. Together, they have helped to popularise Kuchipudi throughout India and the rest of the world. After making several sacrifices for their families and themselves, Kuchipudi legends moved, benefiting Melattur (Kerala) at first and the current movie industry much later. During the first seminar held by the Andhra Pradesh Sangeet Natak Academy on February 28, 1959, Kuchipudi dance was acknowledged as one of the traditional dance styles of India. The base and range of performers grew with the introduction of female dancers to Kuchipudi, which had for centuries exclusively permitted males. The popularity of solo performances and the desire of female dancers to master the dance style helped Kuchipudi spread in many different directions (Seth, 2014). According to Sridhar (2014)-

> avenues offered by art centres like Sangeet Natak Akademi, and measures suggested by UNESCO's Intangible Cultural Heritage List offer great scope for the codification of the art form for the benefit of humanity at large. Scope for further studies related to the genealogy of the traditional families, social anthropology of the area, the study of old manuscripts, documentary films on various aspects, and translation of books into international languages (English, Spanish and Chinese) to cater to international audience/universities/students, study on the village history, etc. could translate to opportunities for NGOs to maintain the heritage and cultural awareness of the region and art form.

Kutiyattam

"Kutiyattam is often described as the oldest continuously performed theatre in the world, with the earliest records documenting the form dated to the tenth century CE. While some have speculated that it began as a secular performance in royal courts, it was definitively incorporated into Kerala's caste-based temple complex in the thirteenth or fourteenth century, where it remained until 1949" (Lowthorp, 2015). Women and men of the *Nambiar*, *Chakyar*, and *Nangiar* castes performed it at the temple as a *kulathozhi*l, or hereditary occupation, in exchange for land, food, and clothing.

Kuti and attam are combined to form the word kutiyattam, with the letter 'y' connecting the two vowels sounds. Attam is a synonym for dancing, and thus acting, whereas Kuti means "tied together." Kutiyattam, then, literally translates to "acting together" or "dancing together." In many various contexts, Kutiyattam refers to acting together, one of which is that it is a type of theatre in which men and women perform together on stage. *Nangyarkoottu*, a related type of kutiyattam, is only practiced by females. Similar to kutiyattam, *chakyarkoottu* is another related form that is only practiced by men. Kutiyattam, which translates to "mixed acting," is a fusion of Kerala's indigenous culture with Sanskrit tradition. Kutiyattam concentrates on the artistic elaboration and expansion of each moment. It is recognizable by its rich narrative representation through *mudra* (hand motions), stylized movements, intensely passionate facial expressions, and minimal discourse of recited Sanskrit. The representation of moods and emotions is called *sattvika*. The actor can create facial expressions that fit a specific mood by using subtle movements of the eyes, eyebrows, lips, and cheeks without using any hand motions. To become professional performers with accurate respiratory control and subtle muscle control shifts of the face and body, actors must go through ten to fifteen years of hard training. The skill of the actor is in completely describing a situation or experience. As a result, a single act could take days to perform and a whole show could run up to 40 days. Due to their religious nature, access to performances was once limited; however, the plays have gradually become more accessible to wider audiences. The Kutiyattam was firstly performed in public outside of temple grounds at Calicut, in 1960, for a limited group of listeners who had been invited by All India Radio. The art consists of three different elements:

- ***Purappad*:** In this section actors give the act's motivation and deliver poems while dancing as part of the *nritta.* The *Purappudu*, or preliminary movements, which are performed by the performer behind a curtain, come after the initial invocatory ceremonies on the first day. Without the audience witnessing any "acting," the first day's performance can conclude with these moves.
- ***Nirvahana*:** The actor then performs the *nirvanam*, in which he uses abhinaya to capture the atmosphere of the play's central character. The play's *nirvanam,* or retrospective, takes the audience back to the play's opening. It is a Kutiyattam-only custom in which the character introduces him by outlining his personal background, sometimes even touching on his past existence. It is up to the actor to decide which of the legends associated with his character to stress, giving him the freedom to develop the role to an extent rare in Indian drama. Introductions of the individuals and events from their life take up the first few days.
- ***Kutiyattam*:** The last is *kutiyattam* which is the play itself, and the conducting element of performance. The characters dress up, enter the stage, read the verses aloud, and then perform them. *Kutiyattam* can have as many characters as necessary to play on stage, in contrast to the previous two acts which are solo performances. On the final day, the entire play is presented, from start to finish. It is not necessary to perform the play exactly as it is written. Even if the play's text is regarded as "holy," the actor improvises and adds to it, strengthening the text's structure with improvised actual and fantasy associations. When an actor utilizes his eyes, face, and body to convey a variety of emotions, the performance is frequently "frozen."

Three interpretations are given to each stanza of the play. It is first uttered and performed extensively in abhinaya (dramatic form using stage conventions to express meaning). After then, it is sung slowly while each word's meaning is further explained. On the basis of essential phrases and concepts, there is then a lengthier, freer improvisation. Great Kudiyattam performers are able to offer the verses immediate significance for their listeners through the use of free Malayalam prose, which not only entertains but also prompts contemplation. In order to bridge the gap between the players and the audience, the *Vidushaka* translates the ancient Sanskrit text into modern Malayalam, explains occult portions, and provides amusing commentary. Because Sanskrit is no longer a spoken language, the Vidushaka's role is crucial in making Koodiyattam accessible to audiences who do not comprehend it.

Traditional Kutiyattam theatres, also known as Kuthampalams, are found inside Hindu temples. It is equivalent to the natyamandapa found in Sanskrit literature. The current Kuthampalam constructions are not much older than three hundred years, although the history of staging dates to much earlier times. More than a dozen such theatres are still present in various temples. The biggest theatre is found at the Vatakkunnatha temple in Trichur. The Kutiyattam was permitted to be performed in agrasha/halls if the temples lacked a Kuthampalam.

There is no standard music in Kutiyattam, but there are several ways to recite the poems or even prose portions. These ways vary depending on the character's kind, the circumstance being described, and the emotions being expressed. Technical names for these recitation techniques include *Indala, Tarkan*, and *Veladhooli*. Even though they have little in common with the ragas of Indian music, these are still referred to as ragas. However, there are specific guidelines for using these recitation ragas: Narration is done in *Antari, Veladhooli* is utilized for shouting and conveys fear and confusion, *Srikarnara* expresses unexpected excitement, *Tarkan* conveys fury, and *Veera Tarkan* conveys enthusiasm. For *hasya* (laughter) and *bibhatsa* (foul language) , use *Kaisika*; for the rainy season, use *Poranir;* and for the words of monkeys, use *Korakurinji*. The typical raga for the *Vidushaka* is *Indala*. The stage manuals contain a few linkages between ragas and talas. The *Vidushaka* in *Vachikabhinaya* would occasionally convey the meaning of even the uttered words' pure tones. Talas, or rhythmic patterns, are crucial to the Kutiyattam performance since music and recitation are both essential components. With the support of the *Kuzhitalarn* cymbals, the female musician *Nangyar* maintains the tala.

There are various musical instruments that are used for the Kutiyattam such as-

1. *Mizhavu*: The copper "*mizhavu*" drums have somewhat different diameters and range in height from 2-3 feet. Calfskin is securely wrapped around the mouth. On seats positioned close to the top of the drum stand, members of the *Nambiyar* community sit facing the audience. They play on them with their hands, one holding the tala while the other uses both palms and fingers to play the *vinyasas*. One *mizhavu* is sufficient for Koothu.
2. *Kuzhithalam:* The *Nangyar* (female musician), who also chants the words for the introductory *Nirvahana,* the *dhruva* melodies chanted at the time of the arrival and exit of characters, uses the *Kuzhithalam*, or a pair of bronze cymbals, to keep the tala.
3. *Kuzhal or Kurumkuzhal*: A double-reed pipe called a *kuzhal or kurumkuzhal* is used to play the *jatis,* propose the rhythm, identify the right tunes, or provide a melodic refrain in the background.
4. *Ldakka*: The standing drummer holds the *ldakka,* or "a tunable, double-faced, pressure drum," using a piece of fabric hanging from the left shoulder. The left-hand controls the tension strings, and the right-hand use a small stick to continue beating. In addition to being used for the *Panchavadya* style of the instrumental symphony, this delicate and sensitive drum is also performed in temples.
5. *Shankha*: When significant figures make their on-stage debuts, the auspicious *shankha* or conch shell is blown. Hinduism regards the **shankha** as a precious and important object. It is a symbol of holiness, good fortune, and the presence of the divine.

Aharya refers to clothing and cosmetics. This is similar to Kathakali but less complicated. The headpiece is also smaller, as is the *Chutti* (the lining made from rice flour paste), which is put around the cheek and chin. There are several forms of makeup utilized, including *Pacca, Pazhukkua, Kari, and Katti.* The generous wear the *Pazhukkua* makeup, which features a reddish-colored facial paint. The Katti makeup, which features a painted round ball at the tip of the nose, is worn by arrogant people like *Ravana.* Just before the concert, a rice-based mask is created and worn by the artists. The actors' eyes are painted red by rubbing a seed on them; when they close their eyes tightly while performing on stage, tears start to flow. A Kutiyattam dancer must go through a 3-hour long preparation process before performing.

The system that had kept Kutiyattam an elite, temple-based profession for almost a thousand years collapsed beneath the artists' feet throughout the twentieth century as a huge wave of change swept over Kerala and the developing Indian country. Following the resurgence in the early 20th century, Kutiyattam is currently experiencing a major financial issue, which is harming the industry. In response to this circumstance, the many organizations in charge of transmitting the tradition have teamed up to safeguard the survival of this Sanskrit theatre.

Kutiyattam received official recognition as a Masterpiece of the Oral and Intangible Heritage of Humanity from UNESCO in 2001. In 2008, Kutiyattam was added to the Representative List of the Intangible Cultural Heritage of Humanity in accordance with the 2003 UNESCO Convention, continuing to be supported by the government through Kutiyattam Kendra. To better safeguard and spread knowledge of important intangible cultural heritages worldwide, UNESCO developed its lists of Intangible Cultural Heritage. By establishing a list of the numerous oral and intangible assets of humanity around the world, the program aims to increase awareness of the importance of protecting intangible heritage. The more well-known art forms, such as Kathakali and Mohiniyattam, which are regarded as icons of Kerala culture, continue to dominate Kerala's arts media and larger performance arenas despite the increased media coverage and general interest in the art since UNESCO accreditation. The way many artists relate to their art has been greatly impacted by this increased social acceptance. The impact of UNESCO recognition that was most frequently mentioned by artists was their improved ability to support themselves as Kutiyattam performers as a result of an increase in institutions and money, which is indicative of a post-recognition rise of the institution. The art's rising institutionalization further incorporated it into the existing national frameworks of heritage and state sponsorship, with institutionalization serving as a means of making it visible to the state. Many artists obtained a stable, living wage for the first time in their lives after Kutiyattam Kendra was founded in 2007. The number of organizations getting Sangeet Natak Academy subsidies more than doubled, bringing a significant number of artists into the ranks of Kerala who earn what is regarded as "regular" wages. The artists and their lives have consequently been significantly impacted by this increase in funding. It has helped to raise young men artists' social prestige, increase social mobility, and improve their marriageability while also giving them peace of mind and the boosted confidence that comes with a consistent income.

Ramlila

Ramleela, or Ramlila is a theatrical folk performance that has its roots in north India. Ramlila is the combination of the terms "Ram" and "Lila." Ram is the name of the protagonist of the Ramayana, who is highly regarded in India as the God Vishnu's incarnation, who took the form of the Prince of Ayodhya and vanquished the demon king *Ravana*. In the context of the holy, the Sanskrit word "*lila*" refers to the recognition of the human world as the impulsive, joyful, and playful creation of God. Ramlila, often known as God Rama's play, is an interpretation of God's *lila* performed for human purposes. Ramlila is a religious work that combines dramatic and ritualistic aspects.

The Hindi-speaking region of north India has an annual outdoor performance of Ramlila, a cycle drama that lasts ten to thirty-two days. Its peak period is from September through October, around the *Dusshera* vacations. It is accessible to everyone, free, and filled with religious significance. The vast majority of Hindus in North India attend a Ramlila at least once in their lives, and many do so consistently year after year.

The Ramayana is believed to have been written in Sanskrit for the first time by Sage Valmiki between 700 and 500 BC. The Ramayana has been recited orally and in writing in almost 300 different ways. However, with the decline of Sanskrit dramas from the 14th to the 19th centuries, folk theatres began to perform in various regional languages. Ramlilas gained popularity in North India due to the Ramayana in Avadhi, also known as "Ramcharitramanas." (The Lake of Rama's deeds), written by Goswami Tulsidas in the 16th century (Mahabir & Chand, 2015). Although the exact origins of Ramlila are unclear, it is believed that Tulsidas himself may have envisioned his poetry as a performance in order to reach a bigger audience. According to tradition, a Tulsidas disciple choreographed a performance of the scene depicting Ram and Bharat's reunion after 14 years of Ram's banishment in the forest. The drama, which is presented in Nati Imli near Ramnagar, is still staged there each year and draws large crowds of viewers, including the monarch of Ramnagar. On successive evenings, grandiose night spectacles took the place of day performances.

Rama, the monarch of the 7000-year-old kingdom of Ayodhya in Northern India, is the main figure of the Ramayana. Ram is more respected as a moral example and a teacher of social and political ideals than any other popular Hindu deity. His most famous epithet is ***Maryada Purushottam***, the ideal representation of appropriate behaviour. He is the perfect husband and king; Sita is the perfect wife; his realm is the perfect nation; and his interactions with his brothers, parents, gurus, subjects, and devotees show the ideals of family and society. The culture is actively promoting these principles. Boys are encouraged to imitate Ram, while younger brothers look up to Lakshman. Girls are instructed to be like Sita. *Ramraj*, or the dominion of Ram, is the Hindu model of social and political perfection. For many Ramlila devotees, Ram stands for the moral pathway, or *dharma*, and Ravan for the perverse path, or *adharma*. Although spectators appreciate Ramlila's ancient message of truth triumphing over deception and its ritualistic function in society, for many individuals, the event's entertainment value is what draws them to the Ramlila grounds. Romance, pride, adventure, and complex characters abound in its narratives. It is a potent manifestation of people's beliefs.

In India, the epic Ramayana, or the narrative of Rama, has a long oral tradition dating back more than two millennia. The sacred drama, or lila, tells the story of Rama's magical birth, youth, marriage, exile, and wife Sita's abduction by the demon king of Lanka, Ravana. It also shows Rama's struggle to save Sita from Ravana, the killing of Ravana, and Rama's triumphant return to his throne in Ayodhya. As soon as Ramlila season begins, followers excitedly anticipate all the intriguing *lilas* or moments in Ram's life. The Manas serves as the foundation for many Ramlila performances in North India. The entire Manas text is narrated by a group of reciters known as Ramayanis, and each day's performance is a dramatization of the recited book. Fundamentally, Ramlila derives both its narrative and performative strength from the text's oral reservoir, and it is remarkable to witness the dynamic environment and group energy when the audience joins in on the epic's recitation while the performance is taking place. Perhaps this ritualized public reading practise is what sparked the creation of Ramlila as a performance. Ramlila's framework incorporates religious rituals, starting with the *arti* ritual, in which the *svarups* (divine embodiments) are worshipped live or on record on stage. This ritual was previously performed after the show but is now more often performed at the beginning.

Ramlila requires attractive music, poetry, dramatic acting, intensive training, and the coordination of many community members behind the scenes, just like so many other North Indian performing genres. For characters like *Ravana*, masks with ten linked heads are employed. Masks of the Ramlila are made of paper mache, metal, and fabric. These artists get their supplies (costumes, masks, makeup, props, and costume jewelry) from the same specialized stores that serve the vernacular theatre market. These businesses only exist and continue to be open because they provide costumes and other supplies to persons involved in Ramlila and other closely connected theatre and dance performances. The effigies used during Ramlila are gigantic, occasionally reaching a height of 50 feet. Largely, effigies are made of *Ravana*, his brother Kumbhkarna and Meghnad. On the final day of Dusshera, which signifies the conclusion of the yearly cycle of Ramlila, it is common practice throughout India to burn the effigies as a symbol of the triumph of virtue over evil. On designated "Ramlila grounds" with temporary or concrete platforms, some Ramlilas are performed. Ramlila stages may be incorporated into the façade of a building in metropolitan areas, opening to the exterior and forming a straightforward proscenium. Ramlila uses hand-painted, illustrative backdrops and vibrant curtains. Usually, musicians take a seat towards the bottom or on one side of the stage.

Even though it is regarded at Ramlila as *daan* (a religious gift), audience members frequently provide money and occasionally award talented performers with monetary rewards. They receive financial support from local consumers, and occasionally local volunteers also work on it. Rich and successful families have started funding private performances in recent years, and troupes (*mandalis*) have also popped up in major cities like Mumbai, Delhi, and Calcutta, increasing the art's appeal throughout India. In 2005, UNESCO designated Ramlila as a Masterpiece of the Oral and Intangible Heritage of Humanity. There is no admission fee, so audience members can come and go as they like while socializing with friends and family and having a fun night out. There are frequently whole fairs or at least a few food and tea stalls, which add to the joyful ambiance. At Ramlila, there are also vendors selling trinkets, particularly miniature bows and arrows and masks. Additionally, they have a significant social impact. In the age of mass media, new media, and global media, when individuals frequently feel emotionally distant and isolated, Ramlila gives them a sense of connection.

Today, amateur, and professional troupes are contracted by community associations to perform Ramlilas in cities and villages throughout North India. Ramlila continues to influence many people's imaginations today, despite the growth of mass media like television and film. During thrilling times, crowds of 10,000 to 15,000 can still be observed at select Ramlila locations. Ramlila, however, continues to evoke an emotional connection between people and their local towns and cultures in this media-saturated environment. When consumers witness these performances directly, they are convinced that it is truly crucial in today's "connected" world. In India, there are numerous renditions and adaptations of the performance, most of which are based on regional interpretations of the narrative and performance practices. This variety is possibly the most important syntactical element of the language used in this performance because performances in different places modify them to their regional variations and include local adaptations, devotional tunes, and performative techniques. Every region's Ramlila follows its own set of theatrical standards that help the story to develop day by day.

Bhand Pather

The majority of north Indian languages use the word "bhand," which comes from the Sanskrit word "bhaand" and means funny behaviour or imitation. Dramatic performance with a strong undertone of imitation and exaggeration is referred to as bhand. The combination of the two Sanskrit terms bhand and pather gives rise to the expression bhand pather. The word Bhand means "comedian" and the word pather means "patra," which means "actor." However, in Kashmiri, bhand means folk actor while pather means dramatic performance with more imitation and exaggeration. Bhands perform in groups and depict current political, economic, and social issues or the lives of some legends in a very humorous, straightforward manner.

The first evidence of Bhand Pather dates to the sixth century. Before the Muslim rule in Kashmir, Bhand Pather was performed in temples on religious holidays, but afterwards it was performed in shrines and khankas. By highlighting cultural similarities and elaborating on distinctions between Hinduism and Islam, Bhand Pather illustrates Kashmiriyat. When a natural disaster occurred, Bhands were asked to offer prayers for the local populace at the shrines of Sufi saints (Shaika & Mishra, 2020). It is a sort of outdoor street play that honours the life of *Rishis* (Hindu and Muslim Sufi sages) while primarily addressing social issues of which everyone can connect to. The Kashmiri Bhands lived by performing around villages and collecting food, money, and clothes from the locals. They were often invited to royal, affluent, and landlord weddings to perform for days, gaining social status. As Bhand Pather gained popularity, it was performed during social gatherings as well as religious and agricultural festivals, as well as the first snowfall of the season. Additionally, this Pather was typical of royal families, who would perform and dance to background music to appease the entire empire.

Surnai, Dhol, Nagara, and Thalij are the musical instruments played during this performance. *Saaz-e-Kashmir,* a musical instrument, is played by some Bhand Parties. The oboe-like *swarnai,* a tiny one-sided stick drum (*nagari*), and a *large dhol* are the three key instruments in Bhand music. Pather begins with the beating of the drum or *Nagara*. *Dhol* is played after the *Nagara* to make the melody more intense. The artists sing hymns and offer prayers for the audience's well-being when the musical prelude, known as *catusak*, comes to end. The introduction to the Pather is then presented in the form of a short conversation between the three lead characters, in which the story's central concepts are briefly hinted at. The *magun* (leader), *sutardhar* (commentator), *vidushak or maskhari* (jester), and *pariparsok or kurivol* (lasher) are the main actors. The *magun* directs the play and offers prayers for the populace; the *sutardhar* observes what is happening; the *maskhari* amuses the audience with ridiculous activities; and the *kurivol* punishes the jester if he loses control. Every pather possesses two highly valuable items: a bamboo stick and a whip. These items are utilised as an embellishment to provide dramatic imagery to the story in order to symbolise oppression in the culture. The majority of the acts are presented in Punjabi, Gujjari, Kashmiri, Dogri, Persian, and English. Other languages may also be employed. There are several Pather plays that need to be performed by Bhands. There are roughly ten different varieties of Pathers. While their fundamental structures are somewhat similar, each Pather deals with various themes. The earliest pather is thought to be Wattal Pather, and the most recent to be Angrez Pather. Some of the Pathers include:

- Dard Pather: The drama highlights the dictator Dards-Afghan kings' brutality toward Kashmiris. It also shows the monarchs' epicurean ideology, opulent lifestyle, and alcohol's effects.
- Gosaine Pather: The Pather concentrates on the religious faith of Kashmiris and ridicules those who use religion to deceive others.
- Pather Buhir/Bata: This Pather depicts the characteristics of the Pandit community. It depicts how the average person gets punished for no wrongdoing while the government celebrates the criminal using humour.
- Shikargah Pather: This is the sole Pather in which Bhands discuss ecological balance while wearing animal masks, and where themes like soil erosion, deforestation, environmental pollution, and wild animal conservation are addressed.
- Raaze Pather: Raaze, meaning King, talks about Afghan dominance, its subjugation of Kashmiris, and other cultures' negative impact on the Kashmiri community.
- Aarem Pather: The Pather discusses the way of life of the Kashmiri society's farmers. It also addresses forced labour and child marriage.

- Waatal Pather: This Pather focuses on themes such as polygamy, child marriage, breach of trust, abusive language, and promise-breaking while also portraying the way of life of the Waatal tribe.
- Bakarwal Pather: Illustrates the exploitation of the lower class Bakarwals by the merchants.
- Angrez Pather: Kashmiris' disdain of English and their affection for their native language is discussed in the Pather.

Bhand Pather is inherited from generation to generation. This theatre is a crucial component of both present and historical cultures. It can be an excellent means to unite people and affirm their cultural identities because it is a part of the universal heritage. However, this folk tradition has been lost somewhere in all these places, creating a significant cultural hole. The moment has come for us to acknowledge the greatness of Bhand Pather as a contribution to Kashmiri culture. Therefore, significant steps should be taken to bring back this folk culture. These Bhands should first and foremost be allowed to perform at national events that should be organised to get exposure across the country. Additionally, the international society needs to support these folk performers. There is a huge amount of potential for incorporating it into our cultural tourist industry. Tourists from different climates and countries are sick of fake life and are constantly yearning for something native, natural, and indigenous. To preserve and protect their identity and increase Pather's appeal to the younger generation, the artists of Pather should get frequent awards. They should receive financial assistance so they will not have to choose to work at different occupations to support themselves. Different institutions, such as Sangeet Natak Academy, State Cultural Academy, and Indian National Trust for Art and Cultural Heritage, national academy of Music, drama, and Dance must do everything in their power to popularise this legacy among the younger generation to reconnect Bhand Pather with the evolving cultural patterns of the Kashmiri people. Additionally, Bhand Pather ought to be incorporated into school curricula so that students can learn about their native folk art.

Puppetry

Puppetry is the most popular subgenre of theatre, in India.

Puppetry is a type of theatre or performance in which puppets are used. The term "puppet" originates from the Latin word pupa, which means a doll. The Tamil classic *Silappadikaaram*, which was composed in the first or second century B.C., has the oldest mention of puppetry. In traditional entertainment, puppetry has always had a prominent position. The Indian traditional puppet art, as seen in the *Orissi* puppets, was primarily intended to celebrate the accomplishments of our forefathers and all those notable individuals who had contributed to the advancement of human civilization. The puppets were crafted into a variety of fantastic and unusual characters. Indian puppetry places a strong emphasis on stylization and symbolism in order to make the puppet's emotional appeal potent and long-lasting. As a result, a puppet character has a greater influence on the audience than a human figure when they are performing. Their restrictions and weaknesses in terms of size, action, motions, and autonomy have their own science and are guided by principles based on the Indian traditional puppeteer's experience and research. Another feature that adds to the puppet's efficacy is its independent personality, which is unlike that of a human performer. A puppet character is built and designed specifically for a role, but a real actor merely has to be dressed and made up to portray that role. Themes for puppet theatre typically draw from epics and legends, just like traditional theatre. A puppeteer controls a moving doll as a puppet. Visual impressions are created by bodily movements; a puppet, for instance, can express thoughts and emotions by moving its head and hands. The puppeteer may also provide a voice for the puppet. Puppets are inanimate objects brought to life by the control of a puppeteer. Hand puppets can be directly controlled with one hand because to their open interiors. For instance, marionettes have strings and rod puppets can be controlled using sticks. India is the home of almost every kind of puppet. Throughout history, puppetry has played a significant role in traditional entertainment. The identities of the puppets from various regions in the country are distinct. They exhibit regional representational painting and sculpture styles. Throughout the nation, there are puppets with distinctive features.

As a very old and widespread traditional art and craft, puppetry can be found everywhere. Puppetry is a versatile form of traditional folk art that contributes to psychological therapies and serves a societal function as well. The significance of puppetry as a means of public communication is immense. If we look at the history of puppetry in India since Mohenjo-Daro, we will see that it was used in plays and fables, as well as in religious ceremonies around the world, such as in Egypt and Rome for the Osiris festivals, where women priests carried puppets on strings that depicted the dog-faced God Anubis with animated arms. Puppetry and puppets are also utilized negatively, such as in rural regions and in the past when voodoo and black magic were practiced. Additionally, puppetry has been utilized to encourage students with emotional and physical disabilities to grow in their mental and physical abilities. Puppetry is thus a highly potent medium for both education and enjoyment, and it offers huge prospects to those who choose to pursue it as a separate art form. Puppet is the oldest form of entertainment and is not the same as a human play. It has its own narrative structure, play production, and playwriting techniques. Puppetry may communicate with those who are illiterate or do not comprehend spoken language because it is largely a visual art. To help participants improve their communication abilities, special classes in drawing, creative writing, dance and mime, dialogue delivery, creative speech, and voice modulation are also organized. Without a real theatre stage or script, puppets can also be employed in educational settings. For instance, a teacher can ask students questions and have interactions with them using a puppet. A puppet can also be a useful tool for confirming children's comprehension when they respond to inquiries and take part in a conversation. Puppets are another instrument used by children and teenagers in the classroom. Students may design their own puppets, put on a puppet show, or just play with puppets at random (Kröger, 2019). Programs to raise awareness about protecting the natural and cultural environment have also been effective. These initiatives seek to increase pupils' awareness of the aesthetic value of shape, music, color, movement, and words. Making puppets and using them to communicate gives children an aesthetic high that contributes to their overall personality development. The creative efforts of numerous persons working together are required for the presentation of puppet programs. It is also a very effective mass communication tool that is frequently used in folk journalism. Being a versatile folk-art form, it serves as both entertainment and a social tool for raising awareness of various concerns by giving audiences useful information. Puppet shows are a very popular and effective method of public communication, both in urban and rural settings. Puppet shows are well-liked even in contemporary media of communication like television and movies.

Puppetry has a special place in people's hearts and minds because of its intimate and personal appeal, familiar format, and use of everyday dialects. Ironically, however, many academic institutions in India do not give puppetry, a common folk art, the credit it deserves in the field of performing arts. On the one hand, scholars agree that India is the source of puppetry, but on the other, when discussing performing arts, they downplay its significance by referring to puppetry as "child's play." Although North East Indian puppeteers and puppet researchers have been working to revive regional puppetry, the rest of the nation is largely unaware of this type of art (Sarma & Devi, 2013).

Puppetry is undoubtedly the most notable traditional media, and it requires support and experimentation. Puppet performances are now using elaborate music, shifting styles and settings, unique lighting effects, smoke screens, miraculous appearance and disappearance, and other techniques to maintain their popularity as times change. Folk media must intersect with electronic and new media, including television and the internet, in order to flourish and survive in the modern world. Puppetry may advance both as a kind of traditional entertainment and as a means of support for puppeteers. It is true that the puppeteers' financial situation has typically been quite poor. They occasionally receive invitations to perform at wedding ceremonies as well as at festivals and hamlet fairs.

Modern puppetry has entered the cities, yet the art form of traditional puppetry is slowly fading. On the other side, contemporary puppetry is gaining popularity, although slowly, and is frequently employed as a method for disseminating social themes. Today, puppeteers narrate tales about anything. Puppetry must be promoted responsibly and with specific goals if it is to avoid becoming just a museum exhibit, because museums are the custodians of our past which preserve our history and heritage. Apart from preserving our heritage, museums also try to connect folks with day today life, to create awareness. Museums organize puppet shows to keep alive this intangible cultural form among masses. The potential of puppetry as a communication tool has recently come to the attention of educators throughout the world. In India, a lot of organisations and people use puppetry to explain educational concepts to students and teachers.

There are numerous varieties of puppetry, but in India there are primarily four: rod puppets, glove puppets, string puppets, and shadow puppets, which are all practised in various regions of the country.

1. **String Puppet:** String puppets, often known as marionettes, have a long and storied legacy in India. A figure with numerous joints that is suspended by a string and is controlled is referred to as a string puppet. Rajasthan, Orissa, Assam, Tamil Nadu, and Karnataka are among the states that use string puppets. In this, the puppeteer's manipulative abilities are more highlighted. Examples of string puppets are as follows-
    - ***Kathputli*, Rajasthan:** *Kathputli* are the name given to Rajasthan's traditional marionettes. These puppets are like enormous dolls with colourful outfits and are made from a single piece of wood. Their attire is modelled after Rajasthani clothing from the Middle Ages, which is still popular today. The local melody is accompanied by a heavily dramatised version in the *Kathputli*. Some of the distinctive facial characteristics of these string puppets are oval faces, huge eyes, arched eyebrows, and large lips. These puppets lack legs and feature long, trailing skirts. They are often controlled by puppeteers using two to five strings that are linked to their fingers rather than a prop or support.
    - ***Kundhei*, Orissa:** The Orissan string puppets are referred to as *Kundhei*. The Orissa manikins are made of light wood and have no legs other than their long, flowing skirts. They feature more joints, making them more flexible, intelligent, and easy to manipulate. The puppeteers typically use a wooden fiddle-shaped device with three sides and strings attached for control. The *Kundhei* ensembles reflect those that are frequently employed by *Jatra* traditional theatre performers. The music is inspired by well-known songs from the area and occasionally has Odissi dance music in it.

- ***Gombeyatta*, Karnataka**: Karnataka's string puppets are known as *Gombeyatta*. They have a design and layout modelled from the *Yakshagana* characters, which are the typical venue types there. The *Gombeyatta* manikin figures have joints in the elbows, shoulders, hips, and knees and are extraordinarily well-adapted. Five to seven strings that are connected to a prop are used to manipulate these manikins. Some of the manikin's more complicated movements are coordinated by several puppeteers at once.
- ***Bommalattam*, Tamil Nadu:** *Bommalattam* manikins from Tamil Nadu combine the tactics of both pole and string manikins. They are made of wood, and the control strings are connected to an iron ring that the puppeteer wears on his head like a crown. Several of the manikins have joined hands and arms that are moved by poles. The *Bommalattam* manikins are the biggest, heaviest, and finest of all conventional Indian dolls. A manikin might be roughly 4.5 feet tall and weigh around ten kilograms.

2. **Glove puppets:** In Orissa, Kerala, and Tamil Nadu, glove puppets are most common. Puppeteers wear them on their hands and use their fingers to move their heads and arms. The visual thread is provided by the puppets while the puppeteer tells his tale in verse or prose. You can create your own glove puppet with a little creativity and work. Sleeve puppets, hand puppets, and palm puppets are other names for glove puppets. Two hands rise from the bottom of the neck of the head, which is either constructed of papier-mâché, material, or wood. The long, flowing skirt makes up the rest of the body. Although these manikins resemble limp dolls, a skilled puppeteer may use them to produce a wide range of behaviors. The control process is simple, and human intervention limits developments. The two arms of the manikin are the middle finger, the thumb, and the main finger that is attached to the head. The glove manikin awakens with the aid of these three fingers. In India, different regions have different names for puppets. For example, in West Bengal, a glove puppet is

called a *Benerputul.* In Orissa, the glove puppet is known as *Kundahei Nach.*

- ***Pavakoothu,* Kerala:** The traditional glove manikin play is known as *Pavakoothu* in Kerala. Due to the influence of Kerala's famed classical dance-dramatization, Kathakali, on manikin displays, it first appeared in the eighteenth century. A manikin's height in *Pavakoothu* varies from one foot to two feet. The arms and head are made of wood and joined together with thick material before being chopped and sewn into a little pack. The essence of the manikins is enriched with paints, tiny pieces of plated tin, peacock quills, and other materials. The controller moves the manikin's hands and top by slipping his hand into the bag.

3. **Rod puppets:** An extension of glove puppets, rod puppets are frequently much larger. They are attached to large, heavy bamboo poles that are attached around the puppeteer's waist. These are animated, three-dimensional moving figures that are controlled by rods. These days, West Bengal and Orissa are the main locations for this type of puppetry.

   - ***Kathikundhei Nach,* Orissa:** In Orissa, the rod puppets are known as *Kathikundhei Nach* (rod doll dance). The popular story of *Mahishasurmardini*, which tells the tale of Durga killing the demon *Mahisha*, is also frequently performed by the Orissan rod puppeteers. The rod puppets are roughly 60 centimetres tall, with painted and wood-carved heads. The Orissa Pole manikins are considerably smaller, typically measuring between twelve and eighteen inches.
   - ***Putul Nautch,* West Bengal:** *Putul Nautch* is the name of the traditional pole manikin type found in West Bengal. They are made of wood and are designed in accordance with various regional artistic trends. The Bengal pole manikins, which persist, are around three to four feet tall, and they are dressed as the *Jatra* performers, a traditional theatre structure widespread in the State. These manikins typically have three joints. Two hands attached to bars are coupled at the shoulders, and the heads, which are

supported by the basic pole, are joined at the neck. The control approach is compelling and extraordinarily dramatic. The linguistic content and music are very similar to the *Jatra* theatre. These rod puppets can weigh between 5 and 10 kilos and reach heights of up to 1.25 metres. Their faces are painted in the **pata** fashion, and then a layer of clay or cloth is applied on top. The performances are characterized by lavish costumes, high-pitched singing, and dialogue delivery. Typically, the ensemble comprises of a lead singer and 18 other members.

- ***Yampuri,* Bihar:** *Yampuri* is the name of Bihar's traditional rod puppet. Wood is used to construct these puppets. These puppets are in one piece and devoid of joints, in contrast to the conventional rod puppets of West Bengal and Orissa. These puppets cannot be manipulated like other Rod puppets since they lack joints, which call for higher dexterity.

4. **Shadow puppets:** In this form, black-and-white or coloured puppet shadows are used. The flat figures, which are typically made of leather, are lightly rubbed against a transparent screen that has a bright light source behind it. Thus, the projection of an image is made, forming a barrier between the audience and the puppet. With darkness all around, the effect on the audience is rather intense. In India, a plain sheet stretched over a flexible frame serves as the screen. Shadow puppets are a type of puppetry that may be among the earliest still used today. They are used in the states of Karnataka, Andhra Pradesh, Maharashtra, Kerala, Orissa, and Tamil Nadu. The two most well-known shadow puppet theatre genres in India are *Ravan Chhaya* from Orissa and *Tholpavai Koothu* from Kerala. As a free performance, the shadow puppet is presented outside. Shadow puppets are typically found at the well-known village of Pinguli on the border of Maharashtra, Goa, and Karnataka. Indian shadow puppeteers continue to practise various customs and traditions related to ritualistic religion. Even today, the majorities of traditional puppeteers start their performances with prayers and bow to the puppets at the conclusion of the performance.

- ***Togalu Gombeyatta*, Karnataka:** *Togalu Gombeyatta* is the name of Karnataka's shadow theatre. The majority of these manikins are quite little. In any case, the manikins' sizes differ according to their social standing; for instance, rulers and severe characters are very large, while regular people and workers are smaller.
- ***Tholu Bommalata*, Andhra Pradesh:** The most lavish and rooted tradition is seen in *Tholu Bommalata*, Andhra Pradesh's shadow play. The manikins are enormous in size and have movable elbows, shoulders, and knees. They have colour on both sides. As a result, these manikins cast colored shadows on the screen. The district's traditional music has a significant influence on the music, while the themes of the manikin performances are taken from the Ramayana, Mahabharata, and Puranas.
- ***Ravanachhaya*, Orissa:** The Orissan *Ravanachhaya* is the most dramatically stimulating. The manikins are unjointed and in one piece. They cast black shadows on the screen because they are not coloured. Since there are no joints, the control must be extremely smooth. The manikins are fabricated from deer skin and posed in sensual poses. In addition to human and animal characters, several props are also used, including trees, mountains, chariots, and so forth.

These four different sorts of puppets have different levels of flexibility. The most adaptable type of puppet is a string one, followed by a glove and a rod puppet. Shadow puppetry's somewhat inflexible nature prevents it from being applied in a variety of ways.

Ventriloquism

The art of "throwing" the voice, or speaking so that it appears to be coming from somewhere other than the speaker, is known as ventriloquism. Furthermore, the voice is hidden simultaneously (partially due to its raised pitch by using puppets to play their sketches characters. The term "ventriloquism" comes from the Latin words, "venter" and "loqui," which refer to the stomach's particular usage during inhalation. "Belly-speaking" (Encyclopaedia

Britannica, 1998). Ventriloquism first appeared among the Ancient Greeks and Romans as a form of religious practice. The oldest recordings of ventriloquism are from England around 1753. The history of ventriloquism in India dates back to the middle of 1916-1917 by Prof. Yeshwant Keshav Padhye, and it was popularized by his son Ramdas Padhye in 1967. Today Satyajit Ramdas Padhye son of Ramdas Padhye is a third-generation puppeteer and ventriloquist who is reviving this art form in India. The ventriloquist is both a puppeteer and an actor, playing a role in the show he presents. Some Young individuals from diverse backgrounds are also entering into the field of ventriloquism driven by their passionate interest. Notable emerging talents include Vignesh Pande hailing from Mumbai and Indushree Raveendra from Bangalore, who are gaining popularity in the world of ventriloquism. The term "dummy" or "vent figure" is frequently used to describe the most prominent form of ventriloquist puppet. Traditionally, wood was used for creating the figurine. Modern materials that replicate the look and feel of wood include Celastic, latex, synthetic wood, and fibreglass.

References

1. Akhtar, W. (2017). Bhand Pather (The folk theatre of Kashmir*). International Journal of Academic Research and Development,* 2(5), 976-978. ISSN: 2455-4197.
2. Alam, R, N., Khalid T. (2021). Semantics of Qawwali: Poetry, Perception, and Cultural Consumption. *Journal of Development and Social Sciences,* 2(4), 822-834, doi:10.47205/jdss.2021(2-IV)65
3. Amruta, P. (n.d.). *Koodiyattam - UNESCO's List of Intangible Cultural Heritage - Art and Culture Notes.* Prepp. Retrieved from https://prepp.in/news/e-492-koodiyattam-unesco-s-list-of-intangible-cultural-heritage-art-and-culture-notes
4. Arif, A. (2018). Indigenous Folk Theatre of Kashmir and It's Relevance in Contemporary Society. *Journal of Indian Research,* 6(2), 33-37.
5. Banerjee, U. K. (2006a). *Indian Performing Arts.* Penguin Random House. ISBN- 81-86622-75-6
6. Basa, M., & Bijina, K (2021). Inheritance and Growth of Kuchipudi Dance. *Dogo Rangsang Research Journal. 11* (03).
7. Bhattacharjee, A., & Alam, S. (2012). The Origin and Journey of Qawwali: From Sacred Ritual to Entertainment. *Journal of Creative Communications,* 7(3), 209-225.

8. Centre for Cultural Resources and Training. (2020). *Carnatic Classical Music.* Ministry of Culture. Retrieved from https://ccrtindia.gov.in/carnatic-classical-music/

9. Chaitanya, S. (2007). *Kutiyattam: The Oldest Living Theatre Tradition.* Boloji. Retrieved from https://www.boloji.com/articles/5490/kutiyattam-the-oldest-living-theatre-tradition

10. Chattopadhyay, A. (2017). Puppetry as a form of Mass Communication: Indian perspective. *Journal of Content, Community & Communication, 5,* 78-80.

11. Chavali, R. (2018). Men in dance with special emphasis on Kuchipudi, a south Indian classical dance tradition. In *Article Presented at International Word Congress of Dance Research.* Retrieved from *http://2018congressathens. cid-world. org/cloud/Mr.% 20Rajesh% 20Chavali_USA_23362/Men% 20in% 20Dance_WCDR_.*

12. Courtney, D. (n.d.). *Kathakali.* Chandrakantha. Retrieved from https://chandrakantha.com/articles/indian_music/nritya/kathakali.html

13. *Creative Arts in India.* (2016). Scribd. Retrieved from https://www.scribd.com/document/466508478/Creative-arts-in-India

14. *Folk music in India.* (2023). BYJUS. Retrieved from https://byjus.com/free-ias-prep/folk-music-in-india/

15. Goyal, S. (2022). *List of Folk Dances of Different States in India.* Jagranjosh.com. Retrieved from https://www.jagranjosh.com/general-knowledge/lists-of-states-and-folk-dances-of-india-1466770456-1

16. Gramin Vikas Seva Sanshtha (GVSS). (2013). *Evaluation Study of Tribal/ Folk Arts and Culture in West Bengal, Orissa, Jharkhand, Chhatisgarh and Bihar.* SER Division Planning Commission, Govt. of India, New Delhi. Retrieved from https://niti.gov.in/planningcommission.gov.in/docs/reports/sereport/ser/ser_folk2211.pdf

17. Hajra, V. (2015). Role of Indian Folk Culture in Promotion of Tourism in the Country. *Paripex - Indian Journal of Research, 4*(2), 231–235. ISSN - 2250-1991

18. Hess, L. (1988). The Poet, the People, and the Western Scholar: Influence of a Sacred Drama and Text on Social Values in North India. *Theatre Journal, 40*(2), 236-253.

19. https://www.delhidanceacademy.in/folk-dance/

20. *Indian Folk Dances.* (n.d.). IndiaNetzone. Retrieved from https://www.indianetzone.com/1/indian_folk_dances.htm

21. *Introduction to Folk Dance of India.* (n.d.). NewKerala.Com. Retrieved from https://www.newkerala.com/india/Dance-Forms-of-India/Introduction-to-Folk-Dance-of-India.html#.VKxyotKUcQY

22. Irfan, M. et al. (2021). Performing Arts as a Domain of Intangible Cultural Heritage With Special Reference To Indian Folk Theatre. *International*

Journal of Recent Scientific Research 12(02), 41069-41072. DOI: http://dx.doi.org/10.24327/ijrsr.2021.1202.5823

23. Kathakali - Research. (2015). Retrieved from https://ibtheatre201416.weebly.com/journal/kathakali-research
24. Centre for Cultural Resources and Training. (2020). *Kathakali Dance.* Ministry of Culture. Retrieved from https://ccrtindia.gov.in/kathakali-dance/
25. *Kathakali in a Nutshell.* (n.d.). Retrieved from https://www.imsc.res.in/~ksomnt17/Kathakali-Introduction.pdf
26. *Kathakali.* (n.d.). keralaculture.org. Retrieved from http://www.keralaculture.org/kathakali/31
27. *Koodiyattam.* (2023). In World Encyclopedia. Retrieved from https://www.newworldencyclopedia.org/p/index.php?title=Koodiyattam&oldid=1103102.
28. Kothari, S. (n.d.). *The Tradition of Kuchipudi Dance-dramas.* https://www.sahapedia.org/sites/default/files/2019-03/The%20Tradition%20of%20Kuchipudi%20Dance-dramas%20-%20Sunil%20Kothari.pdf
29. Kröger, T., & Nupponen, A.M. (2019). Puppet as a Pedagogical Tool: A Literature Review. *International Electronic Journal of Elementary Education, 11*(4), 393–401. https://doi.org/10.26822/iejee.2019450797
30. Centre for Cultural Resources and Training. (2020). *Kuchipudi Dance.* Ministry of Culture. Retrieved from https://ccrtindia.gov.in/kuchipudi-dance/
31. *Kuchipudi.* (2023). In Encyclopedia Britannica. Retrieved from https://www.britannica.com/art/kuchipudi
32. Kumari, A. (2014). Changing forms of folk media in Kashmir. In A, Ambrish Saxena (Ed.). *Ambrish Saxena.* 1st ed. Kanishka Publishers. ISBN No.978-81-8457-586-6.
33. Lowthorp, L. (2015). Voices on the Ground: Kutiyattam, UNESCO, and the Heritage of Humanity. *Journal of Folklore Research. 52*(2-3), 157-180. 10.2979/jfolkrese.52.2-3.157.
34. Mahabir, K., & Chand, S. J. (2015). The phenomenon of Ramleela/Ramlila theatre in Trinidad. *Nidan: International Journal for Indian Studies, 27*(1_2), 1-21.
35. Meaden, W. (2013). *An introduction to Kathakali - Document - Gale Academic OneFile.* Retrieved from https://go.gale.com/ps/i.do?p=AONE&u=googlescholar&id=GALE|A332247601&v=2.1&it=r&sid=AONE&asid=e3f0c91a
36. Mishra, A. (2019). *A Presentation on Kutiyattam (Or Koodiyattam).* Retrieved from https://www.researchgate.net/publication/332275814_A_PRESENTATION_ON_KUTIYATTAM_OR_KOODIYATTAM/citation/download

37. Nair, C.K. (1967). *The Kathakali and the Dance-Drama of India*. The United Nations Educational, Scientific and Cultural Organization.

38. Nair, R. B., & deSouza, P. R. (2020). *Keywords for India: A Conceptual Lexicon for the 21st Century*. Bloomsbury Academic.

39. Pandit, F. (2021). Impact of local arts; Bhand Pather and ladishah, on the people of Kashmir. *International Journal of English Literature and Social Sciences (IJELS)*, *6*(1), 10.22161/ijels.61.35

40. Centre for Cultural Resources and Training. (2020). *Puppet Forms*. Ministry of Culture. Retrieved from https://ccrtindia.gov.in/puppet-forms/

41. Indian Culture. (n.d.). *Qawwali*. Retrieved from http://indianculture.gov.in/intangible-cultural-heritage/performing-arts/qawwali

42. Raina, A. (2015). The art of creating a Kathakali performer's 'Presence'. *Theatre, Dance and Performance Training*, *6*(3), 323-338.

43. Raja, K. Kunjunni. 1974. "Kutiyattam: A General Survey." *National Centre for the Performing Arts: Quarterly Journal 3*(2): 1–14.

44. S, A. (2021). A Study on Cultural and Heritage Tourism of India. *International Journal of Creative Research Thoughts (IJCRT), 9*(5), 149-152. ISSN: 2320-2882

45. Safeguarding Intangible Heritage and Sustainable Cultural Tourism: Opportunities and Challenges. (2008). *UNESCO-EIIHCAP Regional Meeting*. ISBN: 978-92-9223-217-7 Retrieved from https://unesdoc.unesco.org/ark:/48223/pf0000178732

46. Sarma, S., & Devi, B. (2013). Using Puppets Making to Promote Engagement and Motivating in Educational Study. *IOSR Journal of Humanities and Social Science, 13*(6), 21–28. https://doi.org/10.9790/0837-1362128

47. Satpathy, B. B. (n.d.). *Indian Culture and Heritage*. Retrieved from https://ddceutkal.ac.in/Syllabus/MA_history/paper-8-N.pdf

48. Schechner, R., & Hess, L. (1977). The Ramlila of Ramnagar [India]. *The Drama Review*, *21*(3), 51-82.

49. Seth, D. R. (2017). *Oral and Written Traditions in Documentation of Dance Notation in Indian Classical Dances*. Ministry Of Culture. Retrieved from https://indianculture.gov.in/research-papers/oral-and-written-traditions-documentation-dance-notation-indian-classical-dances

50. Seth, R. (2014). Development of Kuchipudi Dance in the Context of 20th Century Dance Renaissance in India. *Research Process*, *2*, 62-74.

51. Shaika, S., & Mishra, K. D. (2020). Folklore and mass media in Kashmir: A quantitative analysis. *Int. J. Sci. Technol. Res, 9*(2), 4447-4451.

52. Sharma, D. (2020). Community, Artistry, and Storytelling in the Cultural Confluence of Nautanki and Ramlila. *Asian Theatre Journal*, *37*(1), 107-132.

53. Singh, Y., Aggarwal, R., K., V., & Aggarwal, L. (2020). An Attempt to Explore the Various Challenges and Success Factors in Performing Arts

Sector in India. *International Journal of Computer Applications*, *176*(25), 1–6. https://doi.org/10.5120/ijca2020919473

54. Singha, M. (2018). *The Journey of Qawwali through the Indian Subcontinent*. Sahapedia. Retrieved from https://www.sahapedia.org/the-journey-of-qawwali-through-the-indian-subcontinent
55. Sridhar, S. (2014). *Revitalising Kuchipudi art and heritage*. Narthaki. Retrieved from https://narthaki.com/info/articles/art370.html
56. UNESCO. (2003*). Intangible Cultural Heritage Domains*. Retrieved from https://ich.unesco.org/doc/src/01857-EN.pdf
57. UNESCO. (n.d.). *Kutiyattam, Sanskrit Theatre*. Retrieved from https://ich.unesco.org/en/RL/kutiyattam-sanskrit-theatre-00010
58. UNESCO. (n.d.). *Performing arts (such as traditional music, dance, and theatre)*. Retrieved from https://ich.unesco.org/en/performing-arts-00054
59. *Ventriloquism and Puppetry in India: The Story of Ardhavatrao*. (2021). Puppet Place News. Retrieved from https://puppetplace.wordpress.com/2021/02/02/ventriloquism-and-puppetry-in-india-the-story-of-ardhavatrao/
60. *Ventriloquism*. (2016). World Encyclopedia of Puppetry Arts. Retrieved from https://wepa.unima.org/en/ventriloquism/
61. *Ventriloquism*. (2019). In Encyclopedia Britannica. Retrieved from https://www.britannica.com/art/ventriloquism
62. *What Is a Ventriloquist?* (2020). Wonderopolis. Retrieved from https://wonderopolis.org/wonder/what-is-a-ventriloquist
63. *World Dance Day 2021*. (2021). The CSR Journal. Retrieved from https://thecsrjournal.in/world-dance-day-indian-traditional-culture-indigenous/
64. Yasir, B.B. (2009). *The Traditional/Folk Theatre (Bhand-Pather) of Kashmir*. Retrieved from http://bbyasir.blogspot.com/search/label/Articles
65. Zarrilly, P. (1984). *The Kathakali complex: actor, performance & structure*. Abhinav Publications.

Chapter - 3

Social Practices, Rituals and Festive Events

From ancient times, people have always held festivals or ceremonies according to their culture to express their happiness, sorrow, and joy. Festivals and rituals are both components and products of a community. This is one of the most diverse and active Intangible Cultural Heritage (ICH) categories, which covers the secular and religious, everyday day and extraordinary practices. People from all around the world and throughout time have interpreted and carried out rituals and festivals in diverse ways. According to UNESCO Domain of 2003 Convention of Intangible Cultural Heritage-

> Social practices, rituals and festive events are habitual activities that structure the lives of communities and groups and that are shared by and relevant to many of their members. They are closely linked to a community's worldview and perception of its history and memory. They vary from small gatherings to large-scale social celebrations and commemorations. Each of these sub-domains is vast, but there is also a great deal of overlap between them. Rituals and festive events often take place at special times and places and remind a community aspect of its worldview and history.

Social practices, rituals and festive events include a variety of forms such as traditional legal systems; culinary traditions; rites of passage; wedding, birth, and funeral rituals; seasonal ceremonies; kinship and ritual kinship ceremonies; worship rites; oaths of allegiance; traditional games and sports; settlement patterns; activities exclusive to either men or women include hunting, fishing, gathering involvement, and many others. They encompass a diverse range of expressions and physical elements, including unique gestures, vocabulary, recitations, songs, dances, distinctive attire, processions, animal sacrifices, and special cuisine. Social, ceremonial, and celebratory customs are employed to mark life milestones, agricultural calendar events, and the transitions between seasons.

A festival is a public gathering that attracts participants from a specific social or religious group. Festivals reflect important historical or mythological moments and honour the heroes and legends that are fundamental to a community's identity. Festival celebrations include specific rites, the practice of specialised crafts like the depiction of ritual motifs and symbols, and the ceremonial preparation of specific dishes. Consequently, public rituals and social practices are a crucial component of festivals.

Social Practices and Rituals

Indians have followed a variety of rituals and traditions over the course of their daily lives since the beginning of time. Social practices or customs are unwritten laws or norms that have been followed from the dawn of time and are passed down from one generation to the next by ancestors. "Rituals are repetitive patterned interactions that are practiced in a variety of settings. The settings range from daily, routine activities such as dinner-time to more stylized practices linked with religious observances" (Fiese & Tomcho, 2001). Rituals are actions that are carried out in accordance with set guidelines and now become part of our cultural heritage. Indian houses have practised countless rituals and traditions for millennia.

Every culture has a unique collection of rituals that represent facets of life and human endeavour and serve to define the community and its place in the cosmos and in relation to the natural world. Sometimes when we are not entirely aware of it, rituals constantly communicate our beliefs about life and ourselves. They enable us to communicate who we are as individuals and how we envision our lives to develop. Rituals and social practices convey our identity as members of a certain clan, tribe, ethnicity, country, religious movement, or denomination. Every level of ritual enables us to recognize and express the enigmatic aspects of existence that we are unable to fully comprehend or explain. The rituals used in India also seek to harmonise the body, mind, and spirit on a whole. Because of the depth of our legacy, the entire globe is fascinated by our traditions.

Ritualistic practises have been connected over time to specific religions in our country. Every householder was required to perform specific fire rituals during the Vedic era. In the past, rituals were cult behaviours centred on nature, community well-being, illness prevention, and the defence of livestock and crops. Agriculture was the centre of the ancient people's lives. An essential event was the planting of a new crop. People prayed for a prosperous harvest and used various rituals to convey their hopes. Man, who was ruled by the natural elements, ascribed the mysteries of nature to different universal forces, including the sun, wind, rain, fire, and earth. These powers were later connected with gods and goddesses. Various purposes were attained through rituals. They could be routines, traditions, practices you have made up yourself, or even daily activities. The milestones that define our existence—from sunrise to dusk, from winter to summer, from birth to death—are rituals. Rituals are not just shown; they also help us define and verify our identities. Some of the different categories of rituals are as follows;

- Birth Rituals
- Rituals to Appease Gods
- Rituals of Fertility
- Initiation Rites
- Wedding Rituals
- Grief Rituals etc.

Most of these categories, however, overlap and are adaptable so that a single event might be seasonal, agricultural, and religious at the same time. The Christian ceremonies of christening, baptism, and confirmation, the Hindu *samskaras*, the Jewish Shabbat, commemoration *(Azadari)* by Muslims during *Muharram*, *Nowruz* by Parsis, etc. are some common rituals (Zarrin & Farha, 2022).

Through rituals, the community's elders tried to transmit their knowledge by word of mouth. These might involve performances by an individual or a group. One's home or a public location, such as a river bank, well, hill, field, tree or water tank, may serve as the performance location. It might simply affect a single community or it might open doors for communication between multiple groups that are situated in various hierarchies. In our lives, rituals serve a variety of functions. Some individuals primarily identify religious practises with the word "Ritual." They are important because they establish the identity of persons who practise them. Ritual provides us with security, comfort, and a predictable schedule. These practises calm us down and give us greater energy for crucial tasks. Rituals might be used to manipulate knowledge, power, wealth, and the consumption of food and drink. They help us to comprehend better who we are and who we want to be throughout life. They support us in expressing our individuality, core convictions, and dedication to God, our work, and the environment. Rituals also aid in our healing. There are many unusual practises and traditions in Indian culture, some of them are as follows:

SOME IMPORTANT SOCIAL PRACTICES AND RITUALS OF INDIA

Namaste Greeting

The greeting commonly referred to as *Namaste,* alternatively known as *namaskar or namaskaram*, which translates to "I bow to the divine in you," is one of the widely recognized practices and traditions in Indian culture. The hands are held together in a prayer position in front of the chest with the fingers pointed upwards, and a modest bow is made. Another well-known proverb is "*Atithi Devo Bhava*," which translates to "the guest is similar to god" and is found in Hindu scriptures. In Indian culture, guests are traditionally accorded the utmost respect and honor, often considered akin to gods.

Sparsh Charan

The *Sparsh charan* is described by the word touch. When combined, they signify "to touch one's feet." The Atharva-Veda places much emphasis on this kind of greeting. The respect for the elderly is shown in this situation. The human body emits vibrations and receives them from those who are nearby, according to the science behind *Charan sparsh*. The body's energy flow is aided by this. When someone touches an elder's feet, they express respect and ask for blessings. The older person could respond by bestowing blessings, resting their hand on the person's head, or offering encouragement and wisdom.

Tilak

Both men and women apply a *Tilak* to their foreheads as part of Indian custom. It is placed on the principal nerve point in the human body—the area in the middle of the forehead between the two brows that serves as the control centre for the entire body. Sandalwood, red *kumkum*, clay, rice grains or ash from *Yagya* are traditionally utilised.

Aarti

Aarti is a type of prayer in Hinduism in which prayer is chanted in homage to the Deity while the flames are waved. When performing *aarti*, the performer faces the idol of God (or any other divine object, such as the Ganga River). *Aarti* is waved in a circular manner clockwise around the deity. God is not the only subject of *aarti*. It can be performed on inanimate artefacts that advance civilization as well as on all living things. To invoke the love, power, and blessings of the Deities, lit wicks are waved in front of the holy pictures during the *aarti*. With the use of musical instruments like drums, bells, gongs, and a conch shell, this prayer is joyfully recited. The blowing of a conch shell (*shankh*) is frequently used to start and end performances. Following a brief prayer, lit wicks are passed around the assembly so that everyone might benefit from the blessings contained within the flames. The devotee has now received the purifying blessing that the Deities had given to the flame. The *Aarti* is conducted twice a day, in the morning and the evening, at smaller *mandirs* and at shrines at devotees' homes. The traditional Hindu way of honouring a particular guest, extending a warm welcome to a friend, wishing a loved one safe return, or offering homage to the Lord is through an *aarti* ritual. Whether at home or in the temple, it is essential to the act of worshipping a deity. There is no better place to do one than by the banks of the sacred Ganges River, where a bath in her waters can erase lifetimes' *karmic* burdens. The holy cities of Rishikesh, Varanasi, and Haridwar are the three most well-liked pilgrimage destinations for *aarti* along the river.

Use of Coconut

The coconut in Sanskrit is alluded to as *Sriphala*, signifying "The God's fruit." Coconut symbolises fertility, society, culture, taboos, and religious rites. It is used in rituals on a regular basis. Pregnant women are forbidden from breaking coconuts since doing so is equivalent to killing a life form, and the coconut is a sign of life. According to ancestral knowledge, the coconut is also widely used in several *Gond* and *Bhil* wedding rituals as well as funeral customs in Rajasthan, Gujarat, and Madhya Pradesh. A common custom at temples is the offering of coconuts. The coconut is broken and offered to the Lord before being received as *"Prasad"* at "*Pandals*." Coconuts are also positioned on auspicious occasions. It is offered and broken when beginning new endeavours, such as starting a business, purchasing a car, house, etc. According to Hindu mythology, coconuts were used in place of slaughtering/killing animals to satisfy people's wishes. Coconut is stored in leaves in a copper container called a "*Kalasha,*" which is also a sign of spiritual consciousness.

Practice to Ring the Bell in Temples

In the Hindu religion, we ring the bell when we visit the temple and when we pray at home. The idols erected in the temple are said to awaken consciousness by ringing the bell. The bell's endearing and resonating tone has the capacity to inspire spirituality. It is an essential component of Hindu traditions and practices.

Fasts

Fasts, also known as *"Vrats" or "Upvas,"* are a significant aspect of Indian culture and a social practice. These gestures are not only used to convey determination and sincerity but also to express gratitude to deities and goddesses. Fasting is done to cleanse one's body and mind, keep bad thoughts and energies out of one's mind, and cultivate the moral, spiritual, and ethical qualities that will guide one to salvation. Indians observe fasts on a variety of days and for a variety of religious reasons. The fasting method is like yoga that aids in strengthening one's willpower and mental control. In India, fasting is practised during some of the important occasions like: During Karva Chauth, married women observe a fast in hopes of extending the health and lifespan of their spouses. Many individuals fast during the nine-day Navratri festival, especially in honour of Goddess Durga. Muslims fast throughout the auspicious month of Ramadan. On Janmashtami, Lord Krishna's birthday, people fast. In the month of Muharram, several Muslim communities fast. Some people keep a fast on Dussehra, which commemorates Lord Rama's triumph over Ravana.

Rituals related to *Mannat* (Vow)

The practise of bringing someone's wishes before the gods are common among Indians, particularly those who are South Indian in origin. The followers must observe a fast for a few days before placing "camphor" on their palms and lighting it on fire. They then slip into a trance and communicate their demands to their gods. The palm suffers a full-thickness burn as a result of these injuries. In many Indian religious traditions, rituals comprising prayers, offerings, and pleas for deities' blessings are common. To show their devotion and ask for divine guidance or favour for their dreams and desires, worshippers frequently conduct fasts, participate in meditation or worship, and give offerings. People also visit the *dargah for* offerings like flowers, incense, and *chaddars* (a textile sheet) to drape over the dargah (tomb). The *chaddar* is a sign of reverence and an expression of prayer or appeal for the saint's assistance. In India, it is popular to tie threads around trees or at different spots to fulfil vows, and this practice is frequently related to folk or nature-based spirituality. In addition, Indians use various techniques to fulfil a *mannat*, such as shaving their heads upon accomplishment, pouring coins into wishing wells etc.

Practice to Ward off Evil Eye

One of the oldest and most well-known superstitions, the evil eye belief has been practiced since the Stone Age and has been documented throughout history. It is a long-held and widespread belief that the evil eye has negative repercussions. Man has believed that almost every adversity throughout history was the direct result of a fatal glance brought on by jealousy, envy, or frustration. Unusual eyes might be harmful to the thing they are focusing on. Many methods, including amulets, talismans, inscriptions, sayings, and customs, have been used to ward off the evil eye's potent effects on both the living and the dead. A superstitiously worn item to ward off the evil eye is called an amulet. It was thought crucial to deflect the gaze away from the subject or target that might be hurt in order to neutralise a malevolent stare. In addition, the use of lemon and green chillies and, a painted pot with black colour and a picture of the *Kaali* Goddess, the sacrifice of animals in the name of the person to protect him/her from the evil eye are some practices that are used to ward off the evil eye.

Baptism

In Christianity, people perform baptism. The sacrament of baptism is the means through which we are reborn as God's children. It is a sacrament of admission to the church by pouring/sprinkling water on the head or immersion in water. The phrase "I baptise you in the name of the Father and of the Son and the Holy Spirit" is spoken during the ritual. Our sins are pardoned and restored to God's righteousness via baptism. As a result, we receive a share in God's life and join God's people. Water is a symbol of life and purification. When someone is baptised, the words used denote that they are entering the life of God the Father, God the Son, and God the Holy Spirit.

Azadari

Azadari is an Urdu phrase that refers to mourning rituals remembering Imam Hussain (grandson of Prophet Mohammad PBUH) and his companions' martyrdom in Karbala, Iraq, roughly 1350 years ago. These rituals are observed by the Shi'ah, and some Muslims from other sects, as well as some non-Muslims, also take part in the remembrance during *Muharram* (the first month of the Islamic calendar). Replicas of Imam Hussain's mausoleum are created throughout the month of Muharram; these are known as *ta'ziya* in Urdu. *Ta'ziyas*, or processions, are used to carry out poems grieving the tragedy of Karbala. Throughout the month of Muharram, Shia Muslims take part in *Juloos*, processions in which they may carry *alams* and *ta'ziyas* (symbolic replicas of the tombs of Imam Hussain and his companions) while also reciting elegies, mourning songs, and narrating the events of Karbala. Shia Muslims participate in these processions to demonstrate their mourning, solidarity, and dedication to the principles of righteousness and fairness embodied by Imam Hussain's sacrifice. Many events associated with the rituals, such as *Marsiyakhwani, Majils, Alam* (flags) raising during the procession, etc., take place in congregation halls or buildings known as *Imambaras*.

Parda System

Indian family life is heavily influenced by *parda,* or the veiling and seclusion of women which is restricted to certain areas and communities. Hindu and Muslim women observe intricate restrictions regarding the covering of the body and refrain from making public appearances, especially in front of married relatives and unfamiliar men, in most of northern and central India, particularly in rural areas. Practices related to the *parda* are associated with patterns of power and harmony in the family. Even a young daughter-in-law hides herself behind a veil. These customs place a strong emphasis on respectful interactions, restrict unauthorized contact, and strengthen family hierarchies. However, Due to reasons including rising levels of education and urbanisation, the *Parda System* is progressively changing, which is leading to a change in views regarding covering up. Women's empowerment, exposure to different cultures, and the impact of journalism and global trends in fashion all contribute to changing practices. And now this system is gradually diminishing.

Dowry System

One of the worst social practices that has had an impact on our culture is the practice of dowry. Traditionally, dowries have been provided by a bride's family members at the time of her marriage in several societies. In India, women have a very limited voice when it comes to making decisions regarding their future spouses as well as the customs and rites that would be observed during their weddings. Even though there are now significantly more women working, dowry is still widely used in society. One of the main causes of the high prevalence of dowry in many communities is hypergamy, which is the practice of marrying a spouse whose social position is higher than her own. Greater dowries reflect a higher social status for the family. In addition, families are encouraged to give their daughters a sizable dowry in order to guarantee her safety and the respect of her in-laws. Because the Indian marriage system is largely based on arranged weddings, parents of daughters are frequently prepared to pay a good dowry to find a suitable spouse for her, to minimize the possibility of the daughter becoming permanently dependent on the parents.

Culinary Practices

Cooking is one of our favourite Indian cultural practices and traditions. In India, each region has a unique cuisine with a distinctive dish or ingredient, each serving them differently. The culinary traditions of the Indian royal family, including Rajas, Maharajas, Nawabs, Mughals, and the Marwari community, vary greatly throughout various states and regions of the country. With unique flavours and cuisines, each group has added to the rich texture of Indian food. It is widely considered one of the best countries in the world for vegetarian cuisine, particularly in Gujarat and Rajasthan. Rajasthani cuisine was influenced by Rajput royalty. Dal Baati Churma, Gatte ki Sabzi, and Ker Sangri are among the traditional Rajasthani vegetarian dishes from the Marwari people. Mughlai, Bengali, North Indian, and Punjabi cuisine heavily emphasise non-vegetarian alternatives. A rich culinary heritage left by the Nawabs of Awadh, notably in Lucknow, includes foods like *kebabs* (*Galouti Kebab and Seekh Kebab*), *biryani*, and numerous recipes cooked at low flame. North Indian cuisine continues to be influenced by the Mughals' gastronomic legacy. Popular Mughlai cuisine includes Butter Chicken, Rogan Josh, and Mughlai Biryani. The royals and nobles were renowned for their lavish feasts, frequently including various delicacies and intricate culinary methods. These meals have become essential to India's diverse and extensive culinary history. Kerala in South India is well known for its delectable seafood cuisine. India has a long-standing history of drying seafood, highlighting the nation's diverse culinary heritage and creative approaches to preserving and utilising its plentiful marine resources. The preservation of fish and other marine food by drying ensures a longer shelf life and offers a rich source of protein. There are usually sufficient fresh ingredients available, including exquisite spices and herbs used for flavour and aroma, enhancing colours, and their medicinal capabilities. Every spice used in Indian cuisine is essential for maintaining good health. They not only give food flavour, but they also function as antibiotics and antiseptics. An essential part of Indian culinary practices is the drying and grinding of unique spices, especially when making authentic and delicious meals. The traditional sun-drying process involves spreading the spices out in the sunlight until they are thoroughly dried. Mortar and pestle were commonly used in the past, but nowadays, electric spice grinders or blenders are frequently utilised for convenience. Each spice mixture, or masala, has a specific function and is mixed in various ratios to produce the distinctive flavours of India's numerous regional cuisines. These freshly ground spices play a crucial role in preparing traditional and genuine Indian meals, contributing to the fresh and varied flavours for which Indian cuisine is known. This knowledge of preparing spices has been passed down from generation to generation. Pickling has a long history as a culinary practise in India. It is a crucial component of Indian cuisine, with various regional varieties of pickled foods. Fruits and vegetables are preserved using this method, sometimes in vinegar and other times in a delectable combination of spices, salt, and oil. The pickles (*achar*) are essential to Indian meals because they add a burst of strong and sour flavours that go well with other foods. During the harvest season, many people have yearly rituals for preparing huge amounts of pickles. Every area of India has its special pickle recipe, which typically reflects the regional flavours and ingredients available. These recipes are essential to maintaining the nation's culinary tradition. Food has traditionally been served on the floor in banana leaves since ancient times. It is more than just a representation of our culture. It also offers health advantages because it contains natural antioxidants that shield us from various ailments. It also indicates a sustainable approach towards nature.

Rituals of Child Birth

Rituals of welcome and blessing are performed to commemorate the birth of a child, and they are often much more extensive for boys than for girls. Although social inequality exists throughout the world, the caste system in India may be the only place where it has been so carefully built. In India, castes are ranked, named, and intermarriage social groups that are acquired via birth. Here, hundreds of millions of people belong to thousands of castes and sub-castes. There are distinct social practices, customs, and traditions for each caste and subcaste.

Historically, a person's marriage, social connections, occupation, and social position were determined by their caste. South Asia's social system is mostly centred on these large kinship-based groups. Being a caste member gives one a sense of belonging to an established group from which they can expect support in various circumstances. The traditions surrounding childbirth in India vary greatly amongst different communities, cultural backgrounds, and regions. Following are some common childbirth rituals and customs in India: The term Baby shower (*Godh Bharai)* is also referred to as *Valaikappu* in South India. The expecting woman receives presents, blessings, and good wishes. In many Muslim communities, it is tradition to recite the *Azan* in a baby's ear as soon as it is born. This practise ensures that the first words heard by the child are the words of the call to prayer, emphasising the significance of religion and belief in the child's life from the start. The most important aspect of childbirth rituals is naming ceremonies. The infant's name is typically selected based on astrological factors, family customs, or religious significance. The naming ritual in Hinduism is known as *Namkaran*. A ceremony called *Aqiqah* that involves animal sacrifice to commemorate the birth is frequently performed by Muslim families. An *Annaprashana* in Hinduism commemorates a child's first foods, usually when teething starts. The first haircut ritual, *chudakarrana or mundan*, is typically given between the ages of one and three.

Practices and Rituals of Weddings

Indian weddings are marked by a vast range of folk songs sung using *dholak*. Many of which captures the culture, customs, and regional flavours of the many states and communities throughout the nation. In Indian weddings, the *haldi* (turmeric) ceremony is a significant pre-wedding ritual. It is a joyous and colourful ritual in which a paste of turmeric, oil, and water is spread to the bride and groom's bodies. The *haldi* ceremony could incorporate additional traditions in certain areas, such as tying a protection thread around the bride's wrist. During the Haldi ceremony, the bride and groom dress simply in white or yellow. However, in recent years, it has been a growing trend for people to select unique attire for the Haldi ceremony that looks good and highlights the event's joyous and celebratory aspect. *Henna* is applied on the bride's hands and feet before the wedding. In our nation, this practice has been prevalent for a long time. It has several medical effects in addition to being a means of dressing that gives the hands and feet a lovely colour.

Rituals like *Kanyadaan, Jaimala, Mangalphere, Sindoor, and Saptapadi* are performed during Hindu weddings. A *"pandit"* or priest conducts the religious rites and chants Sanskrit hymns and mantras in front of the sacred fire (*agni)* during these events. The *Saptapadi* rite, in which the bride and husband must take seven steps together while facing north before the bride turns to the groom's left, is the most significant part of Hindu marriages.

In India, it is traditional for the groom to apply vermilion *Sindur* (a mixture of lime, turmeric, and mercury) to the bride's hair partition during the wedding. A woman's vermilion signifies good fortune and her married life, indicating her transition from a daughter to a housewife. The pair is now legally married. However, during Muslim weddings, the Nikah ritual is performed. The *Doli* (departure of the bride) to the groom's home is the completion of every wedding.

Death Related Rituals

The goal of existence, according to Indian philosophy, is to merge with the Divine, who is Reality itself. After-death practices are carried out with the assumption that the *atma* (soul) continues to exist. The rites' main goal is to free the soul from its ties to the planet and help it unite with the supreme and free from the cycle of rebirth by obtaining *moksha*. According to Hindus, cremation is the most certain method to achieve spiritual emancipation. Because of this, the group performs particular Hindu funeral rituals. These rituals are typically carried out at a Hindu funeral rite. Arranging flowers and rice balls (*pindas*) around the body, setting up a lamp close to the body's head, providing food, and praying over the body before cremation. It is believed that the smoke rising up towards the sky from the pyre symbolises the soul's freedom and unification with heaven. Such cremations support the notion of a good funeral. Hindu funeral rites also emphasise water bodies like rivers and oceans. Therefore, historically, manual cremations took place on *ghats* (public open-air pyres), frequently situated next to rivers and oceans. Such places serve as spatial constellations and "holy gates". Any cremation according to predetermined rules is likewise regarded as a good funeral. The decedent's family will start 13 days of mourning after the cremation. Family and friends are welcome to pay a condolence visit during this time. After the deceased has passed away, there is frequently another ritual held during the period of grief. Supporting the spirits of the deceased as they embark on their next journey is the ceremony's goal.

Rudaali Tradition

Rudaalis, or female professional mourners, were widespread throughout India, but they were especially prevalent in the western Indian state of Rajasthan. In modern India "*Rudaalis* of Rajasthan," also known as the "Weeping Women of India". Women from the lower caste known as *rudaalis* were employed as professional mourners to express the family's sorrow at the loss of the deceased member. Hiring a *rudaali* increases family pride and is a status symbol. Women from high castes do not cry in front of commoners. They must uphold their dignity even in the event that their spouses pass away. *Rudaalis* wept on their behalf and on behalf of everyone else who felt the need to weep but was forbidden to by society. Most mourners at funerals are female, and they dress in black or white. But even though their only job is to sob for someone they do not even personally know, "Every time a guest enters, the *rudaalis* scream louder in a show of irreplaceable sadness and loss," as the saying goes. They exhale heavily, sob loudly, throw their heads back, and scream aloud while pounding the ground in front of them and raising their voices to the sky. Hiring a *rudaali* is a sociocultural practise that sheds information on the dialectical relationship between the upper and lower castes in *Rudaali*. As time passes, less and fewer people continue the *Rudaali* tradition. Due to their poor social status, these women are more susceptible to exploitation. They are now restricted to Marwar's villages. People prefer sophisticated and peaceful funerals as many traditional procedures and traditions are altering considering this.

Snake Charming *(Practiced by Saperas)*

The practice of snake-charming is regarded as an age-old art that is now credited to India, notably to *saperas* who would demonstrate their capacity to hypnotise snakes. It is a traditional Indian folk art. The act would consist of a healer holding a cobra in a box while strumming a *pungi* (bansuri) while keeping the snake fascinated by the instrument.

Thulaja (2004) stated that "*Snake charmers are street performers who hypnotise and coax their snakes to dance and sway to the music they play on their flutes.*" In the past, many *saperas* performed it in front of their local communities, and it was seen as an enchanted or miraculous act. The reality of snake hypnosis can differ significantly from what you may believe or imagine. Snakes are not conscious of the instrument's sound; rather, they concentrate on the *pungi* and the person playing it, sensing them as potential dangers. As a result, the snake keeps a fixed gaze on the instrument and pays great attention to how the musician moves, particularly how their hands interact with it.

The *Saperas* are the predominant group among the several communities in India that traditionally connect themselves to the snake for commercial reasons. This caste is not the only one that engages in the practice of snake charming; other groups include "the *Bede* people in eastern West Bengal and Bangladesh, the *Kattu Naicker* caste in the Tamil region, and the *Vadi* tribe in Gujarat." Numerous sub-castes and clans are collectively referred to as being in the *Sapera* caste. Every community that considers itself to be a part of the group can trace its origins to ancestors who left present-day Rajasthan as nomadic people. The *Sapera* caste is still present today, with members living in Haryana, Rajasthan, Delhi, Uttar Pradesh, West Bengal, Madhya Pradesh, and other places. In addition to this renowned tradition, they perform shows, hunt, and catch snakes wandering into homes, and engage in other livelihoods like playing the *dhol*. Most snake charmers are skilled hunters, and the main form of snake charming involves seeking and trapping a snake, most frequently an Indian cobra. The cultural heritage of being a *Sapera* includes passing down cures for illnesses, particularly snake bites, from one lineage to the next (Sundar, 2018).

Snake charmers once regularly featured in Indian marketplaces and celebrations, luring people with their talent for handling some of the most dangerous animals on the planet. India, regarded as the "land of snakes," faces the same ongoing threat of human-caused extinction that other nations do to snakes and other creatures. These days, even during *Nag Panchami,* the annual Hindu celebration honouring the king cobra, it might be difficult to find a snake charmer. This most well-known traditional art is in danger of disappearing, and animal rights groups believe this must happen soon. According to them, it is a brutal form of art. Snake charmers are taking advantage of the increasing tourism industry, which would not necessarily be negative if it did not involve cruelty, harm, or confinement. However, it is sad that some *Saperas*, but not all, grab wild cobras, brutally remove their fangs, and stitch their mouths closed, rendering them defenceless. However, these snakes endure months of agonising anguish before starving to death.

The government of India has made an effort to provide space for *Saperas* and their current snakes and prevent them from collecting additional snakes. Identification chips have been implanted by the government under captivity snake skin, enabling scanning and confiscation of newly captured animals without chips. The "Wildlife Protection Act" (1972), which imposed restrictions and cracked down on snake charmers, has sadly led to the near-extinction of tribal snake charmer groups. Thus, the efficient establishment of "tribal snake charmers" cooperative societies" like the "Irula Cooperative Society" (ICS), founded in 1978 in Tamil Nadu or comparable institutions, which might be an Indian example of an appropriate way to safeguard biological diversity concerning cultural diversity, has become imperative for the resurgence of sustaining both snake society as well as tribal snake charmer communities (Konar & Modak, 2010,160).

Festivals

Every country in the world celebrates a variety of religious and cultural holidays. India is a country with many festivals, as well as a variety of cultures and religions. Indians hold festivals to honour their values, way of life, and traditions. Every festival has unique traits of its own. The major goals of these festivals are to bring happiness and solidify relationships between family and friends. India has more festivals than there are days in a year, which is not surprising in a place where modest village rites of devotion and propitiation are celebrated with the same zeal as highly sacred days across the country, celebrations that can bring crowds of up to 500,000 people. According to Tribhuwan (2003)-

> festivals are occasions that strengthen the role of religion in people's lives and tie families and individuals to their neighbours.

Additionally, these are the times when young people can learn about and participate in ancient customs that are still alive.

People celebrate the joys of life at these festivals with rituals, music, hymns, dances, fasts, and fests. Some festivals have definite dates, whereas most holidays follow the calendars used by various religions. Local festivals abound and are conducted on various yearly days. Few events are planned using the lunar calendar. In India, festivals may serve to commemorate a god at a specific temple, the agricultural cycle, a religious story, or event, or all three. In addition to the idea of consecrated time, there is also the idea of sacred space, which extends beyond of the local vicinity of a temple, church, gurudwara, mosque and *imambaras*. The banks of a river, the point where two bodies of water converge, mountains, the seashore, a sacred bank, forests, and the tomb of the beloved Pir or Saint are all gathering places. Here, fasting, feast, song, and dancing are performed after rites involving prayer, sacrifice, oaths, and blessings.

India is known as the 'land of festivals' and has a rich and varied cultural past. The festive season begins immediately following the harvest season and brings people joy and happiness. Festivals certainly have social and economic consequences, but they also have an influence on the healthcare system (Yeolekar & Bavdekar, 2007). The glory of a Culture may be found in its festivals, one can determine the greatness of a nation like India by taking a quick look at its colourful and vibrant list of festivals. So is the greatness of Indian culture—such many cultures, culminating in such diverse festivals, and all under the banner of a single nation. These festivals are observed with utter fervour and devotion, with the primary source of this diversity being the great variety of religions, occupations, and beliefs present in the nation.

As India is a tremendously culturally varied nation, and this is reflected in its festivals. They can be categorised broadly into three groups: national, religious, and seasonal. We can understand how the Indian holidays differ from one another by dividing them into national, religious, and seasonal celebrations. National holidays are typically held to honour illustrious figures and occasions. The religious ones adhere to religious myths and tenets. Every season we encounter, which differs from region to region, is celebrated along with the seasonal ones. Independence Day, Republic Day, Gandhi Jayanti, and other such holidays are considered as national holidays. India celebrates these events irrespective of their social status, belief system, religious affiliation, or gender identity; every person in the nation observes them. All of them are cherished with great passion. Everywhere throughout the nation, these festivals are observed as holidays and are quite popular.

One of the most well-known celebrations is the religious festival, which is celebrated not only in India but also around the world. Religious Festivals demonstrate the people's affiliation with their own religions. Among the important religious celebrations are Diwali, Holi, Raksha Bandhan, Mahavir Jayanti, Janmashtami, Dussehra, Buddha Purnima, Maha Shivaratri, Durga Puja, Eid, Christmas, Easter, and Guru Nanak Jayanti etc. The two most well-known Hindu holidays are Diwali and Holi. They are incredibly vibrant and illuminated. Additionally, regional communities of the nation observe seasonal celebrations. For instance, Assam celebrates Bihu as a festival. Tamil Nadu observes Pongal. Whereas Basant Panchami is a festival that is observed throughout North India and West Bengal.

SOME IMPORTANT FESTIVALS IN INDIA

National Festivals

India's national festivals are a vibrant tapestry made of the nation's deep cultural diversity, unbreakable sense of solidarity, and history. The diversity of India, a country where tradition and modernity coexist, and traditional ceremonies combine with modern festivities, is reflected in these festivals. These national celebrations serve as a reminder of India's rich and harmonious cultural heritage while also showcasing its traditions and ideals. Some of the main festivals are given below-

Republic Day

It is observed on January 26th of each year throughout the nation. Indian constitution came into effect on this day in 1950. This day is important as it symbolises the start of the process of transforming our country into a democratic republic and giving political and voting rights to every citizen of the country. A multi-hued representation of the nation's rich cultural legacy and military power is displayed every year, a unique event (grand parade) takes place in New Delhi on Rajpath. The national anthem, "*Jana Gana Mana*," plays around the country on this day. The President of India is in authority of this event. One of the primary goals of the Republic Day Parade is to honour those who have given their lives as martyrs for the nation and to bestow bravery medals on members of the armed forces, citizens, and young people for their bravery. In honour of every member of the armed services who gave their life for the nation, the Indian Prime Minister first places a wreath at *the Amar Jawan Jyoti* at India Gate. Then, the national anthem is sung, the flag is raised, and a 21-gun salute is fired. Following that, the recipient of the gallantry medal receives honours such as the *Ashok Chakra, Paramvir Chakra, and Vir Chakra.* A colourful parade featuring tableaus from various States and patriotic schoolchildren performing cultural dances follows. States and various departments and ministries display their accomplishments or cultural traditions with corresponding tableaux that incorporate instruments, costumes, and cutting-edge technology. Every exhibit highlights India's diverse and rich cultural heritage.

Independence Day

On August 15 of each year, the nation commemorates its independence. On August 15, 1947, India achieved freedom from British colonial rule. It serves as a reminder to all Indians that a new age of freedom from more than 200 years of British colonialism is about to dawn. On this occasion freedom fighters have been honoured who gave their youth up in order to secure our independence. The prime minister hoists the country's flag at Red Fort (New Delhi), before a heartfelt performance of *"Jana Gana Mana,"* India's national anthem, and 21 honorary gunshots that signal the start of the main event. The Prime Minister delivers a speech to the country recalls the occasions leading up to freedom of India, and closes the speech with a reflection on the future of the nation to remind his or her people of the country's struggle for freedom. In addition to patriotic parades and pageants honouring the liberation heroes, events often feature schoolchildren performing and a march-past led by the Indian armed forces and paramilitary forces. All around the nation, such celebrations are held. The national anthem is sung while the flag is raised by the chief minister of each state's capital. Flag-raising ceremonies and cultural events that highlight India's diversity are held at government and non-government organisations, schools, universities, and housing complexes.

Gandhi Jayanti

India observes Gandhi Jayanti as a national holiday. Throughout our nation's struggle for independence, Mahatma Gandhi upheld the idea of nonviolence. Every year on October 2nd, Gandhi Jayanti is marked to honour the life and legacy of Mahatma Gandhi, often known as the "Father of the Nation." Mahatma Gandhi's tireless efforts contributed to India's success in achieving freedom and independence. Worldwide, as declared by the United Nations General Assembly, this day is commemorated as International Day of Nonviolence. People hold prayer gatherings, cultural events, and numerous other social gatherings to celebrate Gandhi Jayanti. On this day, portraits of *Bapu* (Mahatma Gandhi) are adorned with flowers and garlands, and speeches by well-known people at the ceremonies reiterate some of his most inspirational sayings.

Religious Festivals in India

Diwali

Diwali, an autumn festival, is celebrated on the darkest new moon of the year, occurring typically between October and December. It is also known as the "Festival of Lights" because on this day, everyone, especially Hindus, lights candles and *diyas* inside their homes. Diwali festivities vary depending on different regions and cultures. The most widely embraced Hindu custom entails illuminating *diyas*, small earthen lamps filled with oil, on the night of the new moon to invoke the goddess of wealth, *Lakshmi*. The Bengali people revere the goddess, Kali. In North India, the festival also marks the celebration of Rama's victory over Ravana, the ten-headed demon king, and Rama's homecoming to Ayodhya with Sita, Lakshman, and Hanuman, connecting it to the Dussehra festival. In South India, the occasion commemorates Krishna's triumph over the demon Narakasura.

Rangoli, intricate patterns crafted from colored rice, sand, or flower petals, are employed to adorn residences and embellish floors, both indoors and outdoors.

Holi

One of India's most revered and popular festivities is Holi. The magnificent Indian festival lasts for a day and a night and starts in the evening of Purnima or the day of the full moon in the month of Falgun. Holi is the name of the festival that is celebrated the first evening *as Holika Dahan or Choti Holi*, and Holi is the festival that is celebrated the next day. On the day before Holi, the tradition commences with the lighting of a bonfire, symbolizing the triumph of good over evil. The next most important ritual is playing with colours where people use colour on each other, enjoy them, and party. Playing with dry or liquid colours, water guns, and water balloons are among the games that children and young people enjoy in groups. On this occasion, you may even see groups of people dancing and singing their way through the streets while carrying drums and other musical instruments. The greatest places to experience the Holi celebration in India are in the state of Uttar Pradesh, more specifically in the towns and cities that have a strong connection to Lord Krishna, such as Braj, Mathura, Vrindavan, Barsana, and Nandgaon. During the celebrations, all these locations experience a spike in tourism.

Raksha Bandhan

The festival of Raksha Bandhan honours the lovely bond between a brother and a sister. According to the lunar calendar, it is observed on the full moon of the *Sravana* month. *Raksha*, which means guarding, and *bandhan*, which means to tie, are two related words. Sisters customarily tie a strand of thread (*rakhi*) around their brother's wrist to honour their union. The brother is reminded of his duty to care, support, and always keep his sister safe by this thread of love. When a woman ties a *rakhi* (bracelet usually created from a combination of red and golden threads) around a man's hand, it is thought that he has an obligation to uphold his religious duty and defend her. After that, presents and sweets are exchanged. The event has grown nowadays as more people take part in the celebrations as close friends frequently exchange *rakhis*. Soldiers' wrists are tied in *rakhis*. Women children tie *rakhis* around the prime minister's wrists. Members of the congregation get their wrists bound by priests with *rakhis* and so on.

Durga Puja

One of the religious festivals in India is called Durga Puja, and it is enthusiastically observed all around the nation. To honour the unfathomable might of Goddess Durga, it is especially honoured in Kolkata, the capital of West Bengal. September or October sees the Hindu celebration of Durga Puja, which honours the goddess, Durga. The festival of Durga Puja marks the goddess Durga's return to her maternal home from the holy mountain Kailash. It embraces traits found in everyone and even the universe, including power, beauty, transformation, elegance, and compassion. This festival is observed for a total of 10 days over the whole Navaratri season. On this day, Devi Durga is worshipped. In several *pandals*, Devi Durga's idol is shown alongside those of other Gods and Goddesses. Devi Durga is depicted killing *Mahisasura* (evil demon) with weapons in her ten hands. The priest chants conventional *mantras* while praising the image of Devi Durga. Visitors can see the enormous pandals of the goddess Durga from the sixth day of Navaratri till the ninth day. The goddess Durga's idols are submerged in water on the tenth day of Navaratri, which is known as Dashami. This ritual is known as *Visarjan*.

For the ten days of the Durga Puja, Kolkata comes alive with energy and lights up. Every household celebrates every day with boundless energy, accompanied by the sound of *dhak* and *shankh* (conch shell), as well as the aroma of freshly cooked *bhog*. In the Bengali colonies, radios and televisions all broadcast the same sound in the morning, which is Chandi Path. It is a sensation that people experience daily. The occasion they look forward to all year. In the puja pandal, several cultural components, including theatre, dance, and art competitions, offer captivating visual enjoyment. The pandals are decorated thematically and display excellent craftsmanship in a variety of materials. As a result, the puja draws both, Durga Maa believers and followers of various cultural art forms. People have new dresses and leave their houses to view the stunning *Pandals* that have been embellished with lights, flowers, and other aesthetically pleasing elements. Ladies appear to be one step ahead of the males, dressed in the most stunning outfits, accessorised with the heaviest jewels and thickest bangles, and wearing *sindoor* and *bindis* to visit temples for Durga Puja. For each day of Durga Puja, particular commodities are required. Gathering the necessary materials in advance will ensure a seamless performance of the ritual worship of the goddess. There are different items that are used for the puja for different purposes, such as; **food offerings (***Panchashasha,* i.e., curd, honey, sugar, sugar cane juice, *til* oil etc.), **water offerings (**coconut water, *sarbooushodhi*, spring water, water containing lotus pollen, rainwater, etc.), **Puja items (**powders of five different colours - rice chaff or coconut fibre burnt for the dark colour, rice, turmeric, kusum flowers or red *aabir*, *bel patra* or powdered wood apple leaves, green coconut with stalk, *Sindur*, etc.), **cloth offerings (**a *dhoti* for Vishnu, a *sari* each for *bodhon* and *Chandi*, *Gamcha* or a piece of cloth to cover the pot), Water camphor and perfumed sandal wood paste, *aashon* (a mattress of jute or hay), *chandmala* (garland with circular decorations), Ghat or a pot etc. The renowned Durga Puja in Kolkata has finally been added to UNESCO's list of the Intangible Cultural Heritage of Humanity (ICH) in 2021, considering the many traditional values, labourers, artists, and sentiments connected.

Dussehra

It is also known as Dasara or Vijayadashami. The Sanskrit words *dasha* (meaning "ten") and *hara* (meaning "defeat") were used to create the festival's name. The Dussehra celebration commemorates Lord Rama's triumph over Ravana (10-headed demon king). Lord Vishnu incarnated as Rama, symbolizing the victory of virtue over vice. The malevolent demon Ravana embodied evil in this story. Ramleela, a well-known folk play, draws individuals eager to witness and celebrate the life of Lord Rama. It is a wonderful moment to celebrate Rama's virtues and draw inspiration from them. The nine-day Navratri festival comes to an end on Dussehra, which also falls on the tenth day of the Durga Puja event. In open fields at night, effigies of Ravana—often accompanied by those of Meghnada, Ravana's son, and Kumbhkarana, Ravana's brother—are lit on fire as a ritual.

Eid

Eid is a holy occasion when Muslims gather and embrace one

another while making vows of *Zakah* (almsgiving), generosity, peace, and brotherhood. It is a Muslim celebration, they celebrate *Eid-ul-Fitr* (the feast of breaking the fast) and *Eid-ul-Adha* (Feast of sacrifice) as their principal events. This celebration is not about celebrating your own happiness, but rather about fostering the happiness of others. Muslims from all over the world express their gratitude to Allah for what they have. Eid celebrations are occasions that bring bliss and delight to friends and family members. Ramadan's holy fasting month concludes with food, gatherings, and festivities on Eid-ul-Fitr. Muslims rise early and consume dates to break their fast. However, the gorgeous new apparel *kurta payjama* (traditional dress) that is specifically bought to wear to Salah is what gives this celebration its sparkle. On both the occasions people congregate in large numbers to pray in Jama Masjid (mosque). Eid al-Adha is a three-day festivity observed by Muslims which starts on the tenth day of the Islamic lunar month of *Dhu al-Hijjah*. After the Eid prayer, the *qurbani* (sacrifice) is performed, to mark this day in remembrance of Prophet Ibrahim's sacrifice for Allah, the ritual of *qurbani* entails slaughtering an animal as a sacrifice.

Buddha Purnima

Buddha Purnima, also known as Buddha Jayanti, commemorates the birth of Prince Siddharta Gautama, a Nepalese prince who founded Buddhism and was born between 563 and 483 B.C. It is celebrated annually, usually between April and May. The title "Buddha" is reserved for people who achieve "bodhi," or wisdom, Siddartha was given this name once he gained enlightenment. In Hindu and Buddhist lunar calendars, it is typically observed during the month of "Vaisakhi." Buddha is regarded as Lord Vishnu's eighth incarnation in India. As a ritual, Buddhists follow a longer-than-usual and comprehensive Buddhist sutra, which is akin to a service, as part of the celebration of Buddha Purnima. Buddhists typically wear all-white clothing and abstain from eating meat and dairy products. The Buddha statue is set inside a floral-decorated, water-filled bowl. People go to temples to represent this day as a new beginning.

Mahavir Jayanti

People of the Jain faith celebrate the birth anniversary of Lord

Mahavira, the founder of Jainism. People organise Rath Yatras or peaceful processions on Mahavir Jayanti, bringing the idol of Lord Mahavir on chariots, horses, elephants, etc. On this day, many rituals are performed, one of which is the *abhisheka*, or ceremonial bathing in honey, water, and milk, of the idol of Lord Mahavir. Mahaveer Jayanti is celebrated with enormous grandeur at all Jain temples since it is an auspicious occasion for the Jain community. It is mostly observed in the Bihar temples of Pawapuri, Gujarat's Girnar and Palitana, Rajasthan's Shri Mahavirji Temple, and Kolkata's Parasnath Temple. To obtain the blessings of liberation, many Jains engage in charity. Jains have satvik cuisine, which comprises freshly prepared vegetarian meals made without onion or garlic, on this day and throughout the year. These two root vegetables are not included in the satvik diet, which is also produced with the least cruelty to animals.

Christmas

Annually, on December 25, people observe Christmas, marking the eve of the birth anniversary of Jesus Christ. For Christians, who regard Jesus Christ as the son of God, this is one of the most cherished and esteemed celebrations. Around the world, people adorn their homes, public places, and even trees with various decorations and lights that each have a unique meaning and add to the festive atmosphere. The Christmas tree is the focal point of decorations and is frequently decorated with ornaments, lights, tinsel, etc. On Christmas Eve, it is a tradition in many houses to hang stockings filled with little presents and candy. For a warm and joyful environment, candles are utilised. Not only are these decorations beautiful, but they also have significant cultural and religious meanings. On Christmas Eve or Christmas Day morning, Christians typically attend a religious service at their local church or a greater church. On this Eve, it is also common to read Scripture passages, sing hymns that are connected to the nativity account from the Bible, and attend early morning mass.

Guru Nanak Jayanti

It is among Sikhism's most reverence festivals. Guru Nanak Dev Ji is regarded as the founder of Sikhism. Guru Nanak's Prakash Utsav and Guru Nanak Gurpurab are other names for Guru Nanak Jayanti is celebrated to honour the birth of Guru Nanak, the first Sikh guru.

In Gurdwaras, candles and lights are lit in honor of the Guru. The Gurudwara hosts Akhand Path, or a 48-hour nonstop reading of the Guru Granth Sahib, two days before Guru Nanak Jayanti. One day before Gurpurab, a parade called Nagarkirtan is organised and conducted by the Panj Pyaras. The teachings of Guru Nanak Dev Ji were propagated by leaders. On the day of Guru Nanak Jayanti, followers recite *Katha* and sing hymns. Following that, volunteers at the Gurudwara organse a communal lunch or *langar.*

Harvest Festivals in India (Season-specific)

Makar Sankranti

Hindus all around India celebrate Makar Sankranti, a harvest festival. It signifies the sun's passage from the Tropic of Cancer to the Tropic of Capricorn, or Makar in Sanskrit, and its subsequent return to the northern hemisphere. This event, which honours the purification of the soul and the start of a new stage of life, is observed with various rituals across India. It is referred by various names across the nation, including Makar Sankranti in Bihar, Andhra Pradesh, Rajasthan, Pongal in Tamil Nadu, *Uttarayan* in Rajasthan, *Khichdi Parv or Kicheri* in Uttar Pradesh, *Maghi* in Himachal Pradesh and Punjab, *Magh Bighu* in Assam. The celebration is also known as *Til Sankranti* because the *til laddoos*, made of jaggery and sesame seeds, are the festival's main attraction. A tradition of kite flying is also very common on this occasion. The sacred dip in Prayagraj is the most significant rite performed on this day. The *Magh Snan* is another name for this. Millions of worshipers participate in the holy bath at Sangam on this day (the confluence of the Ganga, Yamuna, and Saraswati rivers). By taking a bath during Makar Sakranti, devotees are said to achieve *moksha* and atone for their misdeeds. Hindus have a special place in their hearts for Arunachal Pradesh when it comes to Makar Sankranti. The sage Parsurama is said to have submerged himself in the waters of the Lohit Lake, a region in Arunachal Pradesh, to atone for his misdeeds, according to the *Kalika Puranas*, *Srimat Bhagwata*, and the *Mahabharata*, three of the oldest Hindu books. Hindus, who frequent this lake, now known as Parasuram Kund, in great numbers from all over the nation to dip into its sacred waters on a yearly basis, view it as having religious significance.

Baisakhi

According to the solar calendar, the harvest festival of Baisakhi (also known as Vaisakhi) is observed on the thirteenth day of April. This day is observed as the first day of the new year across the nation under several titles. When the rabi crop is ready for harvest, it is celebrated across North India, especially in the states of Punjab and Haryana. It frequently occurs on April 13 and only once every 36 years falls on April 14. It falls on the same day as "Pooram Vishu" in Kerala, "Naba Barsha" in Bengal, "Puthandu" in Tamil Nadu, and "Rongali Bihu" in Assam. Sikhs attend Nagar Kirtans the night before Baisakhi and devote the next day to honouring the Khalsa. The Guru Granth Sahib, the Sikhs' holy book, is also honoured by people who recite sacred hymns, sing songs, and perform other acts of worship. People visit the Gurudwaras, dip in the sacred water, and participate in the daily prayers there. Farmers pray for success in the upcoming year and thank God for the abundant crop. In particular, *langars* are held throughout Punjab, and customarily, everyone receives a serving of *Kada Prasad* (wheat halwa). People perform Bhangra (folk dance of Punjab) in the evenings while dressing up in elegant, colourful clothing.

Ladakh harvest festival

One of the most well-known festivals in Ladakh that highlights the diversity of local cultures is the Ladakh Festival. The Ladakh Harvest Festival, as its name suggests, is a celebration of the beginning of the harvest. In Ladakh, the harvest season is a unique time that is celebrated fervently; agriculture is a substantial industry that is valued by the residents. This celebration normally occurs in August or September to celebrate the end of the agricultural season and the imminent arrival of the crops for harvest. Various cultural performances, including traditional Ladakhi music, dance, and drama, are presented throughout the event. These performances frequently portray the local culture, legends, and folklore. Monks and lamas perform rituals and prayers to express their thanks for the harvest and to ask for blessings for the crops of the following year. People dress in traditional Ladakhi attire during the celebration, which includes vivid robes and ornate jewellery. The celebrations include various sporting events, such as archery and traditional Ladakhi games. Performers travel from all around Ladakh to participate in this lavish celebration.

Lohri

The Punjabi people start the New Year to honor the farmers for their toil and labour during the festival of Lohri. Foods like '*gur ki gajjak*' and '*til ki rewari*' are offered to the fire during the celebration as a manner of expressing appreciation to the Sun God. The night of the Lohri celebration, also called as the winter solstice, is traditionally considered the longest night of the year. The festival's pinnacle is marked by the ignition of the bonfire after nightfall. For newlywed couples and parents of new-born kids, this fire is particularly lucky. Couples and parents go around the bonfire while pouring offerings into it, including popcorn, puffed rice, and the sweet winter dessert known as *gajjak*. The flames of this bonfire, according to Punjabi mythology, send the people's prayers to the Sun God on the day of Lohri, who will bless the ground with a good harvest and put an end to the winter. For the people of Punjab, Lohri is more than just a feast; it is an exuberant celebration of their culture and industry. As part of the Lohri celebrations, the event is also an opportunity to prepare traditional delicacies based on recipes that have been passed down through the generations. The festivals of Pongal and Makar Sankranti, which both fall around the same time as Lohri, all convey the same message—thanking God for the wealth we have on earth.

Basant Panchami

Hindus celebrate Basant Panchami, a springtime festival, typically around February. Basant Panchami is a significant day for Hindus in India for various reasons. Many celebrate the harvest and the start of spring, while some celebrate it to honour the goddess Saraswati. On this auspicious day, people worship Goddess Saraswati, the deity of study, music, and knowledge. Even though the occasion may be observed differently in each state in India, some similar patterns continue. A yellow sari, the colour the Goddess wears, is commonly seen on women. Because the mustard crop is frequently picked during festivals, yellow is a significant hue. Additionally, sweets are made, offered to Maa Saraswati, and given out as "prasad." This occasion is frequently linked to wealth and luck. It is thought that Basant Panchami marks the beginning of spring, a favourable season for planting and harvesting. It is celebrated as the first day of spring, which is a time for harvest after the frigid winter. Given that India is primarily an agricultural nation, it stands to reason that this event is very meaningful to Indians.

Onam

The greatest and most significant festival in Kerala is called Onam. It is a harvest festival that is joyfully observed by people from all communities around the state. A popular legend suggests that the occasion is observed to receive King Mahabali, whose spirit is believed to revisit Kerala during Onam. Keralans' devotion is evident in Onam, reflecting their deep belief in their mythological heritage, religion, and the divine power of worship. It demonstrates the elevated character of the people who try to observe the festival in the proper way and in a grand manner. At this time of the Malayalam New Year, Kerala's stunning scenery is visible in all its glory. It appears that the weather wants to take part in the festivities as well. It helps by turning comfortable warm and sunny. A plentiful harvest makes the fields shine. Farmers have a sense of triumph as they proudly observe the results of their labour. The festival's secular structure is what gives it its beauty. All castes, communities, and religions participate in the celebration with equal joy and vigour. By organising several sports teams on the day, Onam also promotes harmony and fraternity. The development of its rich and enduring culture is one of Onam's most amazing features. In the ten-day carnival, we see not just glimmers of it but the full spectrum of it. On one platform known as Onam, you can observe Pulikali, Kaikottikali, Kummattikalli, Kathakali, Thumbi Thullal, as well as many other folk arts and customs. Onam celebrations last for ten lengthy days. The first day, Atham, and the end or tenth day, Thiru Onam, are the two most significant days out of all of these. Atham, celebrations start on the first day. On this day, people take an early morning bath and go to the neighborhood temple to pray. This day is notable for the beginning of the Pookkallam or floral carpet. Girls from the house make Attha Poo in the front courtyard to welcome the divine spirit. It is time for the family to prepare for the large feast known as Onasadya after finishing the morning rituals. The family's oldest member is seated in the middle of the row. A distant brass lamp with a light is set up in front of him. A little plantain leaf is arranged to the west of the lamp, on which food is served. In the name of Lord Ganapathy, this offering is made then everyone gathered is given a supper. The extravagant supper is served on banana leaves and includes 11 to 13 vegan dishes. The meal is served in a prescribed sequence, and the individual dishes are placed in a specific location on the leaf. Onam is a festival celebrated by many people that is marked by celebrations and cultural events all around the state. The Snake Boat Race (Vallamkali) and fun events like Kummatti Kali and Pulikali stand out among them.

Pongal

Tamil people celebrate the harvest with an annual festival called Pongal. It is time to express gratitude to Mother Nature, the Sun, and all of the farm animals that contributed to the successful harvest production. The four-day festival of Pongal marks the beginning of the auspicious Tamil month of Thai. It normally takes place on January 14 or 15 each year. Pongal is the name of the cuisine cooked and eaten during this festival. The main ingredient is cooked sweet rice. It derives from the Tamil verb *pongu,* meaning 'to boil over.' The first day of Pongal is known as *Bhogi.* On this day, people cleanse their homes of unneeded possessions to mark the beginning of something fresh. New clothes are worn, and houses are decorated for the event. The main Pongal day is the second day, which is known as Surya Pongal. This day is dedicated to the Sun God. At auspicious times, each household makes a pot of fresh rice with milk, and kolam, bright and lovely floor decorations, are made at the entrance to their homes. When the milk begins to boil over, everyone in the household shouts, "*Pongalo Pongal*" with great excitement. Once the Pongal offered to the Sun God, they would eat various Pongal meals, especially for that day. The third day of Pongal is known as *Maatu Pongal.* Cattle (*Maatu*) are celebrated and worshipped on this day to honour their work in cultivating the soil. Cows receive baths and are adorned with bells, floral garlands, and beads in various colours. The Pongal festival's fourth day is known as *Kaanum Pongal.* On this day, a focus is put on strengthening ties within the community. Families assemble for a sumptuous meal. Younger family members often approach their elders to ask for their blessing. On this day, people throughout India celebrate with traditional folk dances like the mayilattam and the kolattam.

Ugadi

Karnataka and other South Indian states take great pleasure and passion in celebrating the sacred festival of Ugadi. The Hindu lunisolar calendar observes Ugadi on the first day of Chaitra. The syllables "Yuga" and "Adi," which mean "a new beginning," are the source of the name "Ugadi." Ugadi is thought to have been the first day the universe was created. According to Hindu mythology, Lord Brahma created the universe on this day, followed by days, weeks, months, and years. Ugadi, a colourful festival, is observed to ring in the New Year with plenty, pleasure, and success. The festival holds a special significance for the people as it ushers in the spring season and the start of nature's annual cycle. In anticipation of a bountiful harvest, the farming families prepare for the new year. Ugadi is also regarded as a holy period for starting new endeavours. Devotees from across the state observe the day by attending religious and cultural events and cooking a lavish feast for their loved ones. A unique treat called Bevu Bella perfectly encapsulates the spirit of this holy day. To make it, different components are mixed, including tamarind, neem leaves, jaggery, raw mango, pepper, and salt. The meal represents a variety of human emotions and foresees a year full of bittersweet life events. Another important aspect of this holy occasion is the red clay and lovely string of mango and neem leaves used to decorate the front door. In front of their homes, people also create vibrant designs known as Kolamulus or Rangoli using rice and flowers. The celebration of Ugadi, celebrated for its spiritual significance and vibrant cultural offerings, fills people's lives with hues of happiness, hope, and prosperity.

Vishu

Vishu represents the start of the springtime. Kerala celebrates the Hindu festival of Vishu as the harvest celebration and the astrological New Year for the Malayalis. The sun enters the sign of Aries, also known as the Mesha Rashi, on the day of Vishu, when farmers begin using ploughs and other tools for agriculture. To start the New Year, one should witness the Vishukkani at sunrise on the auspicious day of Vishu. A collection of numerous auspicious objects, such as fruits, grains, vegetables, lamps, flowers, coconuts, gold, mirrors, and Hindu sacred books, is called Vishukkani, which is also pronounced as Vishu Kani. This ritual is called Kanikanal. The people of Kerala celebrate Vishu, also known as the festival of light, by setting off fireworks, lighting *diyas* outside their homes, cooking a special meal called *Sadya*, and engaging in prayers and rituals. Traditional rites are prevalent at Vishu, but there are also many feasting customs. Along with other seasonal vegetables and fruits, special recipes are made with jackfruits, mangoes, pumpkins, and gourds.

Bhogali Bihu

Makar Sankranti is known as Bhogali Bihu or Magh Bihu in Assam. It is one of the greatest events celebrated by Assamese Hindus. The festivities begin the evening before the festival. It is a night of feasting, prayer, sweet-exchanging, and hut-building using thatch, dried leaves, and bamboos. This night is known as *Uruka*. The name *Mejis* refers to these improvised homes. *Dhols* play in the background as people assemble around the *Mejis* and sing religious hymns. The *Mejis* are burned as part of the ceremony the following morning after an early bath for self-purification. In order to obtain the gods' blessings for the upcoming harvest season, rice cakes, also known as *pithas,* and betel nuts are tossed into the burning huts. Then, the burned remains are carried and scattered among fruit trees to foster their fruitfulness. The remainder of the day is spent engaging in or watching cockfights, buffalo fights, and other such amusements.

Wangala

Among the Garos (tribe) of Meghalaya, India, the Wangala Festival is one of the most well-known celebrations. Saljong, the fertility-promoting Sun god, is honoured at the harvest celebration known as Wangala Festival. The Wangala Festival commemoration signals the conclusion of a time of labour, which boosts field productivity. Additionally, it denotes the start of winter. Wangala Celebration, also known as a 100 drums festival, when the tribal people make sacrifices to appease Saljong, the Sun God, who serves as their primary god. The Wangala Festival essentially serves as a means of preserving and promoting the cultural identity of the Garos in Meghalaya. This is one method of showcasing the local tradition and culture. It is often observed for two days; however, it can occasionally last up to a week. The first-day ceremony, referred to as "Ragula," takes place within the chief's home. The second day is referred to as "Kakkat." People of all ages dance to the beat of music produced by long, oval-shaped drums while wearing colourful costumes and feathered headgear. This is the time to unwind, and for days the astonishing beat of drums can be heard in the hills and valleys. A queue of two parallel lines, one of men and one of ladies each wearing festive finery, is the fundamental motif of the popular dance styles that are performed throughout the festival. Both young and old participate in the celebrations with passion. The men are beating the drums as the line advances in time with them. The male "orchestra" includes flutes, gongs, drums, and other percussion instruments.

Ka Pomblang Nongkrem

Pomblang Nongkrem is primarily Meghalaya's harvest celebration. It is the most significant celebration for the state's Khasi population. The celebration is typically observed in November and lasts for around 5 days during the chilly winter months. For those who live in the Khasi Hills, it is one of the most well-known festivals. It is like a large carnival that features the exchange of money, the sacrifice of animals, and a fervent religious atmosphere. The Pomblang Ceremony, which involves the sacrifice (decapitation) of goats, is the most significant rite of the celebration. During this event, tribal members present goats to the Hima's administrative chief, known as the "Syiem" of Khyrem (Khasi State). The famous Nongkrem dance in which young women dance in the shape of a ring, is performed by Khasi people on the fourth day after the religious rites. This maiden dance is performed by the young ladies from the "Syiem" residence under the cover of an umbrella. Young males from the Tribal Khasi communities dress up for the Nongkrem dance in multicoloured silk dhotis, coats, and plumed turbans that are embellished with sparkling decorations.

Nuakhai

The Indian states of Southern Chhattisgarh and Western Odisha are the main regions to observe the well-known agricultural festival known as Nuakhai or Navakhai. It is customary in Nuakhai to welcome the new rice harvest. According to the calendar, it is celebrated the day following Ganesh Chaturthi on *panchami tithi* (the fifth day of the lunar fortnight of the month) of Bhadrapada or Bhadraba (August-

September). The festival holds great significance for the farmers and the agricultural community since it is viewed as a new ray of hope. People overlook their differences and build relationships with one another because of this occasion. Every family in Odia prepares and enjoys eating Aaresha pitha on Nuakhai. This demonstrates both the agricultural value of the celebration and the type of solidarity, fraternity, and ties it fosters within society. Folk songs and dances are performed to mark the occasion, showcasing the culture, tradition, and diverse facets of the community. People of all ages participate in this song and dance tradition and have a great time doing it.

Gudi Padwa

For Marathi and Konkani Hindus, the New Year is marked by the spring festival referred as Gudi Padwa. On the first day of the Chaitra month, the event is observed in and around the states of Maharashtra and Goa. In accordance with the lunisolar Hindu calendar, it signifies the start of the New Year. Following that, the most significant ceremony is performed and the Gudi is built. They buy silk fabric with a *zari* brocade in a vibrant green or yellow colour. Then it is put onto a lengthy bamboo pole is adorned with a cloth, neem leaves, gathi, a garland of red or yellow flowers, and a sprig of mango leaves secured on top of it. Afterwards, a stick with all the decorations is placed on top of an inverted copper or silver pot. The Gudi is ready and is either positioned at the entrance or outside the opening in the window. Rangoli patterns are used to decorate the floor as part of the Gudi Padwa celebration. People pray to Lord Brahma, the clothing worn by the populace, especially by ladies, is quite typical to the area. The saree is draped so that the bottom half, which could be in a variety of vibrant colours, resembles *dhoti* pants more than a long skirt. This outfit is adorned with a garland of mogra flowers in the hair, which is put in a bun, as well as an exquisite gold nose pin. Most men and women even wrap a turban made of cotton fabric in saffron over their heads.

Nabanna

The festival of Nabanna, which is observed in the Bengali month of Agrohyon (November) and is a way of expressing appreciation for good fortune, is a prominent event in the agrarian calendar of Bengal. By paying respects to the Golaghor (storehouse), Nabanna is commemorated. A traditional cake called a "pitha" is made during the celebrations. Typically, it honours the Hindu goddess Lakshmi, who stands for fertility and abundance. According to folklore, a community can't eat its "new food" (or "new rice") until it has first given nabanna to Lakshmi. Farmers will cut and husk a special variety of rice frequently used to make rice porridge. Occasionally, tribute is also made to neighbourhood deities and ancestral spirits. Other customs associated with the occasion include turning on lamps to welcome the moon, gifting children gifts and sweetened milk, and feeding crows rice.

Nowruz

It is also known as Navruz, Nooruz, Nevruz, or Nowruz. Nowruz, which technically translates as "New Day," that refers to the Persian, Iranian, or Parsi New Year. It begins on the first day of the spring equinox, or exactly at the moment of the equinox when both days and nights are of equal length. This is the first day of the Aries constellation and the start of the Iranian solar calendar. On March 21, the Parsi community in India, which follows the religion of Zoroastrianism, celebrated Nowruz, that is considered to be the first day of the New Year. According to the community, the festival represents freshness, renewal, and liberty. Some muslim communities also celebrate Nawruz besides Zoroastrians and Muslims with diverse religious views, Nowruz rites and celebrations have a long history. Nowruz is a celebration of the new year and the arrival of spring that has been held since at least the sixth century BCE (UNESCO, n.d.). Nowruz is mostly observed in Iran, Afghanistan, Turkey, and the Kurdish regions of Iraq and by the Parsis throughout India and other diaspora communities worldwide. This festival is enthusiastically observed in India, where people decorate their homes, make delicious foods, and participate in ceremonies based on the motions of the sun during the day. They also visit the Fire Temple, the Parsi community's worship centre. The Nowruz celebrations last for around two weeks and encompass a variety of ceremonies, rituals, traditional games, special foods, performances, and other cultural events. Muslims offer special prayers in mosques on this day, and Parsis offer prayers in the Fire Temple. Following prayers, people give each other hugs, kiss their heads or hands as a sign of respect, and say "*Sal Mubarak*" and "*Nauroz Mubarak*." Gathering around "The Table," adorned with items that stand for purity, brightness, livelihood, and wealth, to share a special meal with loved ones is a significant activity carried out during this time. A copy of the *Gathas* (songs), a lamp or candle, a small ceramic plate with sprouting wheat or beans, a tiny bowl with a silver coin, decorated eggs, flowers, chocolates, and a bowl of water with goldfish are traditionally placed on a table for this special day. All of this symbolises happiness, prosperity, and wealth. Visits to family members, especially the elderly and neighbours, are carried out while wearing new clothes. Parsis wear *kustis* (sacred cord) and headgear made of gold and silver. A symbolic dinner is shared by communities and their members, and it frequently consists of cooked rice and vegetables with many regional flavours. '*Falooda*' is the primary dish of Nauroz among the Persian community that contains milk and rose water. '*Ravo*' is another well-known dish. It is a sweet delicacy related to *"Halwa"* that is produced by baking *suji* (rawa), sugar, and milk. 'Nadur Fish' and 'turnip chicken' are popular meals in Kashmir. Nadur Fish is made by deep-frying fish, adding hot spices, and cooking it with Nadur, which is a lotus stem. Chicken and dried turnips are deep-fried together to make Turnip Chicken.

Nowruz is also the time for traditional cultural festivities that combine universal and regional rituals. Nowruz celebrations are well known for their poetry, and 'Nowruzi poems' are frequently written, printed, and spoken during this time. Music is also essential, and Nowruz has unique folk songs for the occasion.

Nauroz stands for the triumph of good over evil. On this day, one must monitor their good and negative thoughts and actions to become a better person. These practises promote cultural variety, tolerance, and community harmony. Through involvement and observation, they are passed down from older to younger generations. In 2010, the International Day of Nowruz was established by the UN General Assembly. In the year 2016, UNESCO included it in the Representative List of Intangible Cultural Heritage of Humanity. UNESCO characterizes it as a festival that "promotes values of harmony and brotherhood between generations and between families in addition to reconciliation and neighborliness." Nowruz plays a significant role in fostering human connections based on respect for one another and the concepts of harmony and good neighbourliness.

Nauroz is an amalgamation of uplifting thoughts, feelings, rights, and emotions. This day is about interaction, integrity, peace, prosperity, justice, and happiness.

Every festival has unique traits of its own. Indian festivals are also observed according to the season and the state. Following is the State list of festivals celebrated in the country:

Table 5: State Wise List of Indian Festival

S. No.	State	List of Indian Festivals
1.	Andhra Pradesh	Bhishma Ekadasi, Ugadi, Deccan Festival, Pitr, Brahmotsavam
2.	Arunachal Pradesh	Pongtu, Losar, Murung, Solang, Mopin, Monpa festival
3.	Assam	Bhogali Bihu
4.	Bihar	Chhath Puja
5.	Chhattisgarh	Maghi Purnima, Bastar
6.	Goa	Carnival, Sunburn festival
7.	Gujarat	Navratri, Janmashtami, Kutch Utsav, Nowruz
8.	Himachal Pradesh	Rakhadumni, Gochi Festival
9.	Haryana	Baisakhi, Surajkund Mela
10.	Jammu and Kashmir	Har Navami, Chhari, Bahu Mela
11.	Jharkhand	Karam Utsav, Holi
12.	Karnataka	Mysore Dasara, Ugadi
13.	Kerala	Onam, Vishu
14.	Madhya Pradesh	Lok-rang Utsav, Tejaji, Khujaraho festival
15.	Meghalaya	Nongkrem festival, Khasis festival
16.	Maharashtra	Ganesh Utsav, Gudi Padva, Nowruz
17.	Manipur	Yaoshang, Porag, Chavang Kut
18.	Mizoram	Chapcharkut Festival
19.	Nagaland	Hornbill festival, Moatsu Festival
20.	Odisha	Rath Yatra, Raja Parba
21.	Punjab	Lohri, Baisakhi
22.	Rajasthan	Gangaur, Teej, Bundi, Nowruz
23.	Sikkim	Losar, Saga Dawa
24.	Tamil Nadu	Pongal
25.	Telangana	Bonalu, Bathukamma

26.	Tripura	Kharchi Puja
27.	West Bengal	Durga Puja
28.	Uttaranchal	Ganga Dussehra, Kumbh Mela
29.	Uttar Pradesh	Ram Navmi, Ganga Mahotsav, Navaratri,

Social practices, rituals, and festive events are significantly impacted by the changes communities go through in modern cultures because they rely so heavily on the widespread participation of practitioners and other members of the communities. Festivals and rituals are examples of cultural activities that help to preserve the spirit of interpersonal interaction. With the development of new religious forms and rituals, these prehistoric festivities underwent substantive modification and transformation over time. These traditions are strongly impacted by different elements like individualisation, migration, the extensive acceptance of education, the increasing impact of major world spiritual beliefs, and other repercussions of globalisation.

The occasions that helped to break up the routine of everyday life and provide an interval from rigorous work are either forgotten about or compressed into the shortest time. Holidays, feasts, and festivals are seen as a loss of productivity in the modern workplace, which results in financial loss. Consequently, although some rituals and festivals have totally disappeared, others have experienced significant changes. The urban inhabitants avoid major religious gatherings and are cautious of fairs and festivals. "One of the major characteristics of the postmodern age is that change is both rapid and broad in scope. It is estimated by futurists that our current knowledge base now doubles every 2-3 years. Many futurists believe that by the year 2055, human knowledge will double every 24 hours. The rate of change today is fuelled by many factors- social, technological, and economic" (Oswald, 1999). There is a widespread belief that there are far fewer rituals and celebrations in modern culture. Festivals will inevitably be replaced by other forms of entertainment due to industrialization, secularization, population changes, and a host of other factors.

A society's social, political, and legal structures and procedures, as well as a significant number of people, must frequently be mobilized in order to maintain social practices, rituals, or joyous occasions. In some circumstances, official legal actions must be taken to ensure the community's access rights to the sacred sites, valuable artefacts, or natural resources required for the performance of social rituals, practices, and celebratory occasions. Due to the loss of their traditional surroundings, individuals have created new symbolic elements for their rituals and festivities using the resources at their disposal. As a result, these practices' unique features are becoming more similar. Communities use a variety of strategies to combat this homogenization. For instance, parents actively involved in Hindu communities in the United States enroll their children in weekly scripture reading sessions analogous to Bible reading groups. However, no such sessions are frequently attended by Hindu children in modern India. This example shows how groups seek to maintain their cultural distinctiveness while incorporating aspects of another culture. Marriage, birth, and death ceremonies are likewise condensed and carried out in a condensed manner (Indira Gandhi National Open University, 2017). Our ancient traditions and rituals are magnificent ways of life. It is our responsibility to carry on this legacy of traditions to the next generation so they can live in peace. In the present, both a new approval and assimilation are required. It is necessary to plan celebrations and activities for the communities for instance-cultural performances, culinary fairs, and sporting events with participants of various ages and backgrounds to encourage active engagement. To foster a larger feeling of celebration, encourage individuals to share their experiences and celebratory behaviour online. Utilise the potential of social media and digital platforms to organize virtual events to raise awareness of cultural celebrations, and share cultural memories. To assist in the transmission of traditions and instill a sense of excitement, it is important to involve newer generations, including children and teenagers, in the planning and preparations for the event and the celebrations. In addition, encourage the planning of events, art contests, or cultural performances by schools, universities, and youth organisations. Festivals can be promoted through commercials, articles, or interviews by working with the local media, community organisations, and government organisations. This promotes excitement and interest, which draws more people to engage in the celebrations actively.

References

1. *10 Customs and Traditions in Indian Culture*. (2021). Authentic India Tours. Retrieved from https://www.authenticindiatours.com/2021/02/10/10-customs-and-traditions-in-indian-culture/
2. Aiyyappan, A. (2012). When a Rudaali Raises a Bawandar. *Intersections: Gender and Sexuality in Asia and the Pacific*, (28)
3. Al-Qattan, M. M., & Al-Zahrani, K. (2009). A review of burns related to traditions, social habits, religious activities, festivals and traditional medical practices. *Burns*, *35*(4), 476-481.
4. Ariba. (2023). *A brief history of Nowruz: Celebration of beginnings, assertion of identity*. The Indian Express. Retrieved from https://indianexpress.com/article/explained/explained-culture/nowruz-history-significance-celebration-persians-kurds-indians-8512962/
5. *Aarti: The Hindu Ceremony of Light*. (n.d.). BAPS Swaminarayan Sanstha, London. Retrieved from
6. Bigonah, H. (2016). Nowruz in tradition transition. *IIOABJ*, *7*(3), 491-495.
7. Bohigian, G. H. (1997). The history of the evil eye and its influence on ophthalmology, medicine, and social customs. *Documenta ophthalmologica*, *94*(1), 91-100.
8. *Buddha Purnima*. (2023). National Today. Retrieved from https://nationaltoday.com/buddha-purnima/#:~:text=Buddha%20Purnima%20is%20on%20May,calendars%20can%20be%20interpreted%20differently.
9. Definition of baptism. (2023). In Merriam-Webster Dictionary. from https://www.merriam-webster.com/dictionary/baptism
10. Devi, M., & Ghatani, K. (2022). The use of coconut in rituals and food preparations in India: a review. *Journal of Ethnic Foods*, *9*(1), 1-13.
11. *Different Marriage Customs in India*. (n.d.). India Online. Retrieved from https://www.indiaonline.in/about/culture/different-marriage-customs-in-india
12. *Festivals of India 2023*. (n.d.). Retrieved from https://www.festivalsofindia.in/
13. Fiese, B. H., & Tomcho, T. J. (2001). Finding meaning in religious practices: The relation between religious holiday rituals and marital satisfaction. *Journal of Family Psychology*, *15*(4), 597.
14. Flintoff, C. (2011). *In India, Snake Charmers Are Losing Their Sway*. NPR. Retrieved from https://www.npr.org/2011/08/08/139086119/in-india-snake-charmers-are-losing-their-sway
15. *Four Extraordinary Daily Religious Rituals to Experience in India*. (2019). Greaves India. Retrieved from https://www.greavesindia.co.uk/four-extraordinary-daily-religious-rituals-to-experience-in-india/

16. Ghosh, B., & Bk, A. (2022). From Ritual Mourning to Solitary Grief: Reinterpretation of Hindu Death Rituals in India. *OMEGA-Journal of Death and Dying*, *0*(0). 1-18. 00302228221085175.

17. Government of Meghalaya. (n.d.). *Wangala – The 100 Drums Festival of Meghalaya.* Retrieved from https://meghalaya.gov.in/wangala

18. Grover, N. (2023). *Nowruz - UNESCO's List of Intangible Cultural Heritage - Art and Culture Notes*. Prepp. Retrieved from https://prepp.in/news/e-492-nowruz-unescos-list-of-intangible-cultural-heritage-art-and-culture-notes

19. *Hindu Funeral Services in Livermore.* (n.d.). Callaghan Mortuary & Livermore Crematory. Retrieved from https://www.callaghanmortuary.com/how-to-plan-a-funeral/hindu-traditions/

20. http://londonmandir.baps.org/worship/aarti-the-hindu-ceremony-of-light/

21. Indian Culture. (n.d.). *Lohri: Honouring the Harvest.* Retrieved from https://www.indianculture.gov.in/food-and-culture/food-festivals/lohri-honouring-harvest

22. Indian Culture. (n.d.). *Durga Puja*. Retrieved from https://indianculture.gov.in/stories/durga-puja

23. *Indian Culture.* (n.d.). Retrieved from https://www.indianculture.gov.in/

24. Indian Culture. (n.d.). *Social practices, rituals and festive events*. Retrieved from https://indianculture.gov.in/intangible-cultural-heritage/social-practices-rituals-and-festive-events

25. Indira Gandhi National Open University. (2017). *UNIT- 5 FESTIVALS AND RITUALS. Impact of Technology in Transforming Folk Art to Commodity.* Retrieved from https://egyankosh.ac.in/bitstream/123456789/38963/1/Unit-5.pdf

26. Jacobson, D. (2004). *Indian Society and Ways of Living*. Asia Society. Retrieved from https://asiasociety.org/education/indian-society-and-ways-living#:~:text=India%20is%20a%20hierarchical%20society,seldom%20evident%20in%20daily%20life

27. Jagannathan, M. (2005). *South Indian Hindu festivals and traditions*. Abhinav Publications.

28. Jayalakshmi, K. (2020). The Science behind Indian Rituals, Customs and Traditions. *Journal of Social Sciences & Humanities Researches*, *5*(9).

29. *Ka Pomblang Nongkrem*. (n.d.). Astro Devam. Retrieved from https://www.astrodevam.com/festivals-of-india-ka-pomblang-nongkrem.html

30. Kandhari, M. K. Grieving Women of Rajasthan-The Rudaalis and their Dying Tradition. *CHRONICLE'20 ANNUAL NEWSLETTER ISSUE 5 DEPARTMENT OF HISTORY*, 58.

31. Konar, A. K., & Modak, B. K. (2010). Socialising snake society: An Indian instance. *Social Change, 40*(2), 157-174.

32. *List of Festivals of India 2023 State-wise.* (2023). Dream Big Institution Team. Retrieved from https://dreambiginstitution.com/famous-festivals-in-india-pdf/

33. *Mahavir Jayanti 2023 & Importance.* (2023). GaneshaSpeaks. Retrieved from https://www.ganeshaspeaks.com/festival-calendars/information/mahavir-jayanti/

34. *Major Festivals of India.* (2015). ImportantIndia.com. Retrieved from https://importantindia.com/17423/major-festivals-of-india/

35. *Makar Sankranti in North East India.* (n.d.). Festivalsofindia. Retrieved from https://www.festivalsofindia.in/makarsankranti/celebrations-in-north-east-india

36. Mohapatra, J. (2013). *Wellness In Indian Festivals & Rituals.* Partridge Publishing.

37. National Institute of Open Schooling. (n.d.). *MODULE – VIII. Social Structure. Socio-Cultural Issues in Contemporary India.* 290-299. Retrieved from https://www.nios.ac.in/media/documents/SecICHCour/English/CH.20.pdf

38. *Nowruz Festival in India.* (n.d.). India Tours. Retrieved from https://www.india-tours.com/fairs-and-festivals/nowruz-festival-in-India.html

39. Onalaja-Aliu, Y., & Griffiths, L. (2016). *Here is A Really Important Thing You Need To Know About Snake Charming.* Hand Luggage Only. Retrieved from https://handluggageonly.co.uk/2016/01/26/heres-a-really-important-thing-you-need-to-know-about-snake-charming/

40. *Onam Festival.* (n.d.). Onamfestival.org. Retrieved from https://www.onamfestival.org/

41. Oswald, R. M. (1999). *Transforming rituals: Daily practices for changing lives.* Rowman & Littlefield.

42. *Raksha Bandhan.* (2011). BBC. Retrieved from https://www.bbc.co.uk/religion/religions/hinduism/holydays/raksha.shtml

43. Ray, A. (n.d.). *Nabanna.* Ministry of Culture| Centre for Environment Education. Parampara project. Retrieved from https://paramparaproject.org/traditions_nabanna.html

44. *Rituals and Customs of Vishu Festival.* (n.d.). Society for the Confluence of Festivals in India (SCFI). Retrieved from http://www.vishufestival.org/rituals-and-customs-of-vishu-festival.html

45. Rizvi, S.S.A. (2012). *Azadari.* Al-Islam.org. Retrieved from https://www.al-islam.org/four-californian-lectures-sayyid-saeed-akhtar-rizvi/azadari

46. Sarkar, S. (2022). *UNESCO recognition of Durga Puja a big feat. But it was no easy journey for India.* ThePrint. Retrieved from https://theprint.in/opinion/unesco-recognition-of-durga-puja-a-big-feat-but-it-was-no-easy-journey-for-india/1151796/

47. Sharma, N., Gaur, C. N., Deshpande, P., Pugalia, S., Alekar, S., & Natu, S. Rudaali: The Price of Kohl Drenched Eyes. *MODERN COLLEGE OF ARTS, SCIENCE AND COMMERCE*, 11.

48. Sharma, P., & Yosufi, N. A. (2018). Nowruz-New Year. *Himalayan and Central Asian Studies, 22*(4), 38-0_4.

49. *Sikh festivals*. (n.d.). Sikhism. Retrieved from https://www.sikhreligion.net/sikh-festivals/

50. Soy, N. F., & Sahoo, H. (2017). Marriage arrangements and customs in India. *Social Science Spectrum*, *2*(4), 248-262.

51. Srinivasan, P., & Lee, G. R. (2004). The dowry system in Northern India: Women's attitudes and social change. *Journal of Marriage and Family*, *66*(5), 1108-1117.

52. Sundar, A. (2018). *Saperas: Snake Charming Community of India.* Sahapedia. Retrieved from https://www.sahapedia.org/saperas-snake-charming-community-of-india-0

53. *The Arati Ceremony*. (2018). Heart of Hinduism. Retrieved from https://iskconeducationalservices.org/HoH/further-information-and-teaching-resources-secondary/fact-sheets/the-arati-ceremony/

54. *The Essentials of Durga Puja.* (n.d.). Society for the Confluence of Festivals in India (SCFI). Retrieved from http://www.durga-puja.org/the-essentials-of-durga-puja.html

55. *The significance of AARTI in Hinduism*. (n.d.). ePuja. Retrieved from https://epuja.co.in/blog.php?blog_id=25

56. Thulaja, N. R. (2004). *Snake charmers*. Singapore Infopedia. Retrieved from https://eresources.nlb.gov.sg/infopedia/articles/SIP_601_2004-12-23.html

57. Tribhuwan, R. D. (2003). *Fairs and festivals of Indian tribes*. Discovery Publishing House.

58. *Ugadi Celebrations*. (2023). Karnataka Tourism. Retrieved from https://www.karnatakatourism.org/ugadi/

59. UNESCO - Intangible Cultural Heritage. (n.d.). *21 March: the International Day of Nowruz*. Retrieved from https://ich.unesco.org/en/news/21-march-the-international-day-of-nowruz-13299

60. UNESCO - Intangible Cultural Heritage. (n.d.). *Nawrouz, Novruz, Nowrouz, Nowrouz, Nawrouz, Nauryz, Nooruz, Nowruz, Navruz, Nevruz, Nowruz, Navruz*. Retrieved from https://ich.unesco.org/en/RL/nawrouz-novruz-nowrouz-nowrouz-nawrouz-nauryz-nooruz-nowruz-navruz-nevruz-nowruz-navruz-01161

61. UNESCO. (2003). *Intangible Cultural Heritage Domains*. Retrieved from https://ich.unesco.org/doc/src/01857-EN.pdf

62. UNESCO. (n.d.). *Nowruz: Celebrating the New Year on the Silk Roads | Silk Roads Programme.* Retrieved from https://en.unesco.org/silkroad/content/nowruz-celebrating-new-year-silk-roads

63. *What is the Sacrament of Baptism?* (2018). Apostolate for Family Consecration. Retrieved from https://afc.org/fc_question/what-is-the-sacrament-of-baptism/?gclid=Cj0KCQjw4omaBhDqARIsADXULuUSgI7a5tm3keCVsg1iWR40hTcznZoMPe3xXL8UX7jpgVlyDtRisCoaAolWEALw_wcB

64. Yeolekar, M. E., & Bavdekar, S. B. (2007). Indian festivals: Ethos and health impact. *Journal of Postgraduate Medicine*, *53*(4), 219.

65. Zarrin, A., & Farha. (2022). Intangible Cultural Heritage: A Future Prospect of Heritage Tourism. *International Journal of Interdisciplinary Research in Arts and Humanities (IJIRAH)*, *7*(1), 40–51.

Chapter - 4

Knowledge and Practices Concerning Nature and the Universe

This domain encompasses a wide range of elements, including indigenous knowledge, traditional ecological wisdom, information on local flora and fauna, traditional healing systems, rituals, beliefs, initiation rituals, cosmologies, shamanic traditions, social structures, linguistic diversity, rites of possession, festive celebrations, and visual artistic expressions. It also includes the community's knowledge and practices about nature and the universe, know-how, skills, practises, and representations that have been produced via interaction with the natural world.

The idea of environmental protection is not new to Indians. In the past, conserving nature and wildlife was a deeply held belief that was reflected in people's daily lives and ingrained in traditions, folklore, religions, arts, and culture. The interconnection and interrelationship of all life were some of the cornerstones of ecology that were conceptualised in the Indian ethos and expressed in the ancient text of scripture known as the *Isopanishad* about 2000 years ago. It adds, 'This cosmos is the Supreme Power's creation, intended for the good of all his creatures. Therefore, each individual living form must learn to benefit from it by becoming an integral component of the system and interacting closely with other species. No species shall infringe upon the rights of another.'

The Bhimbetka, Central India, cave paintings, which date back 10,000 years, are among the world's oldest known examples of art, which show birds, animals, and people coexisting peacefully, are the earliest visual representation of human passion, love, and devotion for nature in India. Evidence of human interest in wildlife can also be found in seals with pictures of elephants, rhinos, bulls, and other animals from the Indus Valley civilization. The indigenous people in India generally referred to as tribes or *adivasis* make up a significant portion of the population of the Indian subcontinent. They are primarily confined to areas with abundant natural and mineral resources. Indigenous people, often known as "original dwellers," and tribes are the groups of people who have coexisted for many years in the hinterland or in the forest. The tribal communities have created incredibly effective strategies for preserving the diversity of their environment since the beginning of humankind. Indian tribal people have lived in varied eco-geoclimatic zones with highlands, forests, water, and other natural wealth from the beginning of human history. Through indigenous knowledge and wisdom, they were able to adapt to their environment and form a close relationship with nature.

According to UNESCO "Local and indigenous knowledge refers to the understandings, skills and philosophies developed by societies with long histories of interaction with their natural surroundings". Traditional knowledge is ingrained in communal rituals, relationships, institutions, and practices. The rural areas of indigenous groups in India are a vast repository of indigenous knowledge about medicines, crafts, arts, and farming techniques etc. It originates from a wide variety of cultures and occupational groups, including traditional farmers, nomads, sailors, and other people whose understanding is related to a specific place and is likely to be founded on a significant period of habitation over many generations. First during the Vedic era, then later during the eras of Buddha and Mahavir, Indian civilization developed in the forest. Religious beliefs and practises, which are constant components of the cultural setting, are closely related to ecosystem management. Locals employ indigenous agricultural practices that are mostly based on traditional knowledge, widespread in agricultural systems and important for ensuring sustainable food and health, impacts biodiversity as well as ecosystems. The *Karbis* tribe of Northeast India has an effective indigenous knowledge system for forecasting annual seasons and day-to-day activities using physical elements, flora and fauna traits, and other indicators (Teron & Borthakur, 2009). These methods understand the importance of rural development and nature preservation; they support the upkeep of a certain region's ecosystem, which promotes the sustainable use of biodiversity. Many indigenous methods of water conservation have been employed all over India. They are referred to as traditional water conservation practices. For instance, Himachal Pradesh inhabitants have created their infrastructure and indigenous methods for storing water, including *khads, baudis, nawns, khatris, kuhls, chhrudus,* wells, rivers, *nalas,* etc (Sharma & Kanwar, 2008). The Garhwal and Kumaon region of the Himalayas have historically had water storing and pounding constructions, which contribute to water conservation, much like the trans-Himalayan regions. They used to have water-pounding constructions known as *Khals, Tals, Chals, and Rou*. These structures ranged in size from smaller to larger (Anthwal et al., 2010). The bari system of farming has developed over time in Northeast India and has been extremely significant in terms of biodiversity management, consumption, and conservation (Barooah & Pathak, 2009). Most of the major environmental problems of the modern day, including those related to water management and conservation, can be addressed, and combated with the help of a proper integration of traditional and current scientific knowledge (Borthakur & Singh, 2020). Using traditional knowledge and wisdom, indigenous communities protect and conserve their environment.

The preservation of nature and natural resources was a fundamental component of the Indian psyche and faith. The majority of the religions that have thrived on the Indian subcontinent contain texts and sermons that urge appreciation for environment and discuss conservation. Numerous religions, including Buddhism, Hinduism, Christianity, Jainism, Islam, and others, place a strong emphasis on the principles of respect for nature and the universe's constituent elements. Therefore, people from different communities have praised nature and most of their practices are eco-friendly. The tribal communities of India are protecting the environment using their traditional beliefs and practise, such as totems, taboos, and the maintenance of sacred groves (Bain, 2017). Since the beginning of time, India has revered some patches of highly forest cover as sacred groves. Many rare and endemic wild plant species, many of which have the potential to be useful to man in agriculture, industry, and medicine, have been conserved by sacred groves. In fact, sacred groves are an example of how the ancient Indians preserved genetic variation on-site. Our ancient philosophy was characterised by reverence for all life, whether it be human, animal, or plant. This legacy of spirituality, humility, and understanding of the value of the environment is still present today.

Many Indian cultural practices are in complete harmony with the environment because Indians have historically honoured nature. A lot of festivals are held all throughout the country to appreciate nature and teach future generations the value of protecting the environment. The strong relationship between society, nature, and culture is exemplified by these. When one examines the importance of the many indigenous traditions of India, it immediately becomes clear that most of these ceremonies honour Mother Nature, her strength and abundance. Such ancient customs of nature devotion in India are based on the knowledge that nature is the source of our existence and well-being. As a result, nature is not only something that should be protected but also revered in India. The traditional festival of Sarhul is observed throughout Jharkhand, a predominantly tribal state in central India. During Sarhul, devotees worship trees. The word "Sarhul" has related to the reverence of trees. It is a celebration where nature is honoured. Many tribes in Jharkhand celebrate Sarhul, but primarily the Munda, Ho, and Oraon tribes. Every year in the month of July, during the Van Mahotsav or Forest Festival, thousands of trees are planted throughout the nation. From July 1 to July 7, Van Mahotsav week is observed to raise awareness about protecting forests and the environment. For the planet's ecology to remain in balance and for humans to have access to oxygen, trees and forests are essential. The Van Mahotsav week serves as a reminder of the need to preserve trees putting an end to deforestation. The Velas Turtle Festival is an annual occasion intended to promote Olive Ridley turtle conservation. In the Konkan area of Maharashtra, Velas is a coastal settlement famed for its immaculate beaches. It is situated between the Savitri and Bharaja rivers. Every year, between February and April, thousands of the endangered Olive Ridley Sea Turtles come to the beach to lay eggs. The Velas Turtle Festival was initiated in 2006 by a local NGO to raise awareness of the need to protect these turtles. Following the appearance and release of batches of turtle hatchlings into the sea, an annual festival is now celebrated. Various Indian states, including Uttar Pradesh, Uttarakhand, Goa, Nagaland, and Jammu & Kashmir, observe bird festivals. Every year, the Forest Departments celebrate the Bird Festival with the assistance of some other organisations, like the Eco-Tourism Development Society, in order to raise awareness among the masses about the value of protecting birds and their habitats and to promote the rich avian diversity of various states. Godavari Pushkaram, Nuakhai, Bihu, Gudi Padwa, Raja Parba, Mesha Sankranti, Makar Sankranti, and Pongal are some examples of festivals that have a strong connection to the environment and promote conservation and appreciation for it **(See chapter 3).** Interestingly, as we discussed earlier, concern for biological diversity conservation is being driven by the world's religions. In Hinduism, several rivers are personified as deities and revered as sacred. There are seven most sacred rivers in India, namely Ganga, Yamuna, Kaveri, Godavari, Saraswati, Kshipra and Narmada. India's sacred rivers are legendary pilgrimage sites because they are endowed with religious and historical significance. Acknowledging rivers' religious, cultural, and societal value is now essential because only then can the proper limitations be put in place to slow down river exploitation that exceeds the limits of nature (Agoramoorthy, 2015).

The early inhabitants were acquainted of the medical properties and uses of several plants and other substances. Every culture has a common understanding of what causes illness, how to treat it, and how to sustain health over time. Each population's cultural heritage includes this cognitive growth, and from it, empirical medical systems that rely on the usage of natural resources have developed. People from all social strata who interact with their surroundings on a daily basis practise healing. They range from basic home remedies for mild illnesses and dietary to more complicated practises like midwifery, bone setting, and the cure of snake bites and psychiatric illnesses. In accordance with the social, cultural, and religious foundations as well as the predominate knowledge, attitudes, and beliefs regarding physical, mental, and social well-being, a traditional medical practitioner or traditional healer is acknowledged by the society in which they reside as competent to give health treatment by employing plant, animal, and mineral substances and certain other ways. Traditional healers employ a variety of therapeutic formulations made from various natural ingredients (mineral, animal, and vegetable). They have a good understanding of how to use plants and herbs as both food and medicine (Jaiswal, 2019). For instance, various components of medicinal plants, including fresh leaves, fruits, bark, and stems, that the *Tagin* (a tribe from Arunachal Pradesh) utilised as traditional medicine to cure conditions like fever, jaundice, wound healing, and diarrhoea. Most illnesses, both physical and mental, were attributed to evil spirits throughout the Vedic period in India, and treatments included rituals, charms, mantras, medications, and surgical intervention. *Jhar-phook*, the name of the healing ritual used by the *ojha* to drive out the evil spirit, typically involves the use of a broom to sweep, a bird's wing, and different ritualistic objects such as sacred stones, sacred ashes and holy water. Similar to the tantric tradition, mantras are extremely important in eradicating evil spirits (Wagner et al., 1999). Other formal medical systems have been practised on the subcontinent, including Unani, Rasashastra, Siddha, and Sa-Rigpa. The traditional healthcare system in India consists of two social streams. The first stream encompasses local health beliefs and practices that rely on readily available local resources. The second stream comprises the organized knowledge system that is codified and based on theoretical foundations, such as Ayurvedic, Siddha, and Unani medicine (Bhasin, 2008).

Indian traditional healing practices, also called as Ayurveda, encompass eight clinical branches. One of the eight clinical fields is toxicology, often commonly referred to as remedies of poisonings or *visacikitsa or agadatantra*. In order to serve the needs of patients who have been poisoned by poisonous animals and plants, this branch of poison healing was specifically established in Kerala by native poison-healing practitioners known as *viṣ avaidyas*. Nearly all common poisonings have been treated by this branch's practitioners. They have developed this unique branch inside the Ayurvedic system using their unique knowledge and skills. The seven Sanskrit or Prakrit literary works have traditionally been recognised as the official texts of Kerala's traditional poison-healing system. Common names for these seven works are *Astangahrdaya, Narayaniya, Uddisa, Utpala, Mekhala, Kalavancana and Laksanamrta*. But *Uddisa, Utpala, and Kalavancan* are only recognised by their names today, and no other information is available about these. Therefore, it is important to preserve rest of them (Yamashita et al., 2010). Indian medicine has a substantial body of literature, and there are many manuscripts in private and public collections and libraries that still require documentation and research. They also contain writings on Unani medicine in Urdu and Persian as well as Siddha medicine in Tamil, in addition to works on Ayurveda in Sanskrit and regional languages.

Traditional wisdom and customs form the core of a community's culture and identity, yet they are severely challenged by globalisation. Many traditional practises are vanishing even though some traditional information may be of importance to scientists and businesses, such as the therapeutic properties of indigenous plant species. In the current five-year plan, the Anthropological Survey of India initiated a nationwide project on traditional knowledge. The project's overarching goals are to (i) catalogue and archive India's traditional knowledge systems, (ii) delve deeply into the subsystems of traditional knowledge, (iii) assist the formalisation of traditional knowledge, and (iv) create an electronic database of traditional knowledge (Anthropological Survey of India, n.d.). The government needs to do more to safeguard indigenous peoples' traditional customs and knowledge and to promote them. Additionally, they should be supported in their development and given the chance to pursue education and scientific research in parallel. In order to eliminate redundancy and ensure the smooth implementation of a certain policy, related departments should collaborate. Sensitizing and educating concerned officials, especially at the local levels, to recognise and appreciate cultural differences is another crucial aspect. Involving relevant non-governmental organisations is also necessary because, sometimes, NGOs find it simple to communicate with and relate to tribal people. It is necessary to figure out how to share the advantages of having access to conventional knowledge. While traditional knowledge might offer a more in-depth understanding of the local context, modern science can provide a wider perspective on local sustainability. To preserve biodiversity, excessive harvesting of biological resources by people should be discouraged. Forest and agricultural goods, herbal remedies, ecotourism, scientific tourism, handicrafts based on indigenous knowledge and skills, and cultural heritage or indigenous health-based tourism should all be supported in order to develop alternative means of livelihood products and services. Indigenous people should participate fully at every level of evolving sustainable development policies and strategies. In addition to tolerance and respect for various cultures and traditions, younger generation should be inspired to learn more about their own cultural history.

SOME IMPORTANT PRACTICES OF INDIA CONCERNING NATURE AND THE UNIVERSE

Sacred Groves

The preservation of selected areas of land or forests as "sacred groves" dedicated to a God or a village God, secured, and worshipped, is one of the best examples of ancient traditions in India based on religious convictions that have made substantial contributions to nature conservation. Sacred groves serve as a wonderful representation of in-situ conservation, which is the most efficient method for preserving biodiversity. On-site conservation is done in natural settings. Sacred groves, which may be found practically everywhere in India, are thought to have developed after agriculture was first practised. They are dispersed throughout the nation and are known by various names in various regions of India. In particular, the enormous number of sacred groves in Kerala in the south and Himachal Pradesh in the north are well known. Murugesan, (2016) identified sacred groves as-

(i) *Local village sacred groves*- which are monitored by the entire village, despite the fact that the village may be comprised of various tribal and ethnic groups.

(ii) *Regional sacred groves*- They are maintained by a temple trust and attract people from several districts for e.g., Sabarimala sacred grove at Kanjikkuzhi, Kerala.

(iii) *Pan-Indian sacred groves*- which are substantial and are overseen by a temple trust, where devotees travel from across the nation to adore the deity for instance Garhwal Himalayas.

(iv) *Sacred groves as the abode of ancestral spirits*- may serve as both a cemetery and a place to worship gods and ancestors.

They can be conceived as a small ecosystem that houses a diverse collection of the rare biodiversity seen in nature. The traditional practise of having a temple, a tank, and a sacred grove in every community illustrates how water was once harvested and distributed. They are

also a result of our ancestors' socio-ecological philosophy. The preservation of these small ecosystems has been made possible in part by the old religious beliefs and customs that have been passed down over hundreds of years. They serve as a crucial habitat for endangered and rare medicinal plants. Through bird dispersion, they also serve as a supply of seeds. Additionally, the sacred groves' transpiration creates a favourable microclimate for a number of creatures by lowering local temperatures and increasing atmospheric humidity. Thus, sacred groves are essential for soil preservation. Due to trees' ability to hold onto water and their ability to hold soil, soil erosion is prevented. They are frequently the only supply of water for many animals and birds, and they are also crucial for soil and water conservation. Moreover, they safeguard the wetlands and water supplies. Moreover, they occasionally assist in replenishing aquifers. Ancient cultural and religious practises of diverse ethnic groups have contributed to the preservation and protection of these biodiversity hotspots and ensured that they do not succumb to the unquenchable demands of industrialisation, urbanisation, and the need to build infrastructure. The sacred groves, on the other hand, have performed their function by meeting the social, spiritual, and medical demands of the dependent local populations. They are rich in biodiversity and home to many medicinally important rare and endangered plant and animal species These lush paradise of trees, shrubs, climbers, and herbs are crucial for maintaining the ecology and ecological equilibrium. In conclusion, sacred groves offer us a number of crucial ecological benefits. Preservation of biological diversity is entwined with safeguarding the environment and life support systems. The ancient Indian tradition of in situ protection of genetic variation is represented by sacred groves. In general, sacred groves serve as a breeding ground and storage facility for many of the regional folk, tribal, and ayurvedic remedies. Sacred groves are particularly common in areas of Kerala, Karnataka, Tamil Nadu, and Maharashtra as well as along the western coast and the Western Ghats.

Sacred groves in Kerala: Sacred groves, also known as Kavu in Malayalam, are abundant with biodiversity. They are frequently spotted in the villages on the sites of Hindu ancestral dwellings (tharavaadu). Kerala's sacred groves are the only remaining sections of evergreen forests that are protected and preserved on the basis of religious beliefs. It is a significant repository of numerous indigenous, threatened, and economically significant plant species. Additionally, it is discovered that these solitary patches are self-sufficient ecosystems that function as a closed system and a hub for bioresources for the local area's water and nutrient cycles. People frequently gave the serpent god Naga or the goddess Durga a portion of the ground on which they constructed homes. It was forbidden to cut down trees or remove even a single twig from these territories. Joint families took care of and maintained the groves. The creation of sacred groves was also considered as a part of the villages' customary efforts to protect the environment's biodiversity and water supplies. Since there was always water available in these groves, people could live there. They were also centres of adoration for nature. There are numerous small jungles in Kerala that are devoted to snakes and known as Sarpakavu, Sarpa meaning snake, kavu meaning jungle. There are also Ayyappan kavus devoted to Lord Ayyappa, the most well-known of which is the sanctified hill of Sabarimala with an Ayyappan temple, visited by millions of worshippers every year. Many sacred groves revere various trees, including, the blackboard tree (*Alstonia scholaris),* Upas tree *(Antiaris toxicaria),* Malabar Ironwood tree *(Hopea parviflora),* Strychnine tree *(Strychnos nux-vomica),* Peepal tree *(Ficus religiosa),* Palmyra palm *(Borassus)* and others. The decline of the traditional joint family structure and the division of family assets, combined with the shifting socioeconomic landscape, pose the greatest challenges to the survival of sacred groves in Kerala. The Kavu and its environs will typically be passed on to a generation that has little to no faith in maintaining the Kavu's integrity.

Sacred groves in Himachal Pradesh: The local traditions and folklore concerning sacred groves in Himachal Pradesh play a significant role in protecting the forests from exploitation. It is not permitted to cut down trees or even carry dried leaves outside the groves known as *Dev Van* or *Devta Ka Jungle*. These sacred groves are devoted to the gods Bakhu Nag Devta, Ringarishi Devta, and Devi. The most frequent plant species in the sacred groves are Deodar, Kail, and Oak, with rare Spruce and Silver fir. Leopards, black bears, barking deer, hares, wolves, and many more creatures can thrive in the dense forests.

Sacred Groves in Uttarakhand: Locals in Uttarakhand refer to the sacred groves as *Deo Bhumi* and Bugyal (sacred alpine meadows). In the state, 126 sacred groves have been identified. These groves are devoted to the gods Chandrabadni Devi, Hariyali Devi, Kotgadi Ki Kokila Mata, Pravasi Pavasu Devata, Devrada, and Saimyar. The most frequent plant species in the sacred groves include Himalayan cedar, Sanjeevani, Indian Barberry, Himalayan firethorn, and Indian valerian. The sacred groves of Uttarakhand are a source of a wide variety of plants and act as a gene pool. Threatened animals like the Griffon vulture are fostered in sacred groves through ritual and traditional methods. The Garhwal Himalaya's sacred groves clearly show the connections between the Garhwal community's cultural characteristics and conservation efforts (Anthwal et al., 2010).

Sacred Groves in Rajasthan: In Rajasthan, sacred groves are identified by a variety of names, including Kenkri in Ajmer, Vani in Mewar, Oran in Bikaner, Jodhpur, and Jaisalmer, and Shamlat deh and Devbani in Alwar. The state is known to include 560 sacred groves. These groves are devoted to the gods Bharthariji, Garva Ji, Naraini Mata, Hanumanji, Peerbaba, and Naharsakti Mata. The most frequent plant species in the sacred groves include the Cutch tree, Mukul myrrh tree, Indian mesquite, Salvia leaved cross berry, Indian tree of paradise, Neem, Banyan, Indian plum, and Pipal. Rajasthan serves as a perfect illustration of how to support the practice of protecting the environment. The groves' resources are used sparingly or only in extreme circumstances. Neem *(Azadirachta indica)* is a unique plant that the Gurjar people of Rajasthan plant and venerate as the residence of the Hindu god Devnarayan. Bishnois revere the orans, which are home to khejarli trees (Prosopis spicigera), blackbuck, deer, and nilgai (Bluebull). 363 Bishnoi women committed their life to save trees in the village of Khejadli in the Jodhpur district in 1730, starting the "Hug a Tree" or a well-known Chipko movement.

Siddha

One of the three ancient medical systems discovered in South India is called Siddha; the other two are Ayurveda and Unani. One of the oldest societies in the world, the Dravidian culture, contributed the Siddha System of Medicine. The foremost experts on this technique in ancient times were the Siddhars. The Siddha system of medicine was established by Siddhars, who were primarily from Tamil Nadu. The Siddhars' knowledge was first communicated verbally but was eventually written down in palm-leaf manuscripts, some of which may still be discovered in South India. It is based on concepts resembling those of Ayurveda. The ancient Siddha texts state that the human body is composed of a number of components. The five components of the human body are fire (THEE), earth (MUNN), water (NEER), space (AKASAM) and air (VAYU). There are also three humours known as the *DOSHAS*, namely *Pitta, Kapha*, and *Vata*. According to Siddha medicine, illnesses develop when there is an unbalance or disequilibrium in these humors or if their individual harmony is disrupted. By addressing the underlying dosha through the use of Siddha treatment, the equilibrium can be restored. Siddha medicine's specialties includes Yoga for physical and emotional well-being and Karpa medicines for rejuvenation and disease prevention. It helps in skin disease control, mental health condition management, management of orthopaedic diseases and Varma treatment and management of geriatric illness. Herbal karpam, mineral karpam, life force circulation regulation procedures, yoga, and other integrated therapies are all included in karpa therapy. The practise of Kayakarpam is most strongly emphasised in Siddha healing tradition as a means of revitalising the body and mind and significantly slowing down biological ageing. In Tamil Siddha tradition, Amuri, Muppu, and Guru are highly revered preparations. Stress and strain are also reduced and lifespan is extended by frequent yoga practise. The therapeutically valuable medications used herbs, roots, salts, and even poisons with reduced toxicity to treat a wide range of unusual disorders. Siddha's 'materia medica' includes drugs prepared from metals and minerals. The use of any minerals and metals is not mentioned in Ayurveda. However, the use of mercury, sulphur, copper, and gold as medicinal agents is expressly stated in the Siddha text. The Siddha system of medicine places a greater emphasis on moral advice and moral principles, which are particularly pertinent to our current health-care system. After independence, the government gradually opened schools where indigenous medical systems, including siddha, could be taught. This was carried out in order to support traditional medical practises.

Ayurveda

India's ancient system of medicinal herbs is known as Ayurveda. The term "Ayurveda" derives from the Sanskrit word "ayu," which means "life" or "longevity." Veda is a term for "knowledge," "wisdom," or "spiritual science." The unification of physical, emotional, and spiritual equilibrium to achieve enlightenment is what makes Ayurveda a full body of knowledge and absolute insight about how to live. Ayurveda emphasises prevention and promotes health maintenance by paying particular attention to life balance, right ideas, nutrition, and daily routines as well as the use of medicines. This ability to achieve balance of mind, body, and awareness in keeping with one's physical condition and to make lifestyle changes to maintain this balance is made possible by knowledge of Ayurveda. Flexibility and ongoing adaptation are essential for good health and long life, and life goes on as long as this capacity for adaptability persists. Ayurveda aims to prolong life while regaining health and well-being. The concept of health in Ayurveda is regarded as being complete and dynamic in character. It is explained as a "many sided equilibrium" (*samya*), which in turn emerges from harmonious interaction and interrelationships with living organisms and their environment. It has three primary branches: Nara Ayurveda, which deals with human life; Satva Ayurveda, which deals with animal life and its ailments; and Vriksha Ayurveda, which deals with plant life, its development, and diseases. It is abundantly clear that Ayurveda is both a medical system and a way of life that supports overall wellness and spiritual growth. More than 90% of Ayurveda's treatments are derived from plants. Plants used in Ayurveda have a potent effect on illnesses in the body. They support the body's physiology and change a disease's pathology. These extractions were developed using several years of real-world experience. The finest results are achieved by combining plants. There are polyherbal formulations that are more effective at preventing illnesses. Compared to single herbs, they are more effective in having positive effects on the body. There are 3 to 30 plants included in the polyherbal formulation of plants used in Ayurveda. These components are properly combined and it functions in such a way that a few plants take the lead and other plants support them in the healing process. The supporting herbs can perform a variety of functions, including functioning as catalysts to aid in the absorption and delivery of medicine to various body parts. They can be utilised to lessen toxicity as well. Everything is dependent on the correct combination. If the appropriate balance is created, it can provide remarkable results. A detailed understanding of ayurvedic herbs is required for that.

Yoga

Yoga has its roots in pre-Vedic India. It was practised circa 2700 BCE, according to different yogic symbols and figures found during the Indus Valley Civilization excavations. The Vedic scriptures, written between 1500 and 500 BCE, acknowledge the existence of yoga. In the *Yoga Sutras*, written 2200 years ago by the sage *Patanjali*, the yoga method was codified. Yoga's holistic approach is well-established, it promotes health, and it may manage a variety of lifestyle-related problems since it brings harmony to all aspects of life. In recent years, yoga's popularity has increased not only due to its efficacy in treating particular illnesses but also because of its ability to relieve practitioners of mental and emotional distress and make them feel good about themselves. As a consequence, yoga is now practised worldwide as a component of a healthy lifestyle. Yoga's ultimate goal is self-realisation, which involves overcoming all forms of suffering and entering "the phase of liberation." It is particularly beneficial for spiritual progress as well as for conserving and maintaining one's physical and mental health. The eightfold path is referred to as *ashtanga* in Patanjali's *Yoga Sutra*, which basically translates to "eight limbs" *(ashta*=eight, *anga*=limb). These eight actions, also referred to as the 8 limbs of yoga, essentially serve as instructions for how to lead a purposeful and meaningful life. They act as a guide for moral behaviour and self-discipline, focus attention on health, and assist us in recognising the spiritual elements of our nature. ***Yama*** is the first of yoga's eight limbs, and there are five *yamas,* i.e., *Aparigraha*- noncovetousness, *Asteya*- nonstealing, *Satya*-truthfulness, *Brahmacharya*- continence and *Ahimsa*- nonviolence. The second limb is ***Niyama; the*** five *Niyamas* are practises that promote spirituality and self-control which includes *Santosha* (contentment), *Suacha* (cleanliness), *Tapas*-(heat; spiritual austerities), *Isvara pranidhana* (surrender to God), *Svadhyaya* (study of the sacred scriptures and one's self). The third of yoga's eight limbs is the set of poses known as ***Asanas***. According to the yogic perspective, taking care of our physical bodies is an essential part of developing spiritually. Through asana practise, we cultivate the disciplined habit and the capability for concentration important for meditation. *Asana* is a Sanskrit word that means "posture or position"; which means "seat." Initially, there was only one *asana*—a secure and cosy stance for protracted sat meditation. Yoga movements not only tone and stretch the body, but they also release the energy channels and psychic centres of the body. In addition to helping to detox and maintenance of the body, the postures in yoga can be used to control, calm, and concentrate the mind. ***Pranayama***, this fourth stage, which is typically translated as "breath control," comprises methods for mastering the respiratory process while acknowledging the relationship between the mind, the breath, and the emotions. The fifth limb is ***Pratyahara*** (withdrawal of the senses) withdrawal enables us to logically examine our urges, which are likely to be unhealthy habits that obstruct our personal development. Pratyahara has two different facets. It involves letting go of undesirable impressions, undesirable foods, and undesirable associations. Without a healthy diet and healthy relationships, it is impossible to control mental impressions, but the biggest advantage of pratyahara is the command or withdrawal of sensory impressions, which frees the mind to explore inwards. ***Dharana*** is the sixth of yoga's eight limbs, it is a form of single-pointed concentration. By focusing on one particular mental object or a particular energetic point on the body like the quiet repetition of a specific sound by which we might learn to slow down the thought process. ***Dhyana*** is the seventh step of the ashtanga method. The uninterrupted flow of attention is dhyana, also known as meditation or contemplation. ***Samadhi*** described as Patanjali's eighth and final stage of ashtanga. The word samadhi, which is frequently translated as "integration" or "absorption," truly means "putting together." By overcoming the limitations of the ego, this condition is liberated. You are no longer bound by the shackles of approval or disapproval, condemnation, concern, or fear and constantly become fully immersed in the current moment while maintaining perfect awareness. This is a state of pure existence.

Unani Medicine in India

India has a long and distinguished history behind the Unani System of Medicine. In the seventh century, it was introduced to India by the Arabs and Persians. India presently ranks among the top countries in the world that utilise medicine. It has the most unani educational, medical, and research institutes. As a form of indigenous medicine, the method became popular in the society. In the 1920s, Hakim Ajmal Khan (1868–1927 AD) led research in unani medicine using contemporary scientific standards. Unani practitioners (*hakims*) favoured natural treatment that combined the physical, mental, and spiritual realms by adhering to harmony and balance principles. *Hakims* have preserved their traditional strengths while learning from modern scientific advancements over the years. Ibn-e-Sina, considered to be one of the remarkable Unani Tibb (medicine) experts, defined Unani medicine as "the science in which we learn various stages of the body in health and when not in health and the ways by which health is susceptible to loss and when lost, is likely to be regained." Unani medicine is used in the Middle East and South Asia. It refers to a legacy of Graeco-Arabic medicine, which was developed into an intricate medical system in the Middle Ages by Arabian and Persian physicians and relies on the recommendations of the Roman physician Galen and the Greek physician Hippocrates. It was first developed in Greece almost 2500 years ago with a herbo-animo-mineral origin that is about 90% herbal, 4%– 5% animal, and 6% mineral. It offers healthcare that is promotional, preventive, curative, and rehabilitative. As a result, it places emphasis on the health of the body, mind, and soul and evaluates how an individual relates to his surroundings. Disease diagnosis and therapy place a high value on a patient's temperament, or "*Mizaj*." When determining the best food and lifestyle to promote a particular person's health, temperament is also taken into account. Warmth, coldness, moistness, and dryness are the four fundamental *mizaj* (temperaments). These single temperaments are combined into four more, namely Cold and dry, cold and moist, warm and dry, and warm and moist. All living things in the cosmos, including all plants, minerals, and animals, all possess *mizaj* in varying degrees. An individual's stable constitution, or health, is provided by the equilibrium of their elemental combination and ensuing *mizaj,* as assessed by *tabiyat*. A person's health deteriorates when their natural temperament changes, much as maintaining the right balance of the elements keeps someone in good health. As a result, *mizaj* is crucial to understanding both the nature of a disease and a person's normal state (physical, mental, and social) in Unani medicine. The pharmacopoeia of the Unani system is extensive and rich, containing more than 2,000 medications made from various plant, mineral, and animal sources. Being acknowledged by the World Health Organization (WHO) in 1976, the Unani system of traditional medicine acquired popularity on a global scale. Numerous institutions in India conducted research and teaching Unani. For instance, the Central Council for Research in Unani Medicine (CCRUM), an initiative of the Indian government, made it easier to translate classical legacy, organise clinical testing, enhance drug standardisation, and look into the toxicological and phytopharmacological characteristics of natural products that hakims had long used. Unani medicine prioritises wellness and treats illnesses using a variety of therapeutic modalities, including medication, food therapy, and regimented therapy. Numerous clinical trials have demonstrated the effectiveness and very few side effects of Unani medications.

Shamanism

Shamanism is a traditional kind of spiritual and religious healing practice. Being the first religion practised by humans, shamanism is still widely considered a way of life as it connects with nature and all its creatures (Shamanism, n.d). Shamanism is a captivating technique that teaches us how to communicate and connect with the various forces of the cosmos. It entails developing harmony and links to all beings, living and inanimate, as well as spiritual ones. Shamanism is a spiritual practice that relies on the shaman, who is claimed to possess special abilities due to hypnotic or ecstatic religious experiences. Shamans possess varying abilities that vary across different cultures. Still, they are generally acknowledged to be able to cure illnesses, establish connections with realms beyond the physical world, and often aid in the transition of departed souls to those realms. A shaman is a priest who is summoned to a home to help a family with their troubles and bridges the physical world and the realm of spirits and gods in this religious activity. In such communities, invisible spirits are said to inhabit their surroundings and determine their fate. Although each shaman has their rites and customs, some elements are shared, such as the euphoric trance or soul journey. In different regions of India, a kind of exorcist known as an *ohja, tantric, aghori, baba, bhagat* who possesses supernatural abilities that enable them to recognize evil spirits, lift their curses, and provide cures. A person with an evil spirits suspicion is likely to communicate with an ojha. The Aghori Sadhus, who worship Lord Shiva and Kali Maa, frequently wear actual human skulls and bones as jewellery or as a bowl for eating and drinking. They are a feared spiritual group due to their use of Black Magic, Tantric practises, and other unusual, unnatural practises. Cannibalistic *Aghori Sadhus* in Varanasi eat the flesh and blood of deceased people. As they only eat dead human remains and never kill people, there is no reason to be concerned. A big part of Aghor ceremonies consists of chanting mantras and presenting cannabis and wine to the holy fire. The magical qualities of *tantrik vidhya* made it a practice even of the Gods. Shiva and Shakti are the primary creators of these forces. In India, shamans use some cultic objects, for instance, the **Shaman Drum**, which is used as a means of travel to access the spirit world. **Peacock Feathers** are used in smudging by shamans. Smudging is a ritual to rid a person, a location, or an object of unfavourable spirits, energies, or influences. When the **Shaman Gong** is rung, the evil spirits are disturbed and leave the Shaman alone. The trance state is initiated with the **Finger Bells**, which signify power. There are also several other materials needed for such rituals. These might include symbolic artefacts used in certain rituals or practises to represent different aspects of the spiritual journey, such as ceremonial bowls (*Kapala*; skulls), knives (*phurba*), *Rudraksha* plant, *kaudi, Rudraksha mala, ullu ke nakhoon, Haddi ki mala, sindoor, sher ka daant* etc. One of the most potent spiritual tools a shaman can use to summon all the spirits and travel into their realms is a **Rattle**, which serves as both a healing aid and a gateway to other worlds. In most Shamanic rituals, the shaman will play drums, dance, or sing in order to enter the blissful trance state where he can communicate with the spirit realm. The Shaman then speaks with the "Master Spirits" to ask for instruction on how to cure someone's physical or mental health. It may also end up asking the spirits to carry out healing rituals. Shaman Sadhana, Shamanic Healing, and Shaman Siddhi are the three divisions of shamanism. All forms of healing practices fall under the category of shamanic healing, which is taught to pupils of the Shaman Sadhana. Selected people, especially those who exhibit a Shaman's characteristic, are taught Shaman Siddhi.

Vedic Astrology (*Jyotish*)

Vedic Astrology is the name given to Indian astrology worldwide. It is a traditional branch of astrology that dates back over 8000 years to India. The Hindi word for it is "*Jyotish,*" which means *light from heavenly bodies. Jyotish,* also known as Vedic astrology, is a branch of the Vedas, which are historic Hindu texts from India. It is an analytical and forecasting technique based on astronomical data that enables its practitioners to accurately gauge and comprehend behaviour, estimate the impact of the past, and the effect of the present, and estimate the possibility that events will unfold in the future. Only kings had access to astrologers in ancient times, therefore they used them to make all significant choices. Additionally, it is thought that the first practitioners of this study were sages who had discovered their true natures as well as accomplished astronomers. Vedic astrologers have been studying the night sky and charting the heavens for hundreds of years, accurately recording the movements of the planets and the characteristics connected to various astrological factors. *Jyotish* differs significantly from Western astrology. The main distinction is that in *Jyotish,* the zodiac is based on the fixed, observable positions of the constellations as we can see them in the sky. Contrarily, the tropical zodiac is used in western astrology. The tropical zodiac is based on the relative and mutable position of the sun rather than the fixed, observable locations of the constellations. The palm is employed in Vedic astrology as a support and cross-reference for the astrological chart. Contrary to the Western idea, which separates the two, astrology and palmistry have always been intertwined in India. In India, palmistry is a subset of *Nimitta*, a branch of *jyotisha*. Nimitta is the study of signs and portents, which also includes the examination of physical characteristics. The lines and patterns on your palms are used in palmistry to read your personality, your experiences in the past, and your behaviour. The relative power of the planets in a person's birth chart can be read from their palm. Based on all of these factors, the palmist recommends future actions. If there is any uncertainty regarding the time of birth, it also aids in correcting the horoscope. Additionally, it gives the astrologer more details about character, possibilities in life, trends, and occurrences in the future. *Jyotish* is an excellent system for healing as well. In fact, because it is founded on a comprehensive understanding of the source of suffering, it is possibly the most fundamental healing approach there. In this way, *Jyotish* does not just concentrate on treating the physical body. It covers every facet of life. *Jyotish* uses a variety of uncommon healing techniques. In order to improve the person's profession, finances, relationships, or physical health, the *Jyotishi* (Vedic Astrologer) may advise that person to wear a specific gemstone, chant a mantra, donate money to a charity, or have a *Yajna* (fire ceremony) done. These methods, known as *upayas,* have been handed down through an oral tradition for many ages. There are several branches of Vedic astrology. Observation and calculation related to astronomy, Vedic astrology is used to perform natal astrology, Horary astrology is the practise of providing answers to inquiries without using a natal horoscope, Electional astrology involves choosing the most advantageous periods to carry out a task or launch an event, and the study of omens and their interpretation is known as omenology.

References

1. *Aghori Sadhus of Varanasi.* (2022). India Chalk. Retrieved from https://indiachalk.com/blog/aghori-sadhus-of-varanasi/
2. Agoramoorthy, G. (2015). Sacred rivers: their spiritual significance in Hindu religion. *Journal of religion and health*, *54*(3), 1080-1090.
3. Anthropological Survey of India. (n.d.). *Indigenous Knowledge.* Retrieved from https://ansi.gov.in/indigenous-knowledge
4. Anthwal, A., Gupta, N., Sharma, A., Anthwal, S., & Kim, K. H. (2010). Conserving biodiversity through traditional beliefs in sacred groves in Uttarakhand Himalaya, India. *Resources, Conservation and Recycling*, *54*(11), 962-971.
5. *Ayurveda traditional healing system of India.* (n.d.). Spiritual Education. Retrieved January from https://spiritual.education/ayurveda/
6. Bains, W. (2017). Conservation of Environment through Traditional Knowledge and Wisdom with Special Reference to Beliefs and Practices in Tribal India: An Overview. *Journal of Multidisciplinary Studies in Archaeology*, *5*, 224-243.
7. Barooah, M., & Pathak, A. (2009). Indigenous knowledge and practices of Thengal Kachari women in sustainable management of bari system of farming. *Indian Journal of Traditional Knowledge. 8* (1). 35–40.
8. Bhasin, V. (2008). Gaddis' folk medicine: A source of healing. *Studies on Ethno-Medicine*, *2*(1), 1-27.
9. Biswas. (2020). *The Practice of Shamanism and Indigenous Art of India.* Karwaan: The Heritage Exploration Initiative. Retrieved from https://www.

karwaanheritage.in/post/the-practice-of-shamanism-and-indigenous-art-of-india

10. Borthakur, A., & Singh, P. (2020). Indigenous knowledge systems in sustainable water conservation and management. In *Water Conservation and Wastewater Treatment in BRICS Nations* (pp. 321-328). Elsevier.
11. Carrico, M. (2021). *Get to Know the 8 Limbs of Yoga*. Yoga Journal. https://www.yogajournal.com/yoga-101/philosophy/8-limbs-of-yoga/eight-limbs-of-yoga/
12. Cresswell, J. (2018). *This Female Photographer Spent a Month with India Cannibal Cult*. Refinery29. Retrieved from https://www.refinery29.com/en-gb/tamara-merino-aghor-cannibals
13. *Folk Healing Traditions.* (n.d.). Science and Society. Retrieved from https://www.ncbs.res.in/HistoryScienceSociety/content/folk-healing-traditions
14. Indian Culture. (n.d.). *Knowledge and practices concerning nature and the universe.* Retrieved from https://www.indianculture.gov.in/intangible-cultural-heritage/knowledge-and-practices
15. Indian Culture. (n.d.). *Yoga*. Retrieved from http://indianculture.gov.in/unesco/intangible-cultural-heritage/yoga
16. Jaiswal, A. (2019). Indigenous Knowledge System and Traditional Medicinal Practitioner. *The Open Anthropology Journal. 2* (2). 1-8. 10.23880/aeoaj-16000119
17. *Jyotish - Indian Vedic Astrology*. (n.d.). indif.com. Retrieved from https://www.indif.com/india/jyotish.asp
18. Kumar, S. (2014). Indigenous Knowledge and Indigenous Community in India: A Study in Human Rights Perspective. *International Journal of Innovative Social Science & Humanities Research*, *1*(1), 125–133. Retrieved from https://www.csirs.org.in/uploads/paper_pdf/indigenous-knowledge-and-indigenous-community-in-india.pdf
19. Moniraj, A. J. (2020). An Overview of the Practice of Witchcraft in India. *Hexerei-Anschuldigungen in weltweiter Perspektive Witchcraft accusations in global perspective, 107.*
20. Murugesan, A. (2016). Sacred Groves of India – An Overview. *International Journal of Current Research in Biosciences and Plant Biology*, *3*(4), 64–74. https://doi.org/10.20546/ijcrbp.2016.304.011
21. National Health Portal of India. (2015). *Unani.* Retrieved from https://www.nhp.gov.in/unani_mty
22. National Health Portal of India. (2016). *Ayurveda.* Retrieved from https://www.nhp.gov.in/introduction_mtl
23. National Institute of Siddha. (2021). *Siddha medicine.* Retrieved from https://nischennai.org/main/siddha-medicine/
24. *Overview of Indian healing traditions*. (n.d.). Science and Society. Retrieved from https://www.ncbs.res.in/HistoryScienceSociety/content/overview-indian-healing-traditions

25. *Palmistry - A Brief Introduction to this Branch of Astrology*. (2019). Jothishi. Retrieved from https://jothishi.com/palmistry/
26. *Sacred Groves in Himachal Pradesh*. (2016). CPREEC - EIACP Programme Centre, Resource Partner on Ecological Heritage and Sacred Sites of India. Retrieved from http://cpreecenvis.nic.in/Database/HimachalPradesh_2228.aspx
27. *Sacred Groves in Rajasthan*. (2021). CPREEC - EIACP Programme Centre, Resource Partner on Ecological Heritage and Sacred Sites of India. Retrieved from http://www.cpreecenvis.nic.in/Database/Rajasthan_905.aspx
28. Sacred Groves in Uttarakhand. (2016). *CPREEC - EIACP Programme Centre, Resource Partner on Ecological Heritage and Sacred Sites of India*. Retrieved from http://cpreecenvis.nic.in/Database/UttaraKhand_911.aspx
29. *Sacred Groves*. (2022). Retrieved from http://www.kerenvis.nic.in/Database/SacredGroves_1433.aspx
30. *Shamanism*. (n.d.). ShaGuru. Retrieved from https://shamanisminindia.com/
31. Sharma, N., & Kanwar P. (2008). Indigenous water conservation systems—A rich tradition of rural Himachal Pradesh. *Indian Journal of Traditional Knowledge*, *8*(4), 510–513. http://nopr.niscpr.res.in/bitstream/123456789/6271/1/IJTK%208%284%29%20510-513.pdf
32. Singh, J. (2016). *Siddha System of Medicine*. Ayur Times. Retrieved January from https://www.ayurtimes.com/siddha-system-medicine/
33. *Temples Preaching Tantric Vidhya In India*. (n.d.). Rgyan. Retrieved from https://rgyan.com/blogs/temple-preaching-tantric-vidhya
34. Teron, R., & Borthakur, S. K. (2009). Traditional knowledge relating to use of flora and fauna as indicators in predicting annual seasons among Karbi tribe of Assam. *Indian Journal of Traditional Knowledge*. *8* (4). 518-524.
35. *Unani medicine*. (n.d.). In Encyclopedia Britannica. Retrieved from https://www.britannica.com/science/Unani-medicine
36. UNESCO. (2021). *Local and Indigenous Knowledge Systems (LINKS)*. Retrieved from https://en.unesco.org/links
37. UNESCO. (n.d.). *Knowledge and practices concerning nature and the universe*. Retrieved from https://ich.unesco.org/en/knowledge-concerning-nature-00056
38. Wagner, W., Duveen, G., Themel, M., & Verma, J. (1999). The modernization of tradition: Thinking about madness in Patna, India. *Culture & Psychology*, *5*(4), 413-445.
39. Yamashita, T., Brahmadathan, U. M. T., & Parameswaran, M. K. (2010). Traditional poison-healing system in Kerala: An overview. *E Journal of Indian Medicine*, *3*(3), 101-117.

Chapter - 5

Traditional Craftsmanship

India has been known for different civilisations and customs. Every area has something special or distinctive to offer. A significant portion of the country's rich cultural legacy is represented by the handicraft. For many years, the Indian handicraft has provided the entire world with a variety of wonderful works of art and craft. Traditional crafts, which reflect the culture and tradition of a specific region, are an essential component of any nation. India's traditional craftsmanship is a reflection of the nation's diverse culture, customs, and aesthetic expressions. The term "traditional craftsmanship" in India refers to a variety of crafts, including weaving, embroidery, ceramics, metalwork, wood carving, and many more. The identity and value of the nation are enhanced by these crafts, which also provide many craftsmen with a means of sustenance." Every part of India has its distinctive craft forms, procedures, and aesthetics that highlight the enormous ability and ingenuity of Indian craftsmen, for instance: pottery, jewellery making, Textiles and Handloom Weaving (Saree weaving, carpet weaving), metal work, wood carving, different embroidery work, stone (marble) carving, puppet making, bone and horn work, glasswork etc. In addition to functioning as creative expressions, these crafts also support numerous craftspeople and help to preserve cultural history. In India, selling and creating handicrafts is the second-largest source of employment after agriculture. Instead of just being artistic creations, they encapsulate a part of the creator and a fragment of the cultural heritage. It is evident that similar to other facets of Indian folk culture, local folklore and folktales are deeply ingrained in Indian folk crafts and paintings, as well as the everlasting history of Indian mythological ideas.

India's artisan culture is famous worldwide for its elegance, beauty, dignity, and exquisite creations. The manifestation of intangible cultural heritage that is perhaps most tangible is traditional craftsmanship. Traditional craftsmanship techniques, as one of the five domains of ICH, utilised various materials such as clay, wood, glass, metal, bones, shells, textiles, etc., in creating various artefacts, including furniture, toys, apparel, jewellery, decorative items, musical instruments, terracotta figurines etc.

The main objective here is not the preservation of the objects but rather the protection of their development, which includes the safeguarding of the knowledge, skills, and expertise required to create such objects. To do this, it is vital to provide conditions that allow craftsmanship and transmission of experience-based knowledge to succeeding generations (Sandgruber et al., 2019). As a result, the transmission of knowledge, skills, and production methods from one generation to the next is crucial. By studying tangible handicrafts, one can have a better understanding of the intangible culture that is represented in them. Our country is one of the world's largest manufacturers of handcrafted arts, including jewellery, hand-printed fabrics, leather items, stoneware, paintings, sculptures, pottery, art of metal wares, embroidered and crocheted items, wood wares, textile items, etc. Some of the advantages noted include the country's access to cheap and plentiful labour, the utilization of Localized assets, limited capital outlays, and a distinctive proficiency in product innovation, as well as growing recognition by global consumers. The skills needed to make crafts range from delicate, exacting labour, like paper crafts, to potent, hard tasks, like producing a sturdy basket or thick shawl. The variety of these skills reflects the variety of the product. The art of manufacturing Indian handicrafts has been passed down through families from generation to generation as a traditional craft. Millions of Indians still rely on indigenous manufacturing methods, traditional skills, and techniques to support themselves through the sale of handmade goods. They are distinctive representations of a particular culture or society made from materials and workmanship found there.

Indians have always created objects for utilitarian purposes, religious ceremonies, and aesthetic purposes, which are of extremely high quality and have ancient roots. Handicrafts began as a leisure activity in rural regions; however, it has now evolved into a flourishing commercial activity due to a steadily expanding market demand. As social reformers began to advocate for village-based crafts for India's cultural and economic renewal in the 19th and 20th centuries, handicrafts became one of the key elements of the Renaissance of Indian ideas. This profound idea was personified by Mahatma Gandhi's *"charka,"* which was also a powerful weapon in the struggle for India's independence. Indian indigenous arts and crafts had been successfully ignored during the long years of colonization (John, 2014). During the Mughal era, Indian handicrafts nearly reached their pinnacle of beauty and splendour. However, the expansion of the factory system of mass production with the entrance of the British was the direct, immediate, and primary reason for the downfall of Indian handicrafts. Handicrafts' importance and position in the economic, social, and political landscape after independence became increasingly apparent, and the sector began to recover. In terms of infrastructure, policy scenario, governmental assistance, trade strategy, and industry definition, the handicraft sector stands out (Srivastav et al., 2016).

Craftsmanship is the cornerstone of any community's material culture, and it exhibits the beauty of legacy. A lot of academics have researched the sociological, economic, technical, cultural, artistic, and aesthetic elements of handicrafts, which are a significant sector of our economy and society. The Handicrafts of India have gained popularity throughout the ages for their originality, beauty, and traditional craftsmanship. It serves as a means to safeguard and cultivate the creative and cultural heritage, as various traditional craft techniques and skills are passed down from one generation to the next. Many nations still preserve a major portion of their own cultural heritage in their handicrafts. In addition to safeguarding India's cultural history, it also generates foreign exchange. Indian Handicraft export has grown to a respectable level, making up a sizeable portion of the economy's decentralized sector. Indian folk art and crafts, which are essential to Indian culture and tradition, are quite popular with Western customers. According to Dey & Malhotra, the major importers of Indian handicrafts are the USA, Germany, and the UK. Before the introduction of mass-produced goods, which are frequently less expensive or more readily accessible, these make up the majority of souvenirs that tourists buy, especially in new destinations. "In India, handicraft industry is a major source of income for rural communities employing over six million artisans including many women, men and children belonging to the weaker sections of the society" (Ghouse, 2012). The fact that this industry employs domestic raw materials to manufacture its goods is one of its distinguishing characteristics.

Handicrafts are an essential part of the Indian economy as they are one of the greatest sources of employment. The industry directly and indirectly employs around 7 million people. The industry is economically significant due to its great potential for employment, low capital investment requirements, high rate of value addition, and high potential for exports and foreign exchange revenues for the nation. More than 67,000 Indian exporters and export firms work to promote local artwork and craftsmanship on both the domestic and international markets. India is one of the major producers of handicrafts for the global market; however, it only accounts for less than 2% of global handicraft exports (*Creative arts in India*, 2016). After agriculture, the handicraft industry is frequently the second-largest source of earnings in developing countries. However, this industry has suffered from a lack of adequate data and statistics. There must be some statistical support to take preventative action. Furthermore, handicraft activities are frequently informal in developing countries; yet, measurable evidence of job losses is required in order to take necessary actions to enhance employment opportunities. There are a number of reasons why handicraft-related data is not readily available, including an absence of consensus on the definition of handicrafts and the difficulty in collecting precise data. Additionally, many rural employees are primarily employed in the seasonal agriculture industry, which leaves them without employment for a while. Many workers turn to artisanal labour to cover their daily costs during this time. Thus, it is challenging to get information on work in handcraft. Therefore, it is challenging to implement the required suitable procedures since insufficient data are available. (Yang et al., 2018)

Handicrafts retain great promise because they are essential to supporting not only the current generation of craftspeople but also for an increasing number of new participants in the crafts industry. However, despite the substantial production base, the global market is still untapped. Since the turn of the 20th century, as life situations have changed quickly, the demand for traditional craftsmanship has dramatically reduced, which has led to a decline in the number of practicing craftsmen. The role that the handicraft sector plays in providing a significant number of craftspeople with employment from generation to generation cannot be overlooked. India's handicraft sector is renowned for its long and distinctive artistic history. But this industry is currently seeing a dramatic fall in its exporting business. There are numerous such instances where mass-produced goods take the place of handicrafts. This is primarily due to the quick shift in electricity supply, insufficient advertising and publicity, unprofitable pricing, middlemen's exploitation, untapped regions, consumer tastes and preferences, rising prices for raw materials, and fierce competition on the global market from advanced nations, which pose a serious threat to the age-old craft, competition from machine-made and electronic products, technology, weak institutional foundation and artificial intelligence, as well as an elevated level of unemployment and a rise in the number of unemployed people. However, as globalization progresses, objects become more and more commodity-like, putting local products up against global competitors. Traditional handicrafts are being replaced by machine-made goods as a result of industrialization, and as a result of growing worldwide competition, handicrafts are facing competition from similar alternative goods. This demand for a product and the alteration in its appearance, style, and colour pose a serious danger to craftsmen producers and drive away these deeply ingrained traditional handcrafted goods, replacing them with mass-produced, factory-made, machine crafts. In addition, the transition to a modern lifestyle, diversity in production, distribution, and sales causes a decline in consumer interest in traditional handicraft industries. One of India's main problems is that our markets do not value craftsmanship at its full worth. When this worth is acknowledged and if consumers are ready to pay more for craft-based products, it should result in higher salaries for weavers and artisans and help millions of rural residents who depend on this industry for their livelihoods. Because fewer people are buying handicrafts as industrial products become more sophisticated, craftsmen are forced to close their shops and relocate to urban areas in order to make a living. As a result of the younger generation's lack of interest in studying the tradition, many old artisan skills and techniques have vanished. Due to industrial products' superiority in the durability of materials and their economic values, handicrafts eventually disappeared and lost their position in society while they flourished.

A nation's historical past—its heritage, customs, practices, rituals, ceremonies, and observances—is displayed through its traditional craftmanship. Indian craftmanship's outstanding display on the global market won them many enthusiasts, but the situation needs to be changed in the local market. To enhance the sector's marketing environments, actions must be executed. Continuity of practice and sharing of knowledge between master and apprentice are essential for the preservation of traditional craftsmanship. Numerous factors, including market orientation, technology, current trends, competition, customer demand, and preferences, must be taken into account while choosing a market research strategy. In order to preserve crafts, it is necessary to renew their organic connections with evolving ecological conditions. As low product quality influences consumer demand in the market, quality consciousness is a problem that needs to be addressed. Because of the growing desire for traditional art among tourists, tourism can be a driving force for relationship regeneration. Offering financial incentives to teachers and students to increase the value of knowledge transmission is a worked method of consolidating and enhancing these systems. Local, traditional markets for handmade products can also be supported while at the same time developing new ones.

The popularity of Indian traditional craftmanship cannot be overlooked. The market share of Indian craftmanship is outstanding. If the right promotional, social, legal, and developmental steps are followed, there is a good chance that its market share will rise. While other nations' handicraft industries are organized and geared toward large-scale manufacturing, the Indian handicraft industry is small, cottage-based, and unorganised. Although the government is taking some steps to improve the situation, more needs to be done in order for the Craft people and their businesses to thrive and survive in this competitive world. This includes providing strategic direction and action plans. There is a need for more technological support and innovation in the sector to align supply and demand with quality. The Indian government's Ministry of Textiles has jurisdiction over the handicraft industry. The Ministry of Culture, the Ministry of Small and Medium Enterprises, the Khadi and Village Industries Corporation, and the Development Commissioner for Handlooms are some of the other significant regulatory authorities and government agencies engaged in the growth and promotion of this industry. The UNESCO (2003) Convention demanded that member states create an inventory of ICH with input from the affected communities, develop laws, set up organizations to oversee and promote it, and take other necessary precautions. As with other forms of ICH, the goal of safeguarding is to guarantee the transfer of traditional artisan knowledge and skills to younger generations, allowing for the local production of crafts and support their creators' livelihoods. Numerous craft traditions have long-standing systems of training and apprenticeship. Many craft traditions incorporate 'trade secrets' that should not be given to outsiders. However, if family members or community members have no interest in learning it, the knowledge may perish since sharing it with strangers contradicts custom (UNESCO, Intangible Cultural Heritage domain). Any endeavour to realize the potential for growth and to support the sustainability and vitality of rural communities must include maintaining cultural heritage. Traditional handicraft must be treated with the appropriate safeguarding measures because it is acknowledged as one of the domains where intangible cultural heritage is manifested. These steps are intended to guarantee the heritage's vitality by continual practice, creation and re-creation, preservation of the process of heritage production, and the transfer of knowledge and skills to subsequent generations. A number of specialists in cultural heritage have emphasized the importance of preserving this cultural legacy in order to preserve the community's identity as well as to provide economic benefits and other values. The local folk arts and crafts are highlighted during several tourism promotional festivals held throughout India across the year, such as "the Taj Mahotsav in Agra, the Ajanta Ellora Festival in Maharashtra, the International Folk Festival in Himachal Pradesh, the Gurez Festival in Jammu and Kashmir, the Pinjore Heritage Festival in Punjab, the Kutch Utsav in Gujarat", and festivals specifically dedicated to arts and crafts, such as "the Surajkund Crafts Festival in Haryana, the Ashtamudi Craft and Art Festival in Kerala, the Margao Crafts Festival in Goa etc". Such festivals are the biggest addition to the Indian tourist situation for product differentiation since culture, crafts, and tourism are inseparable partners (Hajra, 2015).

Table 6: State Wise List of Indian Handicrafts

S. No.	State	Handicraft
1.	Assam	Bell Metal Crafts, Brass Metal, Jute Craft, Bamboo, Sitalpati and Cane Crafts, Decorative Candle, Masks, etc.
2.	Meghalaya	Bamboo and cane Crafts, Costumes and Jewelry, Wood Carving etc.
3.	Andhra Pradesh	Kalamkari, Kondapalli Toys, Pearl jewelry, Banjara needle Crafts, Budithi Brassware, Dokra Metal Crafts, Bronze Castings, Lacquer Ware, Folk Paintings, Kalamkari, and Block Printed Fabrics and Wood Carvings etc.
4.	Arunachal Pradesh	Thangka Painting, Bamboo and cane crafts, Wood carving, carpet weaving etc.
5.	Mizoram	Bamboo and cane crafts, Weaving craft, Jewelry making, Clay craft etc.
6.	Goa	Shell handicraft, bamboo craft, woodcarving, brass metals, seashell craft, Papier-Mache, and wooden lacquer ware etc.
7.	Haryana	Woven furniture, artistic sheet metal work, wooden bead making, zari & tilla jutti (leather footwear), lace work, bone carving, wood carving etc.
8.	Uttar Pradesh	Wood handicrafts, Chikankari, Brocade or Kinkab, Stone craft, Carpets, Art metal, brassware, Glassware, Pottery, etc.
9.	Bihar	Madhubani paintings, Pottery, wooden articles, metal wares, stonewares, jewelry, lacquer works, kashida, sikki and moonj wares, wooden and clay toys, zari, artistic textile fabrics and printing on cloth etc.
10.	Rajasthan	Blue Pottery, Stone Carvings, Woodwork, leather craft, lacwork, weaving, metal work etc.
11.	Punjab	Phulkari, Paranda, Basketry, knitting/crochet etc.
12.	Uttar Pradesh	Chikankari, Banarasi Saree, Carpets and Durries etc.
13.	Telangana	Bidri craft, Banjara Needle crafts, bronze castings, Dokra metal crafts, etc.
14.	Uttarakhand	Wood Carving, Pasmina Shawls, Decorative Candles, Copperware etc.
15.	Himachal Pradesh	Wood Carving, Chamba Rumal, miniature paintings, metal crafts, stone carving, Himachali Cap, Kullu Shawl, Pullas, etc.

16.	Manipur	Stone Carving, Cane and bamboo, Wood Craft, Metal Craft/Brass & Bell Metal, Pottery, Black Pottery, Bamboo Root Craft, Doll Making, Dry Flower Craft, Bead Work/ Jewellery, Kauna Craft, Bead Embroidery etc.
17.	Karnataka	Sandalwood craft, Bidri Art, Stone carving, Toy Making, Mysore paintings, ivory carving, wood carving, Chittara folk art, etc.
18.	Orissa	Kalighat Patachitras, Brass work, silver-work, Terracotta art objects, Applique work, Horn works, Stone and wood Carvings etc.
19.	Madhya Pradesh	Leather Crafts, Chanderi Craft, Bamboo and cane work, Metal crafts, Carpets and Dhurries, Folk Paintings, Ornaments and jewellery, Stone carvings, Dhokra handicrafts, Terracotta craft etc.
20.	Maharashtra	Warli Painting, Kolhapuri Chappals, Bidriware, Kolhapur Jewellery, Paithani Sarees, Ganjifa Cards, Silverware, Dhurrie Weaving, Banjara Embroidery, Brass Musical Instruments etc.
21.	Kerala	Kathakali Masks, Coir Products, Brass and Bell Metal Works, Coir and Cane Products, Ivory Works, Lacquer Ware, Sandalwood Carving, Textiles, Wooden Toys, Kathakali Masks, Wood Carving etc.
22.	Delhi	Carpet Weaving, Bamboo Work, Gems, Kundan and Meenakari Jewelry, Ivory Carving, Leather ware, Paper Craft, Pottery, Shellac Bangles etc.
23.	Tripura	Cane and Bamboo Handicrafts, Handloom etc.
24.	West Bengal	Dhokra Metal Casting, Soft dolls and other dolls, Ceramics, Solapith, Clay dolls, Pottery and Terracotta, Conch Shell Craft, Sandalwood carving, Kantha Sticth, Scroll paintings, Patachitra etc.
25.	Chhattisgarh	Bamboo Art, Bell Metal (Dhokra), Godna, Wrought Iron (loha shilp), Terracotta, Tumba, Wall Painting, Woodcarving etc.
26.	Nagaland	Pottery Making, Wood-Carving, Blacksmithy, Cane and Bamboo art, Metal Work, Traditional Ornaments etc.
27.	Jharkhand	Black Pottery, Musical instruments, Tribal jewelry, Lost wax casting, Khovar and Sohrai Painting, Jadupatua Painting etc.
28.	Sikkim	Wood Carving, Thangka Painting, Cane and bamboo work, Hand-made paper making, Carpet weaving, Blanket weaving, Handloom weaving etc.
29.	Andaman and Nicobar Islands	Palm Mats, Wood Craft, Shell Craft, Cane and Bamboo, Crossbows, etc.

30.	Dadra and Nagar Haveli and Daman & Diu	Woodwork, Carpentry,etc.
31.	Jammu & Kashmir	Shawls, Carpets, Paper Machie, Embrodiery, Walnut Wood carving, Crewel work (Ari work), Copper Ware, Calico Painting etc.
32.	Lakshadweep	Crafts of coconut shells and tortoise shells
33.	Chandigarh	Terracotta and clay work (Mitti da Kaam)
34.	Gujarat	Rogan Painting, Embroidery Art, Pottery, Leather handicraft, Wood carvings, Beadwork, Bandhini – Tie and Dye Art, Batik, Ajrakh, Weaving Arts, etc.
35.	Tamilnadu	Tanjore Painting, Bhawani Durries, Nachiarcoil Metalware, Bhawani Durries, Chola Bronze Works, Embroidery of Toda Women, Papier Mache, Pattamadai Mats, Pottery Works, Stone craft, Wood-crafts etc.
36.	Ladakh	Wood Carving/ Carpentry, Carpet Weaving, Basket Making, Dragon Painting, Silver Filigree/ Black Smith, Namda Making etc.

SOME IMPORTANT CRAFTSMANSHIP OF INDIA

Chikankari

Chikankari is an embroidery technique renowned for its play of textures and supreme level of expertise. The Persian term "*Chakin*" is the root of the English word "Chikan," which means to make delicate patterns on fabrics. It is a type of pure needlework that is typically done on soft cotton fabric and is known as "white work" because it is done with white thread on white-coloured fabric. These days, art is offered in a variety of colours and fabrics.

Since its origin and throughout history, chikan has thrived, changed, and fallen, each time reflecting the preferences, trends, and way of life of its customers as well as the output and standing of the artisans who practise the art. This tradition's beginnings are incredibly obscure. Some fantastical interpretations of historical writings claim that chikan needlework originated in the third century B.C. The earliest surviving specimens of chikan needlework are significantly older than 19th-century dates. Courtiers wearing transparent coats adorned with white patterns or rows of flowers are frequently depicted in Mughal miniature paintings (Sharma, 2015).

Lucknow, the capital of Uttar Pradesh, is known for its traditional chikan handicrafts, which are also known as chikan needlework. It was developed here in the late 18th century, perhaps under the Nawabs of Oudh. The chikan tradition reached legendary heights of exquisite beauty in the 19th century in Lucknow. The work is famous across the world for its grace, finesse, and delicacy. Small white embroidery, chikan's monochromatic sobriety is complemented by a rich texture created by combining several stitches in unique ways, all of which are expertly crafted to go with and enhance outfit designs. The most popular themes are the paan leaf and the keiri or paisley. The motifs are primarily floral, with scrolls, trailing branches, and creepers filling compositions. In addition to kurtas, saris, salwar suits, *topis*, handkerchiefs, and *dupattas*, new goods like tablecloths, tray covers, napkins, *lehangas,* etc. are embellished with chikan embroidery.

The unstructured and troubled chikan craft sector has many issues. Chikan embroidery is a beautiful cultural legacy that must be safeguarded. Such a legacy must be safeguarded based on thorough documentation of the craft's history, advances, techniques, and decorative themes. In December 2008, Chikan received the geographical indication title. The GI tag has not given the work any notable advantages or distinctions of any kind. The industry, which is disorganised and safeguards the local cultural heritage by employing for a significant number of people, persists as a result of the craftsmen' traditional skill and knowledge that have been passed down through the years. Entrepreneurial creativity and involvement are now required to revive the current art form and address related problems. The commercialised market version of inferior goods is a fierce competitor for this delicate craftsmanship of pattern making. Because of this, it is uncommon to view the excellent work's intricate motifs and stitches in all their glory.

Phulkari

The rich history and traditions of the Punjab region are inextricably linked to the traditional embroidery known as phulkari. Phulkari is one of the most well-known embroidered crafts made and worn in the Indian state of Haryana and Punjab. Phulkari is a phrase for floral craft that combines the words "Phul" which means flower and "Kari" which means craft. Phulkari workmanship is used extensively in clothing that features intricate design patterns and brilliant colours. It has, however, primarily been used to decorate women's *chaddars* (shawl).

This needlework has been produced continuously since the 15th century in Punjab. The classic motifs used in the border and multipurpose design of phulkari embroidery. Khaddar and Cham fabrics were chosen to have designs applied on them. Numerous techniques, including hand embroidery, machine embroidery, hand painting, and screen painting, were used to create the Phulkari motifs. Equal amounts of needlework were created using threads of varied colours. Black red, chocolate brown, indigo blue, and black were often the most popular colours used while painting the khadi at home before the needlework was done. Yellow gold, purple, orange, green, and white were the most popular hues for embroidery thread. The eye-catching and lavish, design has a strength that comes from the sturdy, joyful temperament of the Punjabi people, whose lives were centred around agrarian pursuits. A golden harvest's abundance represented joy, which was reflected in the fabric's stories, folklore, and depictions of daily life. After finishing their household duties, Punjabi ladies created the traditional Punjab Phulkari. They sat in "Trijan" groups, where all the women participated in weaving, dancing, laughing, and needlework.

The women of Punjab were the only ones who initially practised the traditional Phulkari art. For Punjabi ladies, phulkari has long been a significant part of their lives. Phulkari is an embroidery technique that has been passed down through the generations. Girls have used it to stitch their goals, aspirations, and imaginative worlds onto khaddar canvases. Phulkari has traditionally been a priceless gift given to daughters during their nuptial ceremonies or on other family occasions, such as welcoming a new baby into the family. Many different products are produced using the embroidery technique. As mentioned earlier, the traditional Phulkari was constructed from handcrafted "khaddar" cloth with brightly coloured silk threads. A unique style of phulkari known as "Vari Da Bagh," in which needlework covers the fabric's whole surface, required a year to complete. Three branches of the work include:

- The genuine phulkari, in which the pattern is diapered over the fabric at intervals

- A bagh or garden with a linked design covering the entire surface ornamentation
- Chobes, where only the borders have ornamentation and the rest is plain

Originally, phulkari was done as a hobby, stitched with care for one's personal use or as a gift for family members, and without any thought of making money. However, as a result of expanding marketization and commodification, phulkari needlework increasingly evolved into a commercial enterprise. Innovative products are being created in Phulkari to meet the needs of the modern market in response to changing consumer tastes and preferences. Phulkari had almost become a lost art by the start of the 20th century and was in grave danger of getting extinct. The once-beautiful craft form has degraded in quality and turned into a parody of itself. Magenta, orange, and red, the classic needlework colours, are no longer seen as being attractive. Fine quality fabrics have taken the place of khaddar, such as terri voils, crapes, chiffons, lizzy bizzy cotton, satin cloth, and silk cloth, and other. Embroidery is also done from the front or right side after printing designs on various fabrics and using ring frames to hold the designs in place. With the joint efforts of State and Central Government, NGO's, designers, and businesspeople, new attempts have been made to restore the forgotten skill of phulkari as a cottage industry.

Mysore Painting

In South India's Karnataka, Mysore paintings are a significant subgenre of Indian classical painting. They are renowned for their extensive details, elegance, and exquisite colour illustrations. It began during Vijayanagar's rule (1338-1575). Mixed hues are hallmark of this artwork. Mysore paintings are not just ornamental pieces; they also effectively capture the devotion and modesty that the artists wished to communicate. Its themes centre is on Hindu mythology and deities. The primary characteristics of Mysore paintings include delicate brushstrokes, graceful body compositions, delicate use of herbal hues, brilliant gold leaf tone, etc. In this artwork, numerous faces, wearables, jewellery, etc. are enhanced using the gesso technique. The use of Gesso, which is prevalent in all Karnataka paintings, is one of the main characteristics of Mysore paintings. A mixture of gum Arabic, glue, and white lead powder is used to make the paste known as gesso. Gold is frequently utilised to brighten up clothing, decorations, earthenware, and gods. Traditional gold foils are used to create each painting. Paint colours are resistant to fungus. Every painting must include a border, which is typically done in black and yellow. In order to set the major individuals out from the background, the artist used yellow to emphasise them. The picture endures for many generations. Three categories of paintings exist:

- Plain gold foil paintings without embossing.
- Work by Makki Safeda (After painting the base colour, various shades of white (zinc oxide: super white) are applied).
- Painting that has been embossed.

An old card game from India is known as "Ganjifa." The game is thought to have been introduced to India historically during the Mughal era. The Persian term "*Ganjifeh*," which meaning playing cards, is whence the name Ganjifa originates. These cards stand out since they are typically hand-painted. Typically, the cards are round, though unusual rectangular decks have also been made. Mysore painting still plays a significant role in capturing the culture of southern India.

Madhubani Painting

In India, painting has been a thriving art form since very early times. Indian paintings are distinctive in that they frequently depict and are linked to deeply significant religious practises and cultural events. Indian rural folk art features distinctive, colourful designs with mystical and spiritual themes. In Bihar's artistic community, there is a still-evolving tradition known as Madhubani painting, which sheds light on the state's socioeconomic structure and cultural identity. The Madhubani, commonly referred to as a Mithila painting from the Mithila region of Bihar state, literally translates as "forest of honey." The viewers have always been fascinated by this artwork's extraordinary beauty. Most of these artworks have a religious theme. It is primarily created by women. The primary subjects of the Madhubani paintings are the Hindu Gods and Goddesses.

The Mithila paintings or Madhubani paintings are known as wall or mural paintings. This is a Hindu painting style that has gained international recognition and is mostly practised in Mithila and the northern regions of Bihar. The Bihar Madhubani painting tradition has persisted unbroken to the present and has changed more and more through time. These days, the art form can be found in saris, on trains, in art galleries, on the walls of railroad stations, and in private living rooms. As part of a ceremony, this type of painting is done. Every motif employed by these Maithili artists has a distinct significance. For instance, fish are a symbol of fertility, procreation, and good fortune; peacocks are a representation of fervent religious devotion; and serpents are regarded as divine protectors. Simple housewives who have never attended an art school are the artists of this work of art. The only people who could create this art were women. At a young age, every girl learned this skill from her mother or other family members.

Bright Madhubani artwork has been created for many years in many parts of Bihar, India, although its origins are mostly unknown. However, it is thought that King Janaka, who ruled the Mithila Kingdom in the eighth or seventh century BCE, commanded the creation of these paintings to record the events surrounding the marriage of his daughter Sita to Prince Rama (Singh, 2022). "Origin of this continuity may be traced to the continuous spell of hindu role in Mithila from 1097 AD to 1550AD under the Karnatas and the Oinavaras which continued uninterruptedly under the Khandavala dynasty (Darbhanga raj) till the present day" (Das, 2013). The area of Mithila, the centre of creative activity, remained unknown to the outside world until the 1930s; however, due to the occurrence of a natural disaster, an earthquake destroyed many villages in the old district of Darbhanga in Bihar. William J. Archer a British Civil Servant got a chance to go as a Provincial Census Superintendent to the badly affected region to locate remains of crumbling walls with vibrantly painted murals that are native to the region. He was fascinated by this kind of art and subsequently, in 1949, published an essay in Marg on the graphical tradition of Madhubani painting. At that time, neither this art nor the Madhubani region was known to the outside world. The area of Madhubani experienced a severe drought in the years 1965–1966. The Central government hired a delegate, Bhaskar Kulkarni, to identify the traditional arts of the area that may be practised on a big scale and might be used to provide resources for Maithil people in order to offer economic sustenance to those impacted by drought. Women from nearby villages, including Rashidpur, Leheriagunj, and Harinagar began painting on paper in addition to walls, boosting attention to Madhubani. When painters like Jagadamba Devi and Sita Devi received national prizes from the President of India, the art gained attention on a national level (Ghosh, 2020 & Das, 2012). According to Das the attributes characterizing almost all Madhubani paintings are: -

- Incorporating vibrant natural and artificial hues.
- A double-line border with elaborate flower motifs or basic geometric patterns.
- Utilizing symbols, lines, and patterns to support the central theme.
- Abstract representations of deities or humans.
- The characters' features are defined by large, protruding eyes and a jolting nose that emerges from the forehead.

The walls are covered in layers of cow manure to start. In some homes, the mud walls are used directly as canvases. These folk painters primarily used three different mediums to express their artistic expressions: wall paintings (*bhitti-chitra*), canvas paintings (pata-chitra), and floor paintings (aripana or bumi shoba). Women frequently pray to the deities before beginning their paintings to obtain their assistance as they carry out their rituals or goals. These paintings feature stunning, eye-catching geometric designs for every occasion, including diverse sanskaras and rituals related to different pujas and seasons, childbirth, marriage, Holi, Surya Shakti, Kalipuja, Upanayanam, Durga Puja, etc.

A variety of colours are used in Madhubani Paintings, such as dark red, green, blue, black, pale yellow, and pink. The Madhubani paintings are still created using only natural colours. Black was traditionally created using burnt barley seeds, yellow using turmeric, or lime mixed with milk from banyan leaves, orange using palash flowers, red using kusuma flower juice and red sandalwood, and green using bel leaves. Rice powder and water can be combined to create a white colour. When pipal bark is dried and boiled in water, it turns pink. Berries from a herb known as sikkar are used to produce blue dye. Dark green comes from Siam creepers, and parrot green from gulmohar sepals. Black colours are made from soot, and light brown is made by combining cow dung and gum with fresh water. Clay and pollen both can produce yellow and red. Gum was blended with colour to extend the painting's life and give it vibrancy. Many paintings feature a lot of red. Outlines are created using a bamboo twig. The cotton wrapped around a bamboo stick is employed as a brush for its elaboration. To add visual depth and aesthetic appeal, the outline is typically left uncolored. The border of a Madhubani painting is quite important. Strong linear designs of geometric symbols and various flora and fauna are used by artists to create border patterns that are visually appealing. Since organic dyes require a lot of preparation time, synthetic colours are now also used.

These naturally talented individuals lack any predetermined concepts and guidelines as well as written instructions. Their creativity and ideas had a huge impact on the form of art. The subjects of these paintings typically fall into one of two categories:

(a) collection of heavenly forms, with the occasional addition of the more typical figurines of the bride, groom, and other wedding guests, and
(b) collection of carefully chosen vegetable and animal forms.

The Indian folk-art style of Madhubani has succeeded in establishing a place for itself in the international house of fame and is now known throughout the world, however rural residents who are genuine artists are unable to acquire the attention they deserve. Their financial situation is dire. In order to advance in the world of modern art, the young generation of educated artists needs strong assistance from both the government and NGOs. For their artistic journey to continue, they require appropriate visibility and reliable finances. The joint efforts of Maithil people, who are dispersed worldwide, can enhance the situation of Madhubani art and its practitioners. They must begin to consider how their own culture and artistic practises will develop. One of them is the Office of Development Commissioner (Handicrafts), under the Ministry of Textiles, Government of India. It offers opportunities to showcase one's cultural activity at various locations, making it one of the options. The major goals of these types of organizations are to improve the skills of craftsmen from other states, to provide funding for capacity building, and to provide seminars and workshops to raise awareness among artisans, NGOs, and other groups. The Madhubani art has gained even more popularity and recognition as a result of recent initiatives by the local government,

NGOs, and cultural institutions like museums. Many fashion designers have introduced collections of Madhubani designs, which include traditional clothing (Stoles, Sarees, Salwar Kameez, long skirts, etc.) that is exquisitely crafted in Madhubani art. Other commonly used items, such as pen cases, backpacks, diaries, etc., are frequently painted in Mithila art and are highly appreciated (Singh, 2022).

Tokio Hasegawa, a Japanese traveller to Madhubani, has established a Mithila Museum in Japan. The Mithila Museum at Nigata has about 850 Mithila paintings, more than 300 paintings that Mithila artists created in Japan. The museum concentrates its efforts on the acquisition, research, and promotion of Mithila art.

Bone and Horn Craftsmanship

The act of carving into animal bones is known as bone carving. It may lead to the decoration of a bone and the construction of a figure. There are differences between bones and horns in terms of their physical or chemical composition. Therefore, the method and process used to create objects made of bones and horns are distinct, albeit occasionally, the methods may be the same. This craftwork provides bangles, perfume jars, traditional combs, jewellery, tobacco pipes, and many more artefacts. The horn and bones of dead animals are originally utilized for the horn and bone crafts-producing process, which makes it an environmentally friendly industry.

The city of Sambhal (Sarai Tarin) of Uttar Pradesh is well-known for its distinctive horn and bone crafts, which are exported to many different nations. The bones and horns products of Paralakhemundi (a town in Odisha) are also magical and exquisitely decorated. Stylised animals and birds that appear to be alive are examples of this amazing craftsmanship. Sometimes, to enhance the beauty of the horn items, delicate silver filigree decorations are applied. In Cuttack, filigree and horn work are mixed to create ornamental jewellery. Other significant locations include Thiruvananthapuram in Kerala, Honawar in Karnataka, Jaipur, Ajmer, Bikaner, Jodhpur in Rajasthan etc.

Bone has been used as a medium for artistic creation since prehistoric times. Bone carving has been linked to numerous cultures that value it as a form of expression. Animal bones were frequently used in religious, ceremonial, and ritual art. Bones are frequently carved and used to make vessels, musical instruments, jewellery, and weapons. Many cultures around the world have practised bone carving, often as a less expensive and recently legal substitute for ivory carving. It also had a significant role in ancient art. Additionally, painters and craftspeople, particularly metalworkers, used bone to test out their creations. These pieces are referred to as "trial pieces." People have used horns for a variety of reasons throughout history. Some bovid horns, like the shofar, are employed as musical instruments. The use of drinking horns was widespread in ancient societies. Scandinavians, Greeks, Romans, Thracians, Scythians, and Africans all utilised them. For at least 2,600 years, people have been using horns as drinking vessels. (Farha & Zarrin, 2021).

These handicrafts are valued by many Western nations; however, today's handicraft industry and artisans face many difficulties as a result of the exporters' very low payments to the artisans for these goods. The artists put in much effort but receive little in return, and their situation remains unchanged despite this. This traditional craftsmanship needs to be preserved urgently, particularly with proper documentation. If the necessary steps are taken early to establish this modest sector based on a traditional craft, bone and horn artefacts have a very bright future. The biggest hurdle in maintaining handicrafts is motivating the next generation in craft production. The craft tends to decline as a result of the craftsmen's children abandoning the traditional employment to pursue more profitable careers. This tradition will be strengthened and kept alive if it is preserved and passed on to the following generation. The issues facing by craftsmen must be addressed immediately in order to preserve this priceless tradition. Through substantial government support measures in terms of funding, technological assistance, the removal of middlemen, training and development programmes for the artisans, this craft should be given a boost.

Bamboo and Cane Craft

India has a large prevalence of bamboo and cane craft, which is very beneficial. Bamboo and cane crafts, once used by indigenous societies, are a fantastic source of art and a means of subsistence in India. Over 1200 species of bamboo are known to exist in the globe, and they are enormous woody grasses. Bamboos are among the planet's fastest-growing plants and are a vital component of the cultural, social, and economic traditions of the north-eastern states. Cane is only found in a small portion of the state, although bamboo is abundantly grown throughout.

One of the most well-known crafts carried out in India's North East is that of bamboo and cane. For the people of the north-eastern states, cane and bamboo are an essential component of life. The states of Manipur, Assam, Meghalaya, Tripura, and Nagaland, etc. are very popular for producing this kind of craftsmanship. Bamboo and cane are used in a variety of ways to create a wide range of products, and typically, people use it in a variety of ways to cater their daily needs. An ordinary piece of bamboo or cane can be transformed into a work of art by the deft hands of craftsmen. These lightweight, elegant eco-friendly products each have their own distinct style. These products have a long lifespan and require less upkeep than wooden products. Many different practical and aesthetic products are made from strips of bamboo and different kinds of canes. Attractive user friendly and eco-friendly products made from cane and bamboo such as *moorahs* or small stools, utility items like picture frames, pen stands, baskets and dustbins, fruit and vegetable baskets, beer mugs, hair clips, decorative items like flowers, flower vases, containers etc. People who work in tea gardens in northeast India wear bamboo-made headgear, and an umbrella's handle with intricate flower carvings is also made of bamboo. Cane and bamboo can also be used to create sturdy, distinctive furniture, which is currently highly trendy. The other widely used products of this skill are jewellery, luggage, and handbags. In addition to innovative designs and enhanced technology, bamboo is a good substitute for plastics, steel, and cement for housing, furniture production, and agricultural tools and implements. Additionally, it is a raw material that is environmentally sound and can reduce the need to use up our forests. The products created from canes and bamboo are likewise well-known on the global market. Additionally, different designs of furniture and utility goods are exported to other nations. The items are now also utilised to decorate the interiors of homes, hotels, offices, etc. This time-honoured craft is currently contending with a number of obstacles, including as intense competition from materials made of plastic and fibre, a dearth of marketing activities, and the ever-increasing cost of bamboo. Farmers are having trouble with an erratic supply of raw materials as a result of the destruction of bamboo and cane forests. The artisans are constrained to reduce the prices of their crafts. There is also a shortage of highly skilled craftsmen capable of making fine creative and aesthetic furniture commercially.

Brass Work

The history of Indian Brass, as it is popularly known, dates to the time of the Indus Valley Civilization, which lasted from approximately 2400 BC to 1700 BC. Other locations, such Kalibangan in Rajasthan, Lothal in Gujarat, and Laimabad in Maharashtra, saw the growth of this extraction. Mohanjodaro and Harappa are without a doubt the two most well-known sites. One of the first metal sculptures from the Harappan period to be found in India is a dancer with a carefree pose. The enormous Buddha statue at Sultanganj is a testament to the metalsmithing mastery of Indian craftsmen and may be the largest antique metalwork still in existence. The world's largest producer of brass is India. In India, this technique has been practised for more than five million years (Geeta, n.d.).

Punjab has a long-standing legacy of producing brass and copper kitchenware using a craft practised by the Thatheras of Jandiala Guru. Copper, brass, and some of the alloys utilised are thought to have health benefits. In 2014, UNESCO added the art of producing copper and brass utensils, as practised by the Thatheras of Jandiala Guru, Punjab, to its list of Intangible Cultural Heritage. An Indian traditional craft form has never been included on the UNESCO list. The Jandiala Thatheras' significance does not lay in their singularity; rather, it is in the manufacturing process, which draws on a wide variety of ancient knowledge systems used by the craftsman. The Thatheras use traditional metalworking techniques to make their items, drawing on a wealth of generational experience. The manual polishing of utensils uses conventional ingredients like sand and tamarind juice. The creation of designs involves deftly pounding several tiny dents into the hot metal. Utensils may be produced for communal or individual usage on special events like weddings or at temples, whether for ritual or utilitarian purposes.

These abilities are what make the craft and craftsman living history, and they are acknowledged and cherished in the UNESCO inscription.

It is believed that this will pave the way for acknowledging the cultural relevance of craft and its practitioners as well as emphasising their significance as India's "Living Heritage." From father to son, the manufacturing technique is verbally passed down. For Thatheras, metalworking determines their family and kinship structure, work ethic, and status within the town's social hierarchy. Metalwork is more than just a means of subsistence.

In the area of brass work, various styles can be found throughout India. Brass is produced in the Northern and North Eastern regions of the country at places like Uttar Pradesh's Moradabad, Sambhal, Hathras, Aligarh, and Varanasi; Rajasthan's Jaipur and Jodhpur; Orissa's Mayurbhang, Keonjhar, Dhenkanal, and Sundergarh; Haryana's Jagadhari and Rewari; and Jammu and Kashmir's Samba, and Udhampur etc.

The variety of brass products produced in Moradabad, Uttar Pradesh, is renowned in the world. There are many different household objects created here that are embellished with detailed etching, including pots, trays, bowls, and decorative pieces. In Moradabad, goods made of white metal, electroplated brass, and copper are also produced.

Cast sculptures of Gods, copper and brass household items are popular in Banaras. Varanasi (Banaras), which is in the Uttar Pradesh state, is the leading city in India for the number of casts and sculptured brass and copper mythological images and symbols, as well as domestic objects.

Large amounts of cooking utensils, lamps, and other items are produced for local usage in the Punjab and all major towns using brass and copper as their primary metal. Brass vessels are supplied by Amritsar, Ambala, Ludhiana, and Jullundur to the steep areas surrounding the Punjab and were once exported up the Kabul Valley into Afghanistan.

Kashmir's Ladakh region is well-known for its antique brass and iron pots. Bowls, samovars, plates, and trays with intricate engravings are another speciality of Kashmiri artisans. On copper and silver goods, intricate floral and calligraphic designs are impressive. After that, the pieces are oxidised, which makes the design pop against the background. This art is referred to as *naquashi*.

The primary location in Rajasthan for brass engraving and lacquering is Jaipur, which produces items like bowls, photo frames, plates, boxes, etc. On the surface, hunting scenes, flower motifs, ethnic patterns, and other designs are stamped or engraved. Either the entire body of the object is covered in lacquer or only a portion of it. Bronze sculptures are another speciality of Jaipur. The art of Koftagari, also known as damascening work, is mostly executed in Alwar and Jaipur. A wire is used to encrust one metal into another. Swords, daggers, and shields are common items.

In the Andhra, Orissa, and Madhya Pradesh tribal regions, the Dokra metal craft is well-liked. This craft's distinctiveness lies in the fact that no two pieces are alike. Here, tiny sculptures of horses, drummers, tribal gods, and plaques are created. Most of the brass used to make these things is scrap brass. The centre of the pieces is filled with clay, which makes them unique among metal crafts.

Rogan Art

A four-century-old kind of cloth painting known as traditional **Rogan art,** having Persian roots, is only practised in the Kutch district of Gujarat, India. Around 400 years ago, the Rogan Art arrived at Nirona Village in Kutch, Gujarat. Rogan painting was initially practised in a few locations around the Kutch region. Several forces combined in the late 20th and early 21st centuries to rekindle interest in Rogan art, particularly painting. A rich, vividly coloured paint made of castor oil and natural colours is used in the textile painting known as Rogan. The word "rogan," which in Persian means "oil-based," refers to the thick mixture produced by heating castor oil before pouring it into cold water. Using a metal stylus called a "Kalam," the paste is dragged out into a fine "thread" after being combined with natural colours. The only instrument used in Rogan painting is a short, six-inch stylus that is pointed at the tip, and the artist's left palm serves as a palette for warming, softening, and mixing the rogan. The fabric is then folded by the artist to print its mirror counterpart. The Rogan painting is then finished by the addition of the smaller elements. Persian alphabets were employed as calligraphic themes in the past. Traditional Rogan art uses floral and geometrical patterns. The "Tree of Life" and happiness idea works by Rogan Art are highly well recognised and inspired by traditional Persian designs.

Rogan Art was initially supported by the farming and animal-herding populations in the area. This art used to be traditionally incorporated into these communities' bridal attire. It is thought that this is a time-consuming procedure that demands effort. The Rogan art practice is a slow process in this quick-paced society. Due to the high cost and lack of exposure, this art is not well known. Demand for the art started to decline as machine-made fabrics became a more affordable alternative. The last and original Abdul Gafur family in Nirona village upholds the Rogan art tradition. The efforts of Abdul Gafur Khatri and his younger brother Sumar Daud Khatri's family preserved this craft, which was on the verge of extinction until recently. Since the 1980s, he has been making an effort to restore the art form by painting items other than ceremonial apparel, holding exhibitions, and raising awareness of it. A male descendant of a Rogan artist lineage was must in order to practise the art.

The traditional constraints of Rogan painting, sadly, made the genre particularly vulnerable to extinction. In the past, Rogan art was practised by numerous Gujarati people. Nine people of Khatri descent in Nirona are the only remaining guardians of the Rogan Painting art from Kutch in Gujarat, India. Abdul Gafur Khatri had given up on his ability to support himself through the art form that had been handed down through his family for generations. Fortunately, the Gujarat government provided a project to the family for the revival of this dying craftsmanship. He also acknowledged his significance in upholding his ancestors' legacy. The art would disappear if he gave up on it. He has been practising Rogan art for nearly fifty years as of now. To raise awareness of Rogan Art, the family actively engages in conferences, exhibitions, and workshops. Although the Rogan painting technique is well known for its distinctive fabric painting style, there is only a small market for its products because they are difficult to find in stores. The art does not yield sufficient rewards because it demands high levels of skill and a lot of time to manufacture a single item. In order to overcome this shortcoming of the art, artists might be supported by carefully considered products. To increase public knowledge of this genre of art, a survey based on Rogan art ought to be carried out. Rogan art fabrics should also be utilized to make clothing. It should be promoted to the fashion world through advertisements and other channels.

References

1. Agarwal, R. (2015). Madhubani painting: Women dominated folk art. *Inter J Applied Res, 1*, 736-38.
2. Ahmad, Y., & Anees, M. (2016). Issues of The Lucknow Chikan Handicraft Industry. *International Journal of Multidisciplinary Research in Social Sciences, 2*(01).
3. Bukhari, W. N. The Embroidery of Emotions-Phulkari Bagh's of Punjab. *Journal of Research (Urdu),35*(2), 182-197. ISSN-1816-3424
4. Chaturvedi, D. K. (2022). A study on Traditional Rogan Art of India. *International Journal of Research Publication and Reviews, 3*(6), 1542–1545. https://doi.org/10.55248/gengpi.2022.3.6.12
5. Dang, S. (n.d.). *Mysore Painting Craft Manual*. Craftcanvas. Retrieved from https://www.academia.edu/33246624/Mysore_Painting_Craft_Manual
6. Das, N. (2013). Madhubani paintings: Its existence and possibility. *International Journal of Scientific and Research Publications, 3*(2), 1-7.
7. Das, S. (2012). Glimpses of Madhubani Paintings. *Heritage and Us conserve it for the future, 2*(1), 52-58. ISSN 2319-1201
8. Dey, M., & Malhotra, Dr. S. B. (n.d.). Challenges faced by small scale Craft entrepreneurs due to absence of organised marketing channels.
9. Dhamija, J. (Ed.). (2004). *Asian embroidery.* Abhinav Publications.
10. Farha., Zarrin, A., (2021). Safeguarding of Traditional Craftsmanship of Sambhal Handicrafts with special reference to bone and horn artifacts. *Journal of Research in Humanities and Social Science, 9*(8), 14-22. ISSN 2321-9467.
11. Geeta. (2007). *Brass Industry*. Scribd. Retrieved from https://www.scribd.com/document/348718138/Brass-Industry
12. Ghosh, S. (2020). Madhubani Painting—Vibrant Folk Art of Mithila. *Art and Design Review, 8*(2) 61-78. https://doi.org/10.4236/adr.2020.82005
13. Ghouse, S. M. (2012). Indian handicraft industry: problems and strategies. *International Journal of Management Research and Reviews, 2*(7), 1183-1199.
14. Hajra, V. (2015). Role of Indian folk culture in promotion of tourism in the country. *Indian journal of research, 4*(2), 231-235.
15. Hawladar, M., & Fakaruddin, M. (2021). Indian Paintings: An Analysis of Geographical and Chronological Context. *Asian Journal of Social Sciences and Legal Studies, 3*(3), 75-84.
16. Jadhav, S. (2013). Indian handicrafts: Growing or depleting. *IOSR Journal of Business and Management, 2*(15), 7-13.
17. John, S. (2014). Study on the role of tourism in promoting arts and crafts–a case study on Channapatna Toys. In *Proceedings of the Second International*

Conference on Global Business, Economics, Finance and Social Sciences, 11(13), 1-9.

18. Kapur, H., & Mittar, S. (2014). Design intervention & craft revival. *International Journal of scientific and research publications, 4*(10), 1-5.
19. Karakul, Ö. (2019). The effects of tourism on traditional craftsmanship for the sustainable development of historic environments. *European Journal of Sustainable Development, 8*(4), 380-390. ISSN: 2239-5938
20. Kaur, P. (2011). Revival of Punjab's traditional handicraft: Phulkari. *Asian Journal of Management, 2*(1), 28-38.
21. Kohli, H. K., Lehal, R., Kaur, H., & Sharma, N. (2020). Phulkari Art: A Tool for Women Empowerment in Punjab. *Pramana Research Journal, 10*(9), 176-187. ISSN NO: 2249-2976.
22. Manfredi, P. (2016). Chikan from Lucknow: Origins of a Legend. *Indian Horizons, 63*(2), 47-61.
23. Mubayi, Y. (2020). Craft as intangible heritage: The Thatheras of Jandiala Guru, Punjab. In *Heritage Conservation in Postcolonial India* (pp. 203-218). Routledge.
24. Pandya, A., & Vishwakarma, A. (2010). Rogan, the traditional hand painted textile of Gujarat. *Indian Journal of Traditional Knowledge. 9*(4), 644-650.
25. Ribašauskienė, E., & Šumylė, D. (2016). The role of traditional craft centers in safeguarding cultural heritage. *Vadybos mokslas ir studijos-kaimo verslų ir jų infrastruktūros plėtrai, 38*(4), 412-424.
26. Sandgruber, R., Bichler-Ripfel, H., & Walcher, M. (2019). Traditional Craftsmanship as intangible cultural heritage and an economic factor in Austria. In *Proceedings of the International Conference Theory and Applications in the Knowledge Economy TAKE 2019* (p. 61). Eduardo Tomé.
27. Sharma, N. (2015). Chikan: Beauty of white. *Mumbai: NIFT.*
28. Singh, C. S. B. (2022). *Madhubani Paintings: People's Living Cultural Heritage*. World History Encyclopedia. Retrieved from https://www.worldhistory.org/article/1527/madhubani-paintings-peoples-living-cultural-herita/
29. Sodhi, S., Arya, N., & Yadav, N. (2016). Creation Of Designs by Adaptation of Madhubani Painting Motifs. *International Journal of Humanities and Social Sciences (IJHSS), 5*(5), 89-94.
30. Srivastav, G., & Rawat, P. S. (2012). Indian handicraft & globalization: in context of export. *Indian Journal of Community Health, 24*(2).
31. Steel, F. A. (1888). Phulkari Work in the Punjab. *The Journal of Indian Art, 1886-1916, 2*(17-24), 71-72.
32. Tiwari, S., & Joshi, A. (2021). The Remaining Essence of Rogan Art: In context of Innovative Business Practices of craft Heritage. *International Journal of Creative Research Thoughts, 9*(8), d536–d539.

33. World Tourism Organization. (2012). *Tourism and Intangible Cultural Heritage*. UNWTO, Madrid.

34. Yadav, U. S., Tripathi, R., & Tripathi, M. A. (2020). Strategies for development of handicraft sector (small industries) in India. *SEDME (Small Enterprises Development, Management & Extension Journal)*, *47*(3), 175-193.

35. Yang, Y., Shafi, M., Song, X., & Yang, R. (2018). Preservation of cultural heritage embodied in traditional crafts in the developing countries. A case study of Pakistani handicraft industry. *Sustainability*, *10*(5), 1336.

36. *Traditional Rogan Art*. (2018). Rogan Art. Retrieved from http://roganartnirona.com/rogan.html

37. *Horn & Bone craft*. (2012). JourneyFix. Retrieved from http://www.journeyfix.com/indian-artcraft/hornbone-craft/overview-102-1117.html

38. UNESCO. (n.d.). *Traditional brass and copper craft of utensil making among the Thatheras of Jandiala Guru, Punjab, India*. Retrieved from https://ich.unesco.org/en/RL/traditional-brass-and-copper-craft-of-utensil-making-among-the-thatheras-of-jandiala-guru-punjab-india-00845

39. *Mithila Museum an Introduction*. (n.d.). Mithila Museum. Retrieved from http://www.mithila-museum.com/aboutMM/Findex.html

40. *Phulkari Shawl*. (2012). JourneyFix. Retrieved from http://www.journeyfix.com/indian-artcraft/phulkari-shawl/overview-102-1122.html

41. *Bamboo & Cane Crafts*. (2012). JourneyFix. Retrieved from http://www.journeyfix.com/indian-artcraft/bamboocane-crafts/overview-102-1111.html

42. Gogoi, M. (2020). Cane And Bamboo Based Traditional Handicraft Industry: A Profitable Business for Youth Self Help Group of Assam. *Indian Journal of Applied Research 10*(12), 31–32. https://doi.org/10.36106/ijar

43. Directorate of Handicrafts and Handloom. (2012). *Cane and Bamboo Crafts*. Retrieved from https://sikkimcrafts.gov.in/canebamboocraft.html

44. *Bamboo and cane crafts remain an integral part of Manipur's economy, lifestyle*. (2019). ANI News. Retrieved from https://www.aninews.in/news/lifestyle/culture/bamboo-and-cane-crafts-remain-an-integral-part-of-manipurs-economy-lifestyle20190330191357/

45. *Horn and bone craft*. (n.d.). IndiaNetzone. Retrieved from https://www.indianetzone.com/1/horn_bone_craft.htm

46. Sharma, P. (2020). *Famous Indian Handicrafts from 29 states of India*. Living Art Life. Retrieved from https://livingartlife.com/famous-indian-handicrafts-every-state/

47. *Cane and Bamboo Handicraft*. (2019). Technology Innovation Management and Entrepreneurship Information Service. Retrieved from https://www.techno-preneur.net/technology/project-profiles/textile/Cane.htm

48. *Handicraft (Horn-Bone) (Sambhal).* (n.d.). One District-One Product. Retrieved from https://odopmart.com/sambhal
49. *Creative Arts in India.* (2016). Scribd. Retrieved from https://www.scribd.com/document/466508478/Creative-arts-in-India
50. UNESCO. (2003). *Intangible Cultural Heritage Domains.* Retrieved from https://ich.unesco.org/doc/src/01857-EN.pdf
51. Baral, B., William, A., & Susanth, C. *(2022). Mysore Painting Classical South Indian Paintings.* D'Source. Retrieved from https://www.dsource.in/resource/mysore-painting
52. *Mysore Painting.* (n.d.). JourneyFix. Retrieved from http://www.journeyfix.com/indian-artcraft/mysore-painting/overview-102-1120.html

Chapter - 6

Safeguarding of Intangible Cultural Heritage of India

This chapter provides an overview of the realm of India's intangible traditions, which are intangible components of our cultural history that are intricately woven into our way of life. India has long been home to a rich and intricate tapestry of ancient cultural tradition, which has resulted in a plethora of both tangible and intangible cultural heritage. A community's traditions, customs, tales, music, dances, and other cultural practices are known as its intangible cultural legacy. Many communities in India continue to practise their customs, rituals, oral expressions, and historical legacy. These intangible assets bind communities to their roots by bridging the past and present through these age-old practises. Different peoples and ethnic groups have influenced our ceremonies, rituals, music, folk arts, craftsmanship, folklore, and dance forms, which developed relationships between nature and the universe. This chapter explores the people and organisations tasked with maintaining, transmitting, and fostering these essential customs as the custodians of these intangible cultural legacies. We also learn how India's intangible cultural legacy is alive and thriving, poised to affect the future by examining the guardians of these cherished traditions, their efforts to ensure continuity, and the vital role they play in safeguarding the essence of our diverse intangible cultural heritage for generations to come. According to Boylan (2006), "Intangible heritage is by definition people-orientated rather than object-centred."

In India, safeguarding Intangible Cultural Heritage (ICH) is a difficult and constantly evolving task. These difficulties are a result of multiple reasons. Here are some of the key challenges that India faces in safeguarding its ICH:

The loss of indigenous knowledge systems and the decline of traditional practises are potential consequences of rapid globalisation, urbanisation, and modernisation. Finding a balance between modernization and preservation is an ongoing challenge. A lack of recognition or adequate documentation of many ICH aspects causes a lack of awareness among the general population and policymakers. This can also result in inadequate funding. Traditional practises may disappear as a result of economic pressures, especially in rural areas. Younger generations may be less likely to pursue their traditional occupations when offered better economic opportunities elsewhere. Traditional knowledge and practises that are commercialised or appropriated may pose a threat to ICH. It can be difficult to prevent the exploitation of these resources while still enabling communities to reap benefits from their legacy. India has a very diverse population in terms of languages, customs, and practices. Maintaining such a wide variety of ICH elements can be difficult. Documentation and maintenance of many ICH aspects are difficult because they rely on oral traditions or performances. However, it is crucial to ensure that these components are passed down to the next generations. It is essential to involve communities in the safeguarding process, but ensuring they actively participate and gain from these initiatives can be challenging. Additionally, communities that practise ICH may be uprooted as a result of migration or shifting demographics, which makes it tough to pass on their customs to the following generation. Both human and financial resources are needed to protect and preserve ICH. These initiatives may be hampered by a lack of resources and qualified specialists. Environmental changes also have the potential to endanger ICH activities like fishing and agriculture, which are directly related to regional ecosystems. The sustainability of ICH is significantly threatened by climate change in particular. The understanding and skills connected with traditional arts and crafts are frequently dependent on natural elements like wood, fibres, pigments, stones, and many more, making it difficult to transfer that knowledge and abilities when those basic materials are in short supply or hard to get (Yadav & Panda, 2023). It can also be difficult to digitise and document ICH, particularly in some remote locations with little access to the internet or other forms of technology. It may also be challenging to resolve issues about intellectual property protection and safeguarding due to gaps or discrepancies in the legal and policy frameworks for safeguarding ICH.

When Indian cultural centres, academies, departments and museums fail to strike a balance between the necessity of collaborating with communities, scholars, and experts to safeguard Intangible Cultural Heritage (ICH) and the simultaneous commitment to prioritise the respectful and ethical preservation of ICH while ensuring inclusivity and accessibility to a diverse audience, they encounter significant challenges.

The safeguarding of intangible cultural heritage (ICH) assumes paramount importance due to many compelling reasons. These reasons emphasise the essential role that the preservation of ICH plays in maintaining the rich cultural fabric of human traditions, knowledge, and practices, thereby ensuring their continuity for present and future generations.

Preservation of Cultural Diversity: ICH represents the diversity and cultural identity of various communities, groups, and societies. The continuation of these customs contributes to the rich fabric of human cultures, languages, and customs.

Transmission to Future Generations: Preserving ICH ensures that conventional knowledge, abilities, rites, and practises are passed on to upcoming generations. In doing so, the relationship between the past, present, and future is maintained.

Promotion of Cultural Identity: Communities' senses of identity and belonging are greatly shaped by ICH. A community's pride and belief in themselves are strengthened when these cultural aspects are preserved.

Intercultural Dialogue: Sharing and protecting ICH can foster intercultural communication, mutual respect, and understanding amongst various cultures and communities.

Social Cohesion: Most ICH practices involve group or shared activities. By preserving these customs, communities can become more integrated and socially cohesive.

Cultural innovation: For contemporary innovation and creativity, ICH can serve as a catalyst. Modern art, design, and technology can be influenced by traditional techniques.

Human Rights: Protecting ICH is related to both cultural and human rights. For instance, the right of indigenous communities to practise and preserve their cultural legacy is acknowledged in the United Nations Declaration on the Rights of Indigenous Peoples.

Benefits to the Economy and Tourism: In some cases, ICH has the potential to be used to support local economies and advance tourism. Traditional artistic forms, crafts, or cultural acts have the power to attract tourists and open doors to economic wealth.

Resilience and Adaptation: ICH frequently incorporates information and techniques from traditional medicine, environmental sustainability, and other fields that can be helpful for dealing with current issues like climate change.

Respect and Recognition: Safeguarding ICH shows respect for the wisdom and customs of other cultures while recognising the importance of our cultural expressions.

Here are some suggestions, according to the UNESCO-EIIHCAP Regional Meeting (2007), for safeguarding ICH;

- Intangible heritage should be incorporated into official curricula in formal education.
- Making the intangible legacy more accessible to the broader population (including the youth).
- Creating reward systems like the Living Human Treasure (LHT) system.
- Creating institutions to share knowledge, abilities, or intangible cultural heritage.
- Working with various forms of mass media.
- Fostering intercultural cooperation to appreciate the world's intangible cultural treasures.

Under *Part I (General Provisions)*- Article 2 (Definitions), Paragraph 3, UNESCO 2003 Convention defines safeguarding of ICH as:

> measures aimed at ensuring the viability of the intangible cultural heritage, including the identification, documentation, research, preservation, protection, promotion, enhancement, transmission, particularly through formal and non-formal education, as well as the revitalisation of the various aspects of such heritage.

As mentioned above, the first step in safeguarding ICH is identification. The Convention encourages communities and groups to identify, safeguard, and develop intangible heritage. Recognising these cultures by people from other parts of the world provides a reason for pride and revitalises the youth's interest in them. No scholar, expert, or official may make this determination on the community's behalf; only the community can decide whether something should be considered a part of the community's heritage. In addition, it is an essential principle of the Convention that no order can be established to differentiate a particular society's intangible legacy as superior, higher value, more significant, or more fascinating than any other group's heritage.

After identification, the second step of safeguarding is "Documentation" of this valuable IH; Indians are rapidly losing their oral histories, customs, and ICH. Today's generations are expected to make a special effort to preserve this incredibly rich cultural legacy that conveys peoples' identities and represents the extensive developmental history of humanity. After some last bearers die, their creative and performing characteristics fall apart, emphasising the fleeting nature of such abilities. It is essential to document their performance and skills in the form of photos, videos, cassette tapes, etc. The "translation" of intangible heritage from its oral form into tangible form, such as audio or video recordings, inventories, and archives, is necessary for safeguarding. Although it may seem like this is "freezing" intangible heritage via documentation, it is important to emphasise that this is only one aspect of safeguarding. As we know, digital media and digitalisation are widely used these days. Cultural institutions can record and preserve cultural history with this modern technology. These forms of technology can help the community or society transfer intangible culture into a tangible form, particularly in the case of intangible cultural assets. Digital technology not only aids in maintaining but also in passing down this heritage from generation to generation. These memoirs must be recorded and digitised before we lose them. We shall no longer have the connection between social and cultural knowledge and memories once the older generation has passed. It is necessary to transform the ICH into material form for protection, using techniques like video and audio recording, still photography, inventory, etc., as discussed above. The inspiration behind making the ICH tangible is not to turn it into a static or lifeless document but to develop a powerful platform for raising awareness and creating a more interactive and participatory shared inheritance of the two generations, i.e., past and future, respectively. Each belonging, historical location, and monument carries remembrance, importance, and beliefs associated with symbols that can only be described as intangible. Digital innovations have helped us to promote, preserve, revive, and safeguard the ICH, through different social media platforms.

After proper identification and documentation of ICH, those parts that are vulnerable or on the verge of extinction can be revitalised through proper research, leading to "the protection, promotion, enhancement, transmission, particularly through formal and non-formal education," according to the Convention. A proper case study can be done on specific areas of ICH which are threatened. These kinds of research will increase the attention of the community and government to revitalise it. A recent example is the G20 summit, which took place on September 9–10, 2023, at Bharat Mandapam in New Delhi. In addition to regular economic concerns, this summit also emphasised India's cultural heritage. It gave a forum such as Crafts Bazaar for experienced artisans from around the country to showcase their centuries-old skills. International delegates were invited to live demonstrations by expert artisans, providing a unique opportunity to observe traditional craft skills in practise and also offering new options for exploring and expanding the market potential of these ancient crafts. A notable characteristic was the availability of Geographical Indicator (GI) marked goods, which received praise for their distinct geographical origin and quality, opening up new market potential. Among the showcased GI products were the renowned Madhubani Painting from Bihar, Handicrafts from Naggar village, Himachal Pradesh, fading crafts like Lac bangle work from Rajasthan and many more.

Without proper research, one may not be able to find which areas of ICH need more attention towards safeguarding. Even though we live in a world where there is widespread contact and an exchange of cultures throughout the globe, there are still various living legacies that are growing in each nation and every region of the world. The actions urged by the Convention — at the national and international levels — can assist communities in ensuring that their heritage is preserved for their successors for many decades and millennia ahead. Other forms and aspects are more delicate, and some are even threatened. The agreements, treaties, and proclamations that arise from this invoke rights and obligations, set forth rules, suggest multilateral and normative mechanisms, and request the establishment of committees. These committees offer advice, seek more funding and review requests. Recommendations must be followed nationally and internationally. Each country must inventory its cultural heritage, create policies, and support heritage work. Lists are used to promote awareness and respect for heritage. (Kirshenblatt-Gimblett, 2014).

The 2003 Convention places much emphasis on preserving the resources that facilitate creativity and the transmission of cultural knowledge among the relevant groups, communities, and practitioners because the protection of intangible, or living, heritage fundamentally depends on the people who make and sustain it. Giving the owners of this heritage primary control over how it is used and exploited is necessary for its protection. Documentation to merely record anything before it disappears is not a safeguard; similarly, research to meet researchers' scientific zeal or to discover the origin, characteristics, or specificity of a given element of intangible legacy is not safeguarding unless and until it contributes directly to enhancing the viability of that heritage. According to the convention, people, groups and communities who engage in and protect intangible heritage must serve as its principal custodians. However, State institutions and policies may be used to assist the actions of these custodians. The issues that are faced by these communities and the people who work for them include ensuring that their children and grandchildren will continue to have the chance to learn about the legacy of previous generations., as well as ensuring that measures designed to conserve that kind of heritage are done with the full involvement and the free, prior, and informed consent of the individuals, organisations, and communities that are concerned.

Protecting living heritage means taking steps to make sure that ICH can continue to exist. Trying to ensure that the tradition is practised and transferred within the community or group concerned is what safeguarding entails. Communities must actively preserve and protect their legacy since only they can strengthen its present while ensuring its future. As intended by the Convention, intangible heritage must always be living heritage: this must continue to be constantly generated, maintained, re-created, and safeguarded by the communities, groups, or individuals associated. As a living phenomenon, intangible heritage is always a part of the present and the future, even though it often evokes the past. According to the UNESCO-EIIHCAP (Establishment Initiative for the Intangible Heritage Centre for Asia-Pacific) Regional Meeting (2007), the following ideas are essential for maintaining and boosting ICH based on international experiences and general concepts:

- Respecting the natural, social, and human environments.
- Respecting and promoting cultural diversity because a country's cultural identity reveals its values and image.
- Appreciating and encouraging community involvement in preserving cultural heritage through developing, owning, and disseminating cultural values. It is crucial to increase each community's knowledge of the importance of its unique cultural heritage and the roles that each plays in its preservation.
- Expanding craft products for tourism and reducing environmental degradation in traditional craft regions.

It is also very important to understand how the UNESCO 2003 Convention, different Indian Centres, academies, and departments of museology at different universities and museums play significant roles in safeguarding ICH. In India, these institutions have evolved to become community hubs, actively engaged in the safeguarding of both tangible and intangible cultural heritage due to their greater ability to communicate and collaborate with communities through formal and non-formal education.

Role of the UNESCO's 2003 Convention for the Safeguarding of ICH

The Convention for the Safeguarding of Intangible Cultural Heritage is a multifaceted instrument that goes beyond legal obligations. It serves as a guiding framework that underscores the significance of intangible cultural heritage, sets out clear principles for its protection, establishes mechanisms for recognition and support, assigns responsibilities to States Parties, fosters international collaboration, raises awareness about the importance of cultural diversity, and promotes the active involvement of communities in the preservation and transmission of their heritage. In doing so, it contributes to the global efforts to celebrate, respect, and safeguard the rich and diverse intangible cultural heritage of humanity. The Convention was adopted by UNESCO in 2003 consisting of nine parts with forty articles. Here is a summary of the key provisions in each part;

There are three articles under ***Part I, "General Provisions."*** Article 1 talks about the "Purposes of the Convention", such as safeguarding ICH, respecting groups, communities, and individuals concerned for the ICH, etc. Article 2 discusses definitions of ICH, including five domains of ICH, Safeguarding, and State Parties. Article 3 "Relationship to other International instruments" clarifies that it should not reduce protection for World Heritage properties linked to intangible cultural heritage under the 1972 Convention. It also ensures that it does not affect the rights and obligations of States Parties under international agreements related to intellectual property rights or the use of biological and ecological resources.

Part II,* known as *"Organs of the Convention," comprises Articles 4 to 10. Article 4 focuses on the "General Assembly of States Parties," which serves as the predominant authority within this Convention and operates according to its own set of rules. Regular sessions of the General Assembly are scheduled every two years. Article 5 introduces the "Intergovernmental Committee for the Safeguarding of ICH," often known as "the Committee," which is part of UNESCO. Article 6 outlines the "Election and terms of office of States Members of the Committee." States Parties that are signatories to the Convention, assembled in the General Assembly, elect State Members of the Committee for a four-year term. The majority of the state members of the Committee initially elected have a two-year term limit, and half of the state members must be re-elected by the General Assembly every two years. When vacancies arise, the General Assembly selects new State Members as needed. A State Member of the Committee is eligible for election only once every two years. States that are members of the Committee must appoint individuals with expertise in various aspects of ICH as their representatives. Article 7 outlines the "Functions of the Committee," including- Promoting the goals of the Convention and ensuring its effective execution. Offering recommendations on best practices and suggesting measures to safeguard intangible cultural heritage. Drafting a detailed plan for utilizing the Fund's resources and submitting it for approval to the General Assembly, as per Article 25. Reviewing reports provided by States Parties in line with Article 29 and presenting a comprehensive summary to the General Assembly. Assessing requests submitted by States Parties and making decisions regarding their inclusion in the lists and proposals referenced in Articles 16, 17, and 18, as well as determining the necessity of international assistance, as outlined in Article 22 and more. Article 8 covers the "working Methods of the Committee", including providing reports of all actions and decisions to the General Assembly and establishing its own rules with the agreement of two-thirds of its members. Article 9 discusses the "accreditation of advisory organizations" as follows- The Committee will recommend to the General Assembly the approval of non-governmental organisations known for their expertise in ICH. Additionally, the Committee will put forward the criteria and methods for this accreditation. Article 10 relates to "The Secretariat," highlighting that UNESCO's secretariat supports the Committee. It is responsible for preparing documentation for the General Assembly and the Committee, including the proposed agenda for their sessions. Additionally, the Secretariat ensures that the decisions made are effectively carried out.

Part III, "Safeguarding of the Intangible Cultural Heritage at the national level," encompasses articles 11 to 15. Article 11 focuses on the "role of state parties," which includes taking necessary measures to protect the ICH within their territories. This includes recognizing and defining the various elements of ICH with the involvement of communities, groups, and relevant non-governmental organizations, among other safeguarding actions mentioned in Article 2. Article 12 stipulates that each State Party is responsible for creating one or more inventories of the ICH present within its territory. These inventories serve to identify and safeguard ICH, and they must be regularly updated. Article 13 outlines additional measures for safeguarding and promoting the development of ICH within a State Party's territory. This includes adopting a general policy to promote the role of ICH in society and integrating its safeguarding into planning programs. State Parties can also designate or establish capable organizations to oversee the protection of the ICH on their territory and promote research, technical, scientific, and artistic efforts to preserve the ICH, especially during challenging circumstances. Article 14 is dedicated to "Education, awareness-raising, and capacity-building." to ensure that ICH is acknowledged, valued, and enriched in society, each State Party is obligated to make every reasonable effort. This includes implementing awareness-raising initiatives, educational programs, and training activities for the general public, as well as younger generations. Additionally, it entails developing specific programs within the relevant groups and communities to safeguard ICH and ensure its continued vitality. Article 15 highlights the "Participation of communities, groups, and individuals" in preserving, transmitting, and managing such heritage. This underscores the essential role that communities, groups, and individuals play in the protection and continuation of their intangible cultural heritage. It emphasises their active involvement in maintaining, passing down, and overseeing this heritage.

Part IV, titled "Safeguarding of the Intangible Cultural Heritage at the international level," is comprised of articles 16 to 18. Article 16 is dedicated to the "Representative List of the ICH of Humanity." It aims to enhance the visibility and awareness of the importance of ICH and foster dialogue about it. The Committee is responsible for preparing, maintaining, and releasing a Representative List of the Intangible Cultural Heritage of Humanity. This list is established based on proposals from concerned States Parties and is submitted to the General Assembly for approval. Article 17 addresses the "List of Intangible Cultural Heritage in Need of Urgent Safeguarding." The Committee, in consultation with the concerned State Party, establishes this list and includes intangible cultural heritage that requires immediate protection. The criteria for establishing, updating, and publishing this list are developed by the Committee and submitted to the General Assembly for approval. Article 18 discusses various "programs, projects, and activities for the safeguarding of ICH." The Committee periodically promotes a range of projects and programs at national, subregional, and regional levels. These initiatives are guided by criteria defined by the Committee, based on proposals from States Parties and the approval of the General Assembly. These efforts are all geared towards safeguarding intangible cultural heritage.

Part V, "International Cooperation and Assistance," contains several articles of importance (Articles 19-24). Article 19 focuses on the necessity of cooperation, including the sharing of knowledge and experiences, collaborative projects, and the establishment of a mechanism to assist States Parties in protecting their intangible cultural resources. This cooperation spans bilateral, subregional, regional, and international levels. Article 20 delineates the objectives of international assistance. It includes safeguarding heritage listed on the "List of Intangible Cultural Heritage Needing Urgent Safeguarding," supporting diverse projects, programs, and activities, and assisting in the preparation of inventories as per the provisions in Articles 11 and 12. Article 21 explores various forms of international assistance, encompassing research into different facets of safeguarding, the training of necessary personnel, the establishment and operation of infrastructure, and the provision of equipment and expertise, among other forms of support. Article 22 lays out the conditions governing international assistance. The Committee will establish a procedure for evaluating requests for international assistance, specifying the required information, such as planned measures, needed interventions, and estimated costs. In times of urgency, the Committee will prioritize assistance requests. Article 23 addresses the process of requesting international assistance. Each State Party can request international assistance for safeguarding its ICH, and these requests may also be jointly submitted by two or more States Parties. Such requests must include the information specified in Article 22, along with the required documentation. Article 24 outlines the responsibilities of beneficiary States Parties. It involves establishing an agreement between the Committee and the beneficiary State Party to govern the international assistance provided. The expenses related to safeguarding measures receiving international assistance are to be shared by the beneficiary State Party within the limits of its financial capacity. Additionally, the beneficiary State Party is obliged to provide the Committee with a report detailing how the provided support was utilised to preserve its ICH.

Part VI, which focuses on the "Intangible Cultural Heritage Fund" and comprises Articles 25 to 28, explains the fund's nature and resources. Article 25, titled "Nature and resources of the Fund," establishes the fund's purpose in safeguarding ICH and includes funds-in-trust as per UNESCO's Financial Regulations. The fund is resourced through contributions from State Parties, gifts or bequests from other States, programs within the United Nations system, donations from private or public entities, support from various international organisations, and income generated from the fund's assets. Decisions regarding the allocation of these resources are made by the Committee, following the standards set by the General Assembly. Article 26, entitled "Contributions of States Parties to the Fund," underscores that the General Assembly will establish that States Parties commit to making regular contributions to the fund at least every two years. The specific amount will be determined as a uniform percentage applicable to all States. The General Assembly will make this decision through a majority vote of the States Parties present and voting, excluding those that have not made the declaration. Additionally, a State Party's contribution to the regular UNESCO budget should never exceed 1% of that amount. Article 27, with the subject "Voluntary Supplementary Contributions to the Fund," specifies that States Parties wishing to make additional voluntary contributions beyond those outlined in Article 26 should inform the Committee promptly. This advance notice allows the Committee to manage its operations effectively. Article 28, titled "International Fund-Raising Campaigns," states that States Parties are required to support global fundraising campaigns organised under the auspices of UNESCO for the benefit of the Fund.

Part VII, "Reports," comprises two articles (Articles 29-30). Article 29, "Reports by the States Parties," stipulates that States Parties must adhere to the periodicity and forms established by the Committee. They must submit reports detailing the regulatory, legislative, and other measures to implement this Convention to the Committee. Article 30, "Reports by the Committee," states that during each of its sessions, the Committee must submit a report to the General

Assembly detailing its activities and the reports received from States Parties, as outlined in Article 29.

Part VIII, "Transitional clause," has Article 31 "Relationship to the Proclamation of Masterpieces of the Oral and Intangible Heritage of Humanity". Before this Convention took effect, the Committee added items designated as "Masterpieces of the Oral and Intangible Cultural Heritage of Humanity" to the Representative List of the ICH of Humanity. However, once the Convention was in force, they stopped making such proclamations.

Part IX, "Final Clauses," comprises Articles 32 to 40. Article 32, "Ratification, Acceptance, or Approval," specifies that UNESCO Member States must follow their national constitutional procedures to ratify, accept, or approve this Convention, and these formal instruments should be submitted to UNESCO's Director-General. Article 33, titled "Accession," outlines that any state not affiliated with UNESCO but invited to join by the UNESCO General Conference is eligible to become a party to this Convention. Additionally, this Convention is available for accession to territories with full internal self-governance acknowledged by the United Nations, which have not yet attained complete independence but possess authority over the subjects governed by this Convention, including the ability to enter into agreements in these areas. Article 34, titled "Entry into Force," stipulates that the terms of this Convention will apply solely to the States that have deposited their respective instruments of ratification, acceptance, approval, or accession on or before the specified date. The Convention will come into force three months after the deposit of the 30th instrument. Article 35, entitled "Federal or Non-Unitary Constitutional Systems," addresses the specific provisions to be enforced for States Parties with federal or non-unitary constitutional systems. Article 36, "Denunciation", allows any State Party to denounce the Convention. They must send a written notice to the UNESCO Director-General. The denunciation takes effect twelve months after receiving the instrument and does not impact financial obligations until the withdrawal's effective date. Article 37, titled "Depositary functions," designates UNESCO's Director-General as the Convention's Depositary. The Director-General is responsible for informing UNESCO Member States, non-member States in Article

33, and the United Nations about the deposits of documents related to ratification, acceptance, approval, or accession, as described in Articles 32 and 33. They also notify relevant parties about any denunciations outlined in Article 36. Article 38, "Amendments," allows a State Party to propose amendments in writing, which the Director-General shares with all States Parties. If at least fifty per cent of States Parties agree in six months, the recommendation goes to the General Assembly for potential approval. Approval requires a two-thirds majority. Once approved, the amendments are submitted to States Parties for their formal acceptance, and they come into effect three months after being deposited. Article 39, "Authoritative texts," states that the Convention is written in six different languages and all versions carry the same weight, including English, Chinese, French, Arabic, Spanish and Russian. Article 40, titled "Registration," stipulates that the Convention may be registered with the United Nations Secretariat when requested by the Director-General of UNESCO, in accordance with Article 102 of the United Nations Charter. This Convention, signed on November 3, 2003, in Paris, is archived in two original copies within UNESCO's records. Authenticated duplicates will be furnished to the states referenced in Articles 32 and 33, in addition to the United Nations.

Role of Indian Centres, Academies and Departments in the Safeguarding of ICH

Following are some Indian Centres, Academies and departments that are playing an essential role in the revitalisation of ICH according to the definition of safeguarding given by the UNESCO 2003 Convention;

1 . Centre for Cultural Resources and Training (CCRT)

It is one of the top organisations aiming to integrate culture and education founded by Smt. Kamaladevi Chattopadhyay and Dr. Kapila Vatsyayan in 1979. CCRT operates independently under the direction of the Ministry of Culture, Government of India. By making education culturally relevant, CCRT has helped strengthen the country's foundation. To assist the wide transmission of Indian art and culture, the CCRT has its headquarters in New Delhi and Four Regional Centers in the western city of Udaipur, the southern city of Hyderabad, the northern city of Guwahati, and the central city of Damoh. The CCRT revitalises the educational system by increasing teachers' and students' knowledge of the diversity of India's regional cultures and by incorporating this knowledge into the classroom. To introduce students to the rich cultural heritage of India, educational tours to museums, monuments, and historical places are organised. Some of the main functions of CCRT are below;

- Organises academic programmes concerning Indian art and culture tailored for both teachers and students that are theoretical and theme-based.
- Organises workshops to offer hands-on learning and understanding of crafts that can be put into the curriculum of schools.
- To raise awareness of the regional differences and diversity of cultural manifestations in our country, various performing arts are organized.
- Creates a library of materials, including scripts, digital photos, audio and video recordings, and films, to create culturally oriented educational tools that support the preservation of rural Indian art and craft traditions.
- Produces publications and other media to help people understand and appreciate Indian art and culture.
- Arranges the Cultural Talent Search Scholarship Scheme so that talented children between the ages of 10 and 14 can study one or more art forms.
- It also executes other Ministry of Culture initiatives, such as scholarships for young artists and junior and senior fellowships for "in-depth study/research" in various cultural areas, including New Emerging Fields of Cultural Studies. Under the NICHM Programme, a recent initiative of the Ministry of Culture, the Government of India, the CCRT has begun to organise training programmes in arts management. The Cultural Heritage Youth Leadership Program is another initiative the CCRT is putting into place to encourage young people to get involved in their communities and promote social values.

2. Sahitya Akademi

India's National Academy of Literature, Sahitya Akademi, was founded by the Indian government in 1954. As the foremost literary institution in India, the Akademi protects and promotes literature in 24 Indian languages through awards, fellowships, funding, publications, workshops, literary programmes, and exhibitions. To promote Indian literature outside of India, the Akademi also runs literary exchange programmes with other nations worldwide. The Akademi hosts at least 50 regional, national, and worldwide seminars annually, along with 300 workshops and literary gatherings. It also honours *Bhasha Samman* for noteworthy contributions to ancient and mediaeval literature and languages which are not formally recognised by the Akademi. Akademi has established Institutes for Translation in Bangalore, Ahmedabad, Kolkata, and Delhi and an Archive of Indian Literature in Delhi. On the North Eastern Hill University campus in Shillong, a project office for promoting tribal and oral literature has also been established.

3. Lalit Kala Akademi

Lalit Kala Akademi (National Art Institute), located in New Delhi, was inaugurated on 5th August 1954, and officially registered under the "Societies Registration Act of 1860" on 11th March 1957 which focuses on visual arts. Akademi has conserved and documented a world-class collection of contemporary, modern, traditional, and tribal Indian art. Lalit Kala Akademi New Delhi, together with its Regional Centres in Chennai, Lucknow, Kolkata, Bhubaneswar, Garhi (New Delhi), and sub-centres in Ahmedabad, Shimla, Patna, Agartala, conducts exhibitions, seminars, camps, talks, retrospectives, and other art activities of unmatched prominence.

4. Sangeet Natak Akademi

The country's premier performing arts organisation, Sangeet Natak Akademi, was founded in 1953 with the goal of preserving and promoting the rich intangible cultural heritage of India. Sangeet Natak Akademi has three component units, two of which teach dance: Imphal's Jawaharlal Nehru Manipur Dance Academy (JNMDA) and Delhi's Kathak Kendra. There are currently five centres at the Akademi in addition to the constituent units:

(i) Thiruvananthapuram's Kutiyattam Kendra, which preserves and promotes Kerala's Sanskrit theatre.
(ii) Guwahati's Sattriya Kendra, which promotes Assamese Sattriya traditions.
(iii) Guwahati's North-East Centre for conserving north-eastern Indian folk and traditional performing arts.
(iv) The North-East Documentation Center in Agartala, which records fieldwork and festivals in the region.
(v) Chhau Kendra, Chandankiyari for promoting eastern India's Chhau dances

The Sangeet Natak Akademi Awards are the highest honour for working artists. The Akademi gives Fellowships to distinguished musicians, dancers, and theatrical academics and established the Ustad Bismillah Khan Yuva Puraskar for young artists in 2006. The Akademi's collection of audio and video recordings, pictures, and videos is one of the nation's largest and used for performing arts research.

5. National School of Drama

India's National School of Drama is one of the world's top theatre schools. It was founded in 1959 as one of the Sangeet Natak Akademi's constituent divisions. In 1975, it became an independent institution and was recognised as a self-governing organisation according to the "Societies Registration Act XXI of 1860", while being wholly funded by the "Ministry of Culture", Government of India. The school's intensive training is centred on a comprehensive, well-planned course that includes all aspects of theatre and links theory to practise. Students get a broad understanding of theatre through the methodical study and practical performance of Sanskrit play, traditional Indian theatre forms, modern Indian drama, Asian drama, and western dramatic protocols. In addition to its 3-year training curriculum, the school has used workshops under the Extension Program to investigate new possibilities in the fields of children's theatre and decentralised theatre education. The school possesses two performing companies: the Repertory Company and the Theatre-in-Education Company.

1. Repertory Company; Four artists founded the Repertory

Company in 1964 with the intention of giving School alumni a stage on which to present plays on a professional level. Over the years, it has performed plays by many writers and directors and grown into one of NSD's key institutions, presenting contemporary and modern works as well as experimental material. In addition to putting on plays, it also runs a festival every summer when both old and new plays are debuted. NSD's Repertory Company tours and performs frequently in India and internationally.

2. Theatre-In-Education Company: The second performance branch, the "Theatre-In-Education Company" (Sanskar Rang Toli), was founded on October 16, 1989. It entails a team of actor-teachers working with and entertaining youngsters. The TIE Company's main goal is to produce imaginative, curriculum-based, and interactive plays in schools that are specially created and prepared for youngsters of various ages.

The school also offers a publication section, an Extension Program, and a literary forum called *Shruti*. Since 1978, NSD teachers and alumni have held workshops for adults and children around the country Sikkim, Laddakh, Nepal, and Bhutan under the Extension Programme. The National School of Drama's Publishing Unit oversees bringing out more significant books on theatre as well as releasing key works on theatre that have been translated from English into Hindi.

6. Kalakshetra Foundation

Kalakshetra was formed in 1936 by lively visionary Rukmini Devi Arundale to represent Indian ideas via creative education. She founded it to "impart to the youth the pure spirit of Art, devoid of ugliness and commercialism." The Kalakshetra Foundation, as it is currently known, is an important location for studying and practising the fine arts, covering over 100 acres by the sea in Chennai. Various traditional Indian arts, including dance, music, visual arts, and crafts, are offered in its courses and training programmes. Evening lessons in Bharatanatyam, Carnatic Music, and Visual Arts are offered for students from seven to eighteen after Smt. Rukmini Devi Arundale passed away; the small campus museum became the new home for her enormous and varied personal collection of more than 5,000 artefacts, which included pieces made of metal, stone, wood, cloth, and porcelain as well as paintings, prints, pictures, and furniture. The Rukmini Devi Library houses a collection of 5,219 books from Smt. Rukmini Devi's possessions, however, it is not open to the public. The Sankara Menon Library has 10,830 works in English, Telugu, Kannada, Tamil, Sanskrit, Hindi, Malayalam, and Grantham on dance, music, and fine arts. The Research Library, which is only open to academics, employees, and students, includes a reference collection of 6,000 books on subjects such as painting, music, dance, religion, and Rukmini Devi's dance drama manuscripts.

It also has Kalakshetra TAG Archives Listening Centre, which houses many historical audio and video assets. Additionally, it has a Craft Education and Research Centre, whose objectives are to share knowledge through workshops, research documentation, and publishing while maintaining ancient crafts, exploring natural dye research, and revitalising lost traditional practices. The Repertory is Kalakshetra's performing wing and is formed up of Kalakshetra alumni employed on a contract basis, staff artists, students, and guest artists. The foundation provides a four-year Diploma programme in Visual Arts and a Diploma and Post Diploma in Carnatic Music. In addition, a Diploma programme in Bharatanatyam is offered.

7. Indira Gandhi National Centre for the Arts

In 1987, the Ministry of Culture founded the IGNCA as a research, academic, and dissemination centre for the arts. The IGNCA aims to position the arts in relation to the physical and social environments through a variety of research, publication, instruction, creative endeavours, and performance programmes. This is done in recognition of the necessity to encompass and safeguard scattered elements of Indian art and culture. One of the initiatives of this centre is to employ technology that combines different types of media on computers to create a variety of software packages that circulate cultural information in partnership with UNDP (United Nations Development Programme). Here are some of the aims and objectives of IGNCA:

- to act as a significant hub for the arts' source materials, particularly those that are written, spoken, and visible.

- to carry out research in the arts, humanities, and culture and publish arts and humanities reference materials, dictionaries, glossaries, and encyclopaedias.
- to create a tribal and folk arts branch with a foundational compilation for structured scientific investigations and live demonstrations.
- to foster creative and critical conversation between classical and contemporary arts through conferences, seminars, workshops, performances, exhibits, and multimedia presentations.

The IGNCA is divided into six functioning parts:

(i) *"Kala Nidhi,"* the multifaceted library;

(ii) *"Kala Kosa,"* which focuses on studying and publishing essential writings in Indian languages;

(iii) *"Janapada Sampada,"* which conducts studies on lifestyle;

(iv) *"Kaladarsana,"* the executive unit, which creates exhibitions to make research and studies from the IGNCA available;

(v) "Cultural Informatics," which utilises technological instruments for the dissemination and preservation of culture;

(vi) "*Sutradhara,"* the administration.

8. Zonal Cultural Centres

Between 1985 and 1987, zonal cultural centres were created as cultural distribution networks to promote, develop, and link Indian urban, rural, and tribal arts. These centres are meant to grow into cultural organisations with thousands of folk artists, craftspeople, and Indian audiences. The Zonal Cultural Centres (ZCCs) symbolise the government and people's efforts to preserve and bring our rich cultural history to the people. Each state or Union Territory has at least one Zone Culture Centre to promote cultural exchange and understanding between zones. The seven Zonal Cultural Centres assist Indian folk and traditional artists and artisans.

(i) North Zone Cultural Centre

On November 6, 1985, the late Shri Rajiv Gandhi, who was India's prime minister at the time, officially opened the North Zone

Cultural Center in Patiala's Virsa Vihar Kendra. In accordance with the Societies Registration Act of 1860, the Center has been registered. It is one of seven cultural centres nationwide that strengthen Indian culture and improve composite national culture.

(ii) North Central Zone Cultural Centre

NCZCC was founded in 1986 and is based in Prayagraj. It is a registered society under the 'Societies Registration Act of 1860'. It covers seven states of North Central Zone and has a Sub-centre in Delhi. The primary objectives of the organization revolve around the preservation, innovation, and promotion of arts within the Zone. This involves raising cultural heritage awareness, supporting folk and tribal arts, and launching programmes to preserve endangered art forms.

(iii) North East Zone Cultural Centre

It is a Zonal Cultural Centre for Northeast India, set up in 1986 with its headquarters at Dimapur, Nagaland. It covers the eight northeastern states. Additionally, on January 17, 2006, the NEZCC opened its Shilpgram, or crafts village, in Panjabari, Guwahati. The primary goal of the NEZCC is to promote and protect the North East region's rich cultural legacy.

(iv) South Zone Cultural Centre, Thanjavur - Tamil Nadu

The South Zone Cultural Centre was founded to convey the indigenous traditions of the zone to the general public, particularly the rural and underprivileged, and help them learn, experience, educate, and enjoy our country's cultural diversity.

(v) West Zone Cultural Centre

The famous Bagore-Ki-Haveli in Udaipur, a massive estate featuring 138 rooms, erected in the 18th century by the Prime Minister of the Royal Mewar Dynasty, houses the WZCC's headquarters. After five years of meticulous repair, Bagore Ki Haveli now features a museum showcasing the royal lifestyle, architecture, and culture. The following MINISTRY OF CULTURE GRANT-IN-AID SCHEMES are provided for West Zone Cultural Centre:

- Guru-Shishya Prampara
- National Cultural Exchange Programme

- Documentation
- Theatre Rejuvenation Scheme
- Young Talented Artists Scheme
- Octave Programme of North East regions

In addition to these projects, the West Zone Cultural Centre organises various cultural programmes with funds from other sources. Workshops and displays of modern and traditional tribal artworks are typically included in these programmes. To maintain and promote traditional folk, tribal, modern, and classical art forms, events like festivals, workshops, seminars, explosions, etc. are also organised.

(vi) Eastern Zonal Cultural Centre

The Eastern Zonal Cultural Centre (EZCC) Kolkata is one of the seven Zonal Cultural Centres set up by the Indian government as part of the National Integration Plan to promote cultural unity among the various States and Union Territories. Since 1985, the EZCC has served as a cultural hub for the several ethnic cultural centres/groups of distinction in the East. EZCC's main area has been to assist and strengthen the spirit of rural and tribal India. In its 35-year existence, the EZCC has been able to instil a conscious awareness of the rich cultural legacies of its zone and other parts of the country through a variety of folk, tribal, and classical music and dance events, documentation and publishing, workshops, and arts and crafts displays.

(vii) South Central Zone Cultural Centre

It is one of India's seven Zonal Culture Centres, founded in 1986 and headquartered in Nagpur. It includes the states of Karnataka, Andhra Pradesh, Maharashtra, and Madhya Pradesh, which are all linguistically distinct. These States have thriving folk, tribal, fine art, and artisan traditions. The Centre works to strengthen, advance, and amplify these traditions through various initiatives. India's Ministry of Culture runs the Centre. Here are some of the objectives of SCZCC;

- To conserve, advance, and disseminate *Lalit kala*, folk, and tribal art within its constituent States.
- to find and give national exposure to emerging, skilled artists in the fields of music, dance, drama, creative art, etc.

- to conduct audio-visual documentation of these forms and to resurrect the four participating States of the Centre's vanishing art forms.
- To promote shared understanding and national integration by setting up national cultural exchange events.

9. Department of Museology at Different Universities

In India, departments under different universities offer courses and educational programs of Museology also focusing on intangible cultural heritage, such as the Department of Museology, Aligarh Muslim University, Aligarh; Department of Museology, Maharaja Sayajirao University of Baroda, Centre for Museology & Conservation, Rajasthan University in Jaipur; the National Museum Institute of the History of Art, Conservation and Museology in New Delhi; Department of Museology, Banaras Hindu University, Varanasi, etc. These academic institutions offer students the chance to delve into and study the diverse array of intangible cultural heritage.

Role of Museums in the Safeguarding of ICH

With a growing trend, populations are relocating to metropolitan areas; as a result, there is a rapid fall in preserving local communities' intangible cultural practices. The younger generation is drifting far from the traditions and values practised by their ancestors for generations. Through cultural interpretation of the objects and with the community's help, museums may develop this relationship and close the gap. For this, museums should pay immediate attention to protecting and documenting both tangible and intangible cultural heritage. When it comes to ICH education, embracing cultural diversity means using ICH as a cornerstone for educating marginalised, underprivileged, and remote communities rather than adopting a nostalgic and backwards-looking perspective that dismisses ICH as unengaging and outdated.

The Shanghai Charter, which was adopted at the 7th Asia Pacific Regional Assembly of the "International Council of Museums (ICOM)" in Shanghai in October 2002, urges museums to "develop documentation tools and standards in establishing holistic museum and heritage practises" and "establish interdisciplinary and cross-sectorial approaches that bring together movable and immovable, tangible and intangible, natural and cultural heritage." The 2004 Seoul Declaration was adopted 2004 during the ICOM General Assembly in Seoul. "*The Seoul Declaration of ICOM on the Intangible Heritage*" emphasises the significance of developing strategies for museums to collaborate with IH. The main theme of the ICOM General Conference in October 2004 in Seoul, Republic of Korea, was "*Museums and the Intangible Heritage.*" On the concluding day of the conference, the General Assembly adopted the "*Declaration of Seoul*" as Resolution 1, which considered the indisputable importance of intangible heritage and its function in the preservation of cultural diversity, as follows:

- affirms its support for the UNESCO Convention for the Protection of the Intangible Cultural Heritage, which was adopted in 2003;
- encourages every nation's government to sign and ratify this convention;
- calls on all nations, particularly developing nations with strong oral traditions, to create an Intangible Heritage Promotion Fund;
- requests that all relevant museums engaged in the acquisition, promotion, and preservation of intangible cultural assets give particular emphasis to safeguarding all vulnerable records, encompassing both digital and documentary aspects of cultural resources;
- urges museums to pay close attention to and prevent attempts to manipulate intangible heritage resources, especially where those resources are being commercialised without the consent of the primary custodians;
- calls on regional organisations, National Committees, and other ICOM bodies to collaborate closely with local organisations in the creation and application of such legal instruments as well as in the required personnel training for efficient application;
- suggests that the understanding of intangible heritage be a qualifying criterion for all training programmes for museum personnel and that the value of intangible heritage be emphasised;

- recommends that the Executive Council and the "International Committee for the Training of Personnel (ICTOP)" quickly update the ICOM Curricula Guidelines for Museum Professional Development.
- declares that this Resolution will now be known as the "Seoul Declaration of ICOM on the Intangible Heritage."

The Guidelines for Museum Professional Development as Set by ICOM Curricula were created by ICOM in 2005 and encouraged museum staff to acquire knowledge skills as a component of professional development and training for staff. Museums are a nation's cultural institutions and have long been related to its collections. A significant number of museums are currently playing an important part in carrying out the obligations outlined in the Convention. For instance, since 2006, the "*National Folk Museum of Korea*" has issued the "*International Journal of Intangible Heritage*", the first scholarly journal devoted solely to intangible heritage. The current issue is to organise continuing methods for the exchange of knowledge and for engaging educational programmes that will improve both education and museums with a wide number of diverse stakeholders. However, the foundation of this form of intangible heritage is that these activities must be cautious not to violate the privacy or human rights of people inadvertently. Museums should use both tangible and intangible cultural heritage in their institutional and instructional operations, according to the ICOM definition agreed in 2007 at the 21st General Conferences in Vienna, Austria.

In recent years, indigenous peoples have built museums and exhibitions to reflect their cultures. People's endeavours to build museums and hold exhibitions to reflect their cultural backgrounds is a movement to restore cultural representation rights to the culture's owners or custodians. This movement has pushed cultural institutions around the globe to include the voices of the people they represent in their shows. There is a rising pattern across the world's most prestigious museums to arrange exhibitions via collaborative projects with people from the cultural subject and provide them with a platform to express their culture. This condition makes it abundantly evident that understanding the collection in the museum, or the collective knowledge that may stimulate the objects, is more crucial for a culture's survival than the objects themselves. The museum is a repository for both tangible historical artefacts and intangible knowledge and information that can be used to develop influential exhibitions and programs for visitors. They can serve as a place where people assemble to foster their sense of pride and belonging, learn about their culture, transmit it to future generations, and make an impression on the outside world as a space to keep and nurture ICH. These actions will lead to positive world transformation. A museum can make a significant contribution to the safeguarding and vitality of ICH. It is crucial that all museums (as well as libraries, archives, and monuments services) evaluate how they are now supporting traditional cultures and the intangible heritage, as well as how they may do so in the future regarding all of their activities and programmes. They must actively and publicly attempt to lead in adopting national and local measures to implement the new Convention. The function that museums play in society must be seen from an inclusive, outward-looking perspective, particularly in protecting and promoting intangible heritage; this may be at least as important as the traditional collections of tangible objects, which have long been the primary, or in many cases the sole, focus of museums. Since the beginning of the modern era, museums have worked hard to engage and build connections with the communities in which they are located. However, even with all of their good intentions and efforts, it seems like they have not yet reached the full extent of the significant influence they hope to have. This gap between their goals and accomplishments calls into question the effectiveness of their community involvement initiatives and emphasises the need for improvement in this crucial area of their purpose.

The current boom in museum development stresses the vital need for specialised museums that support ICH. The development of such specialised museums shows a conscious effort to safeguard the intangible elements of our shared human inheritance as well as a recognition of the need to protect our cultural heritage. This effort will allow for a deeper investigation and recognition of the intangible components that define our common cultural identity. The development of such museums should serve as a dynamic platform that actively supports and empowers the keepers of ICH. They should make it a priority to provide monetary assistance to traditional bearers. This assistance may be provided through grants, fellowships, group initiatives, and other sources. These monetary resources may assist in maintaining the living legacy and ensuring their transmission from one generation to the next. These museums should also embrace a community-centric strategy by actively engaging the communities connected to the ICH aspects they showcase. This should include working together to develop and execute exhibitions, festivals, seminars, workshops, educational programmes and so on. By working closely with the local populations, museums can make sure that the promotion and preservation of ICH are in keeping with the interests and needs of those who are the guardians of these traditions, such as in Mehrangarh Fort, Jodhpur, a well-known historical landmark, Mehrangarh Museum Trust, which frequently conducted cultural events and programmes related to ICH while safeguarding the region's unique cultural heritage. These programmes include Rajasthani folk dance and music performed live at the fort. The Trust promotes classical Indian and folk music through concerts in the Fort and the city, partnering with Swar Sudha. The Fort hosts two music festivals annually: Jodhpur RIFF (Rajasthan International Folk Festival), and the World Sacred Spirit Festival for Sufi music lovers. These performances highlight Rajasthan's rich and varied cultural history. They also host conferences and workshops in collaboration with other institutions. This year, from August 4th to 6th, 2023, the Mehrangarh Museum Trust hosted the Annual General Museums Conference of the Museums Association of India. The conference focused on "Indian Knowledge Traditions and Museums." The Mehrangarh Museum Shop is India's sole professional museum store, offering various products, from T-shirts to jewellery and perfumes, and is recognised by Time magazine as one of the "Best of Asia." Tourists may also observe artists and craftsmen showcasing age-old techniques, such as carpet weaving, within the museum shop.

In order to bridge the generational divide and share local knowledge with a wider audience, including various communities and visitors, museums can act as a mediator or communication channel. The New Museology movement of the 21st century has transformed museums' focus from material things to living culture. Due to their social, educational, and cultural obligations to their local communities, which include raising public awareness and preserving cultural identity, museums place a great priority on meeting the academic and cultural requirements of their visitors in order to be more accessible spaces. The new concept of museology altered the relationship between museums and their society. It outlined the role of museums as producers of cultural democracy, tying together people, locations, and artefacts through museum displays. "The National Handicrafts and Handloom Museum (Crafts Museum, New Delhi)" and the Sanskriti Museum both house collections of many kinds of social and cultural artefacts relating to the various communities in India. These museums are renowned for planning a wide variety of programs focused on the age-old art of terracotta in collaboration with skilled traditional pottery artisans in order to serve regular visitors, tourists and various members of the community who wish to convey traditional, cultural, and social knowledge. It is essential that museums should not only organise workshops but also emphasise the intangible elements of terracotta art, such as its significance in religious and cultural ceremonies like *Basant Panchami, Ganesh Chaturthi*, and *Durga Puja*. Understanding how these activities affect a community is important. Additionally, the relationship between the museum and the community at different levels must be acknowledged. The collections of museums in India include a diverse range of spiritual, traditional, and cultural arts and crafts; many of these collections represent the living heritage of particular people. In the past, the elders of these sections of societies have used these artefacts to transmit knowledge and abilities from generation to generation within their families. There are instances when communities develop a sentimental connection to the objects that are on display in museums. It is necessary for museums to identify, document, and depict the intangible characteristics of the collections that they have. Objects in a museum setting cannot convey their full functionality and purpose without being placed back into the context of the original event. While examining an object in its entirety, one must consider how it relates to the performer, accompanying story, ceremonial performance sequences, and the environment in which it first appeared. It is also important to consider the ceremony's time and place.

The "International Committee for Museums and Collections of Ethnography (ICME)" is committed to promoting, protecting, and interpreting the human rights of all world peoples, as well as their cultures, societies, and environments. It also works to preserve the tangible and intangible heritage that is contained in museums and collaborates with partners around the world to enhance intercultural understanding among museum visitors. While UNESCO's focus on Intangible Heritage leans more towards ICH, the International Council of Museums (ICOM) places equal importance on both ICH and Intangible Natural Heritage (INH) within the realm of IH. This balance has largely been achieved through the dedicated efforts of ICOM-NATHIST (ICOM's International Committee on Museums and Collections of Natural History). The documentation of museum collections is the focus of the (CIDOC) International Committee for Documentation. During the CIDOC 2014 annual meeting, "the CIDOC Intangible Cultural Heritage Working Group (CIDOC ICH WG)" was established in Dresden, Germany. The CIDOC ICH WG met for the first time on September 8, 2014, and again on September 9, 2014. The two sessions on 8 and 9 September 2014 determined that the CIDOC ICH WG will share experiences and create methodologies for documenting intangible cultural heritage. The UNESCO Convention for the Protection of Intangible Cultural Heritage 2003 provides the convention, definition, domains, and framework for the working group. Using the 2007 ICOM definition of museums, which includes "intangible," it would investigate ways to archive and link museum objects and ICH. The Working Group would focus on documenting the ICH and associated fields. It is focused on the ICH-related challenges of documentation and information access.

- The working group would develop ICH vocabulary, standards, and guidelines.
- It would begin by analysing and comparing existing guidelines and formats for ICH documentation and tying ICH to museum objects from diverse countries, regions, and museums.
- It would also honour and appreciate knowledge bearers and the community's engagement in documentation and communication. The CIDOC ICH WG will aim to improve ICH documentation, accessibility, retrieval, and communication.

Museums are best suited to safeguarding and preserving intangible heritage because a wide range of cultural heritage research and documentation skills are possessed by museum professionals.

Moreover, students, interns, and enthusiastic volunteers who may carry out activities linked to research and documentation are available at museums. Museum staff are skilled in public presentation, educational programming, community engagement, and respect for traditions and culture. Typically, museums handle the accessioning, cataloguing, storage, preservation, conservation, exhibition, repatriation, and de-accessioning of artefacts pertaining to intangible heritage. When a museum acquires an object, it adds it to the collection that oversees upkeep. Intangible heritage is maintained and passed on through social activity and continuing social connections regulated by those who practise it. Inventories are crucial to protecting IH because they can increase public understanding of the significance of IH for both individual and communal identities, as well as by making those stocks accessible to the general public. The 21st century has seen a global movement towards the documentation of cultural heritage via digital technology. Intangible heritage can be made tangible with the use of digital technologies. Audio and video are the primary digital recording media. Internet and multimedia technology make it simple to record IH and aid in the preservation of unrecorded representations, customs, everyday practices, stage arts, folklore, knowledge and practises. The museum plays a crucial role in preserving cultural landscapes, increasing community involvement in decision-making, and recognising their status as "living heritage." Museums should play a crucial role by collaborating with other cultural institutions, NGOs, and the local community to preserve IH as a living cultural legacy that must be dynamic and sustainable. They can document artists discussing their work, surroundings, and activities, taking a recording of their folk music and songs. In order to engage communities in a continuous process of transformation through the IH collection, museums need to embrace a new paradigm. With cultural interpretation of the items and with the help of the community, museums may develop this relationship and close the gap. For this reason, museums must put a strong emphasis on the appropriate documentation, conservation, and display of both the tangible and IH. It is essential to encourage communities to exhibit their lives and memories in museums that promote traditional values. A key tenet of the idea of safeguarding living heritage is community involvement. The Convention emphasises how local people should take the initiative and be in charge of identifying, documenting, and transforming their living cultural heritage as well as implementing safeguards to maintain it. Community-based Museums are an ideal instrument for improving people's sense of identity, community bonds and values, and the preservation of their natural environment. For example- Arna Jharna Museum displays the stark beauty of Rajasthan's Marwar area. Its location is a sanctuary for desert flora and animals bordered by religious sites, protected forest regions, and waterbodies. The museum's major highlight is its extensive collection of Rajasthani brooms, which represent a vast universe of rituals and beliefs connected to them. In order to sensitise the viewer, a series of videos also emphasises the communities, work, abilities, and even hazards linked with the creation of brooms. The second module showcases an incredible assortment of musical instruments, including those that are no longer in use or being made. Two further sections emphasise pottery and puppetry. In line with Kothari's concept of a "living museum," all aspects of biodiversity, geology, and water-harvesting related to the museum site, aside from the collection, are part of a participatory educational process. The museum honours the local communities and their regional roots of knowledge, art, and culture, which are not relics of the past but rather a source for recreating the present.

Nobody else can decide on their behalf whether a certain expression or activity is their heritage; heritage can only exist when it is recognised by the communities, groups, or people that produce, maintain, and transmit it. To emotionally engage individuals, museums can give communities a chance to narrate their own stories through workshops and outreach programmes. By recreating historical stories, traditional dances and music, festivals, and traditional arts and crafts, museums must embrace the people's collective memory to safeguard the community's cultural legacy. A museum hosts various events, including talks, films, performances, musical performances, dance, theatre, and other cultural activities. Within the framework of the museum's active social program, they assist performing arts organisations and individuals, such as actors, musicians, storytellers, and dancers, to exhibit their performance in the auditorium, garden, or outdoor space. Museums may be utilised to bring the past to life through storytelling sessions, stories about the lives of individuals, tales about nature, storylines about the cosmos, and storylines regarding creatures of all kinds. Traditional stories can also be used to highlight special collections and exhibitions about the local area, such as the epic. Community-oriented educational sessions can be planned as one-day or a number of co-activities where participants can have hands-on experience learning things like traditional arts and crafts, rituals, indigenous knowledge, cuisine, games, etc. The Museum is vital in promoting IH via the media, the radio, the web, the Virtual Museum, and social networking sites. It links IH to its programmes and activities, like events hosting celebrations, lectures, seminars, and workshops. Local communities can be engaged in heritage preservation by working with regional museums to display and create a database of intangible cultural artefacts from the area around the museum. Intangible heritage temporary exhibitions and events should be organised by the museum regularly. Communities should participate and provide their traditions and cultures on the side museum walls. It should create interdisciplinary educational programmes incorporating intangible cultural heritage into museum activities.

In recent years, museums have begun to realise they must expand their aims beyond the simple preservation, interpretation, and display of artefacts. In order to involve communities in a continuous transforming process via the collecting of intangible heritage, museums need to embrace a new model. In 2016, Erika Ribašauskienė, & Diana Šumylė presented a model for safeguarding cultural heritage; this model recommends five primary actions for institutions or responsible bodies put in place to protect cultural heritage-

- A measure of revival that includes reactivating, restoring, and enhancing endangered cultural activities;
- A process of investigation, documenting, and inventorying that entails thoroughly analysing traditional practices
- A measure of marketing, presentation, and recognition, which involves raising ICH awareness
- A method of protection and preservation that incorporates all measures necessary to ensure that ICH practice continues
- Measure of transmission and dissemination refers to disseminating information and abilities outside of a community or passing it along in traditional ways.

Proper consideration of all the above measures ensures a continuing process of ICH protection. India's museums must do a lot to help people understand life in all its facets. Using modern scientific knowledge and indigenous cultural elements, Indian museums must reach all social levels in different regions. Museums can enable communities, organisations, and people to safeguard their intangible cultural legacy by means of the collections that they hold. With the community's assistance, museums can regularly organise exhibitions and educational events like gallery walks, lectures, conferences, and workshops. Museums can serve as cultural platforms for social communities to inform and interact with their ancestors. In order to promote and preserve ICH, museums and community organisations need to team up and work together. It is vital to maintain your unique identity rather than adopt the identities of those around you. The dynamic between Intangible cultural heritage, museums, and educational institutions that all play a part in ICH safeguarding is continually developing. The focus of museums and museums like institutions should mainly be on documentation, evaluation and listing for safeguarding ICH according to the UNESCO 2003 convention. Thus, educational challenges must be addressed in a coordinated manner. Communities, scholars, and institutions are urged to employ mass media and communication technology to disseminate recorded performances to preserve and promote oral traditions and expressions. Through developing audiences and increasing public awareness, cultural media, industries, and organisations can significantly contribute to guaranteeing the continued existence of traditional forms of ICH. To appropriately equip people and institutions for maintaining the complete range of ICH, safeguarding may also require upgrades in infrastructure and training.

In the Indian setting, museums must pay more attention to the cultural education of the general population because rituals and spirituality play a crucial role in defining Indians' way of life. The museums in India must ask themselves what role they may play for the public that has ignorantly deviated from their own cultural advancements and religious glories. Museums should collaborate with local communities to maintain the integrity and originality of cultural heritage. In order to safeguard our local traditions, it is necessary to consider the idea of converting small areas into open-air museums, allowing for their uniform integration and inevitable involvement with everyday activities in the community. The Hasta Shilpa Kala Village in Manipal's Udupi district, Karnataka, is an open-air museum that showcases Indian heritage, antiques, and culture from the golden era. It features a number of traditional homes and shrines in addition to many galleries with toys, kitchenware, fabrics, and other household items, as well as artwork.

As discussed earlier, the intangible values of artefacts are just as significant as their tangible ones. These features of artefacts are still not given enough consideration in museums, and they may require more care for preservation than just focusing on the preservation of the objects' outward appearance, which will eventually deteriorate and disintegrate. Conserving intangible qualities of objects implies maintaining cultural-specific practises, rituals, and traditions, which will provide society members with a sense of pride and identity as direct successors and contributors of a great civilisation. Using collections to build a knowledge of the past's culture and environment is crucial for comprehending the present and building a sustainable future. It must not only keep the things learned in the past but also bring back many old but still useful and beautiful rituals and traditions for the upliftment of the country and its people. Even what is left now faces ignominy since people today are tossing it out as an outdated superstitious behaviour from the past due to a lack of understanding of the underlying implications of these rituals.

Need for Establishing Specialized Museums for ICH

Within the realm of museums, the ICH field has been overlooked for years, and it generally did not get the attention it deserved. After the 2003 Convention, museums started talking about ICH. However, because their emphasis had historically tended more towards material forms of heritage, they frequently found it difficult to understand and express ICH completely. It is important to understand that legacy's tangible and intangible aspects are inextricably connected and cannot be separated. To address this, it is critical to propose the development of some specialised museums completely dedicated to Intangible Cultural Heritage, emphasising the intangible elements. For example, when discussing craftsmanship, it is impossible to interpret it without talking about the object prepared by the craft and the process and techniques involved. Therefore, museums need to seek a balance between exhibiting intangible elements like oral traditions, dance, music, customs, and rituals and the tangible artefacts closely related to them like costumes, masks, musical instruments, manuscripts, cultic objects, etc. These museums will provide a unique opportunity to investigate and appreciate the diversity of human culture, not simply through tangible artefacts but also via the ongoing traditions, values, and manifestations that shape communities. These specialised museums can significantly contribute to the preservation and promotion of ICH by acknowledging the interconnectedness of cultural heritage's tangible and intangible components, ensuring that it receives the consideration and respect it deserves within the broader museum landscape. People should be motivated to honour their heritage and appreciate the diversity of their cultures. This will increase awareness of the value of maintaining and upholding our traditions, particularly among younger generations. It encourages respect and a sense of pride in our cultural heritage and provides a forum for promoting regional customs, talents, and crafts. In order to achieve these objectives, it is crucial to organise conferences and seminars for academicians with the collaboration of stakeholders. These activities may be used as a platform to discuss issues and challenges that communities face and to promote talks on different government programmes that can provide funding to help the preservation of local intangible heritage. Museums can organise different cultural festivals and events that gather visitors from numerous regions, fostering tourism and ICH. Additionally, museums can invite practitioners in oral traditions like Vedic chanting, dastangoi, storytelling, folk music, *keertan,* poetry, and more to participate in cultural events. This not only encourages these people to maintain their oral traditions but also stimulates the following generation to continue their heritage, making these customs available to wider audiences, including tourists and visitors to the country and outside of the country. Moreover, museums can partner with well-known heritage volunteers to promote community well-being and sustainable development. Additionally, they may conduct yoga classes, which come under the fourth domain, and oral history transcriptions within their galleries, enhancing the accessibility and comprehension of these traditions to a larger audience. These museums must be comprehensive and include all five Intangible Cultural Heritage (ICH) areas. To do this, the museum's structure might be carefully planned with various galleries devoted to a certain aspect or area of ICH. A gallery with storytelling, folk songs, chants, and recitations where visitors may fully experience the diversity of "Oral Traditions". The "Performing Arts" section of the museum will offer visitors a captivating journey into the realm of traditional artistic expressions. In this section, the intangible cultural heritage may come alive through the visual and auditory wonders of traditional music, theatre, and dance. It will not only allow visitors to appreciate these art forms but also provide insights into their historical and cultural significance. The exhibits on "social practises, rituals, and festivals" will take on a fascinating trip into the fundamental elements of our society. This immersive experience will provide visitors with a comprehensive understanding of our social conventions, festivals, and rituals via the use of reconstructed ceremonies, exhibits of traditional clothing, and explanations of traditions. Visitors will be invited to participate in hands-on activities, including crafting traditional decorations, savouring festival of foods, and partaking in simple rituals, offering an immersive experience of cultural customs. Visitors could be able to interact directly with these customs through interactive exhibitions. Traditional astronomical knowledge, ecological information, and indigenous understanding of the natural world might all be explored in the gallery. A devoted gallery on traditional craftsmanship will give visitors a concentrated and immersive place to explore the subtleties, history, and cultural relevance of these time-honoured artisanal practices. A gallery like this will hold a wide range of traditional crafts, from textiles to ceramics, as well as instructive exhibits, hands-on activities, and even live demonstrations, all of which will increase awareness and knowledge of these cultural traditions.

In conclusion, museums are essential custodians of cultural heritage, both tangible and intangible, equipped with expertise, resources, and committed staff needed to preserve ICH. Museums should go beyond curation, actively involving communities and educating the public while reuniting people with their cultural origins. They must serve as dynamic cultural platforms, fostering community involvement, storytelling, and tradition celebration through various events and educational programs. Collaboration between museums and local communities is pivotal in preserving cultural authenticity. In India, museums have to play a crucial role in cultural education and preservation, with the potential to transform public spaces into open-air museums. Education and training in safeguarding ICH are of paramount importance, and collaboration between museums and educational or cultural institutions is the key. All ICH domains can be widely shared through technology and mass media, ensuring their continuous existence and greater accessibility. In order to preserve the rich fabric of intangible cultural heritage and ensure its continuation for future generations, museums should serve more than just repositories. They ought to be active and community-engaged organisations.

References

1. Arna Jharna. (n.d.). ArnaJharna. Retrieved from https://www.arnajharna.org/the-museum.
2. Bala, S. (2007). Role of museums to promote and preserve intangible cultural heritage in the Indian context. Commonwealth Museums: Culture, Economy and Climate Change and Youth, 2(1), 1-4.
3. Bala, S. (2012). Digital inventories on cultural memories and intangible cultural heritage: case study of Yadav community of Haryana, India. Incl. bibl, 1, 11-19.
4. Bouchenaki, M. (2003). The interdependency of the tangible and intangible cultural heritage. ICOMOS 14th General Assembly and Scientific Symposium.
5. Boylan, P. J. (2006). The intangible heritage: a challenge and an opportunity for museums and museum professional training. International Journal of Intangible Heritage, 1(1), 53-66.
6. Centre for Cultural Resources and Training. (2022). About Us - CCRT. Ministry of Culture. Retrieved from http://ccrtindia.gov.in/about-ccrt/about-us/
7. du Cros, H. (2012). Intangible Cultural Heritage, Education and Museums. 10.13140/RG.2.1.3217.5522.
8. Hasta Shilpa Heritage Village Museum. (n.d.). Vijayanath Shenoy. Retrieved from https://www.heritagevillagemanipal.org/Founder.html
9. Indian Culture. (n.d.). Kalakshetra Foundation. Retrieved from https://indianculture.gov.in/MoCorganization/kalakshetra-foundation
10. Indian Culture. (n.d.). Sahitya Akademi. Retrieved from https://indianculture.gov.in/MoCorganization/sahitya-akademi
11. Indian culture. (n.d.). North East Zone Cultural Centre. Retrieved from

https://indianculture.gov.in/MoCorganization/north-east-zone-cultural-centre

12. Indira Gandhi National Centre for the Arts. (n.d.). About IGNCA. Ministry of Culture. Retrieved from https://ignca.gov.in/about-ignca/
13. International Committee for Documentation - CIDOC. (n.d.). Intangible Cultural Heritage - ICOM CIDOC. Retrieved from https://cidoc.mini.icom.museum/working-groups/intangible-cultural-heritage/
14. Kamal Mahmoud, H., Omar Abdalla, A., & Abdel Wareth Abdel Meguid, O. (2022). The Preservation and Exhibition of the Intangible Heritage in Museums. International Journal of Eco-Cultural Tourism, Hospitality Planning and Development, 5(2), 117-227.
15. Kirshenblatt-gimblett, B. (2014, January). Intangible Heritage as Metacultural Production. Museum International, 66(1–4), 163–174. https://doi.org/10.1111/muse.12070.
16. Kumar, S. (2014). Indian Ritual Objects in Contemporary Museums and their Contextual Crisis. In Proceedings of National Seminar on Ancient and Spiritual Sciences (25-26 Oct.), organized by Center for Scientific Spirituality Studies, Dev Sanskriti Vishwavidalya, India; Bharti Publications, New Delhi (pp. 366-73).
17. Lalit Kala Akademi. (n.d.). ABOUT LKA. Ministry of Culture. Retrieved from https://lalitkala.gov.in/about
18. Ministry of Culture. (n.d.). Eastern Zonal Cultural Centre. Retrieved from https://ezcc-india.org/about-ezcc.php
19. Ministry of Culture. (n.d.). Intangible Cultural Heritage. Retrieved from https://indiaculture.gov.in/intangible-cultural-heritage
20. Ministry of Culture. (n.d.). North Zone Cultural Centre. Retrieved from https://www.culturenorthindia.com/
21. Ministry of Culture. (n.d.). South Central Zone Cultural Centre, Nagpur. Retrieved from https://www.sczcc.gov.in/index.php?option=commonpage&RID=61&depid=0&lang=Eng
22. Ministry of Culture. (n.d.). South Zone Cultural Centre, Thanjavur. Retrieved from https://szccindia.org/
23. Ministry of Culture. (n.d.). West Zone Cultural Centre. Retrieved from https://wzccindia.com/
24. National School of Drama. (n.d.). About NSD. Ministry of Culture. Retrieved from https://nsd.gov.in/delhi/index.php/about-nsd/
25. North Central Zone Cultural Centre. (n.d). Retrieved from https://nczcc.in/about/
26. Ribašauskienė, E., & Šumylė, D. (2016). The role of traditional craft centers in safeguarding cultural heritage. Vadybos mokslas ir studijos-kaimo verslų

ir jų infrastruktūros plėtrai, 38(4), 412-424.

27. Safeguarding Intangible Heritage and Sustainable Cultural Tourism: Opportunities and Challenges. (2008). Bangkok: UNESCO Bangkok. UNESCO-EIIHCAP Regional Meeting. Retrieved from https://unesdoc.unesco.org/ark:/48223/pf0000178732

28. Sahitya Akademi. (n.d.). About Sahitya Akademi. Retrieved from https://sahitya-akademi.gov.in/aboutus/about.jsp

29. Sangeet Natak Akademi. (n.d.). About Us-Sangeet Natak Akademi. Retrieved from https://sangeetnatak.gov.in/about-us

30. UNESCO. (n.d.). Text of the Convention for the Safeguarding of the Intangible Cultural Heritage. Retrieved from https://ich.unesco.org/en/convention.

31. Yadav, G., & Panda, G. (2023). Suatainability of Intangible Heritage: Challenges and Prospective Solutions. Aalekh Journal of the Directorate of Museums, 2(4). 33-38. ISBN: 978-81-954549-8-3.

32. Yoshida, K. (2004). The museum and the intangible cultural heritage. Museum International, 56(1-2), 108-112.

Appendix - I

Glossary

Agency[1]

The capacity to make decisions that have an impact on *social practices* and *representations* in which individuals and *communities* are involved.

Bearer

A member of a *community* who recognizes, reproduces, *transmits*, transforms, *creates* and forms a certain *culture* in and for a *community*. A bearer can, in addition, play one or more of the following roles: *practitioner*, *creator* and *custodian*.

Community

People who share a self-ascribed sense of connectedness. This may be manifested, for example, in a feeling of identity or in common behaviour, as well as in activities and territory. Individuals can belong to more than one community.

Conservation

Taking measures to preserve *social practices* and *representations* from neglect, destruction or exploitation.

[This notion may not be applicable to all aspects of intangible cultural heritage. Therefore, for the purpose of the future convention, the adoption of the term '*safeguarding*' is endorsed.]

Creativity

The inherent capacity of human beings to invent original meanings, media and imaginaries,

Creator

A member of a *community* who is among those most active in transforming and changing *social practices* and *representations*.

Cultural community

A *community* that distinguishes itself from other *communities* by its own *culture* or cultural design, or by a variant of the generic *culture*. Among other possible extensions, a nation can be a cultural community.

Cultural space

A physical or symbolic space in which people meet to enact, share or exchange *social practices* or ideas.

Culture[2]

The set of distinctive spiritual, material, intellectual and emotional features of a society or a social group, encompassing, in addition to art and literature, lifestyles, ways of living together, value systems, traditions and beliefs.

Custodian

A *practitioner* who has been entrusted by the *community* with the responsibility of *safeguarding* their intangible cultural heritage.

Documentation

The recording of intangible cultural heritage in tangible forms.

Festive event

A collective gathering at which events of significance for a *cultural community* are proclaimed, celebrated, commemorated or otherwise highlighted, usually including dance, music and other performances.

---

1. In the following glossary the terms printed in *italics* are defined elsewhere in this list, or a very similar term is defined.
2. This definition is based on the one suggested at the UNESCO World Conference on Cultural Policies, MONDIACULT, Mexico City, 1982.

Identification

Technical description of a specific element constitutive of the intangible cultural heritage, often done in the context of a systematic inventory.

Indigenous community

A *community* whose members consider themselves to have originated in a certain territory. This does not exclude the existence of more than one indigenous community in the same territory.

Local community

A *community* living in a specific locality.

Oral expression

Aspects of intangible cultural heritage expressed through the spoken word or in song.

Oral tradition

Passing on by word of mouth and memorizing information from the past.

Performing arts

Instrumental and vocal music, dance, theatre, storytelling, sung poetry, pantomime, and other spectacular practices representing the *creativity* of *communities*.

Place

Cultural environment produced by *social practices* through the use or appropriation of built structures, spaces or natural sites.

Popular culture

Social practices and *representations* through which a *cultural community* within a wider society expresses its distinctive identity. These cultural forms are often commercialised or mediated.

Practitioner

A member of a *community* who actively reproduces, *transmits*, transforms, *creates* and forms *culture* in and for the *community* by performing and otherwise maintaining *social practices* based on specialized knowledge and skills.

Preservation

Ensuring that certain *social practices* and *representations* are maintained.

[This notion may not be applicable to all aspects of intangible cultural heritage. Therefore, for the purpose of the future convention, the adoption of the term '*safeguarding*' is endorsed.]

Process

A sequence of *social practices* that are seen as interconnected.

Promotion

Drawing public attention, in a positive way, to aspects of intangible cultural heritage.

Protection

Ensuring that certain *social practices* and *representations* do not suffer damage.

[This notion may not be applicable to all aspects of intangible cultural heritage. Therefore, for the purpose of the future convention, the adoption of the term '*safeguarding*' is endorsed.]

Representation

Visual, aural, gestural or textual signs that stand for a *cultural community* or important aspects of their *social practices*.

Researcher, administrator and manager

Specialists who *promote*, display and mediate *culture* through personal engagement, and in organisations and institutions at local, national, regional and international levels.

Revitalisation

[*If referring to practices developed by the cultural community*:] Reactivating or reinventing *social practices* and *representations*, which are no longer in use or falling in disuse.

[*If referring to heritage policies:*] The encouragement and support of a *local community*, developed with the agreement of that same *community*, in the reactivation of *social practices* and *representations*, which are no longer in use or falling in disuse.

Safeguarding

Adopting measures to ensure the viability of intangible cultural heritage. These measures include the *identification*, *documentation*, [*protection*,] *promotion*, *revitalisation* and *transmission* of aspects of this heritage.

Social practice

Activities, which manifest ever-changing concepts, knowledge and skills, related, among other things, to social relations, status, methods of decision-making, conflict resolution, and collective aspirations.

Sustainability

Meeting the needs of the present without compromising the ability of future generations to meet their own needs.

Traditional culture

Social practices and *representations* which a social group considers to have been derived from the past through intergenerational *transmission* (even if these are recent inventions) and to which the group designates a differentiated status.

Transmission

Transferring *social practices* and ideas to another person or persons, especially to younger generations, through instruction, access to *documental* sources, or by other means.

Appendix - II

STATEMENT - 1

ABSTRACT OF SPEAKERS' STRENGTH OF LANGUAGES AND MOTHER TONGUES - 2011

Presented below is an alphabetical abstract of languages and the mother tongues with speakers' strength of 10,000 and above at the all India level, grouped under each language. There are a total of 121 languages and 270 mother tongues. The 22 languages specified in the Eighth Schedule to the Constitution of India are given in Part A and languages other than those specified in the Eighth Schedule (numbering 99) are given in Part B.

PART - A

LANGUAGES SPECIFIED IN THE EIGHTH SCHEDULE (SCHEDULED LANGUAGES)

	Name of Language & mother tongue(s) grouped under each language	Number of persons who returned the language (and the mother tongues grouped under each) as their mother tongue		Name of Language & mother tongue(s) grouped under each language	Number of persons who returned the language (and the mother tongues grouped under each) as their mother tongue
	1	2		1	2
1.	**ASSAMESE**	1,53,11,351		Haijong/Hajong	71,792
	Assamese	1,48,16,414		Rajbangsi	4,75,861
	Others	4,94,937		Others	2,83,900
2.	**BENGALI**	9,72,37,669	3.	**BODO**	14,82,929
	Bengali	9,61,77,835		Bodo	14,54,547
	Chakma	2,28,281		Kachari	15,984

	Mech/Mechhia	11,546
	Others	852
4.	**DOGRI**	25,96,767
	Dogri	25,96,763
	Others	4
5.	**GUJARATI**	5,54,92,554
	Gujarati	5,50,36,204
	Gujrao/Gujrau	15,431
	Pattani	16,510
	Ponchi	13,812
	Saurashtra/ Saurashtri	2,47,702
	Others	1,62,895
6.	**HINDI**	52,83,47,193
	Awadhi	38,50,906
	Baghati/Baghati Pahari	15,835
	Bagheli/Baghel Khandi	26,79,129
	Bagri Rajasthani	2,34,227
	Banjari	15,81,271
	Bhadrawahi	98,806
	Bhagoria	20,924
	Bharmauri/Gaddi	1,81,069
	Bhojpuri	5,05,79,447
	Bishnoi	12,079
	Brajbhasha	15,56,314
	Bundeli/Bundel khandi	56,26,356
	Chambeali/ Chamrali	1,25,746
	Chhattisgarhi	1,62,45,190
	Churahi	75,552
	Dhundhari	14,76,446
	Garhwali	24,82,089
	Gawari	19,062
	Gojri/Gujjari/Gujar	12,27,901
	Handuri	47,803
	Hara/Harauti	29,44,356
	Haryanvi	98,06,519
	Hindi	32,22,30,097
	Jaunpuri/Jaunsari	1,36,779
	Kangri	11,17,342
	Khari Boli	50,195
	Khortha/Khotta	80,38,735
	Kulvi	1,96,295
	Kumauni	20,81,057
	Kurmali Thar	3,11,175
	Lamani/Lambadi/ Labani	32,76,548
	Laria	89,876
	Lodhi	1,39,180
	Magadhi/Magahi	1,27,06,825
	Malvi	52,12,617
	Mandeali	6,22,590
	Marwari	78,31,749
	Mewari	42,12,262
	Mewati	8,56,643
	Nagpuria	7,63,014
	Nimadi	23,09,265
	Padari	17,279
	Pahari	32,53,889
	Palmuha	23,579
	Panch Pargania	2,44,914
	Pando/Pandwani	15,595
	Pangwali	18,668
	Pawari/Powari	3,25,772
	Puran/Puran Bhasha	12,375
	Rajasthani	2,58,06,344
	Sadan/Sadri	43,45,677
	Sirmauri	1,07,401
	Sondwari	2,29,788
	Sugali	1,70,987
	Surgujia	17,38,256
	Surjapuri	22,56,228
	Others	1,67,11,170
7	**KANNADA**	4,37,06,512
	Badaga	1,33,550
	Kannada	4,35,06,272
	Kuruba/Kurumba	24,189
	Prakritha/Prakritha Bhasha	12,257
	Others	30,244
8	**KASHMIRI**	67,97,587
	Dardi	25,600
	Kashmiri	65,54,369
	Kishtwari	39,748
	Siraji	1,24,896
	Others	52,974

9.	**KONKANI**	22,56,502
	Gorboli/Goru/ Gorwani	50,259
	Konkani	21,46,906
	Kudubi/Kudumbi	17,209
	Malwani	23,617
	Nawait	13,123
	Others	5,388
10.	**MAITHILI**	1,35,83,464
	Maithili	1,33,53,347
	Purbi Maithili	11,116
	Tharu	53,575
	Thati	1,65,420
	Others	6
11.	**MALAYALAM**	3,48,38,819
	Malayalam	3,47,76,533
	Pania	22,808
	Yerava	26,563
	Others	12,915
12.	**MANIPURI**[1]	17,61,079
	Manipuri	17,60,913
	Others	166
13.	**MARATHI**	8,30,26,680
	Are	53,879
	Koli	13,809
	Marathi	8,28,01,140
	Others	1,57,852
14.	**NEPALI**[2]	29,26,168
	Nepali	29,25,796
	Others	372
15.	**ODIA**	3,75,21,324
	Bhatri	3,34,258
	Bhuiya/ Bhuyan[Ori]	32,126
	Bhumijali	34,651
	Desia	2,27,313
	Odia	3,40,59,266
	Proja (Ori)	1,56,354
	Relli	12,969
	Sambalpuri	26,30,381
	Others	34,006
16.	**PUNJABI**	3,31,24,726
	Bagri	16,56,588
	Bhateali	23,970
	Bilaspuri Kahluri	2,95,805
	Punjabi	3,11,44,095
	Others	4,268
17.	**SANSKRIT**	24,821
	Sanskrit	24,709
	Others	112
18.	**SANTALI**	73,68,192
	Karmali	3,58,579
	Mahili	26,399
	Santali	69,73,345
	Others	9,869
19.	**SINDHI**	27,72,264
	Bhatia	22,409
	Kachchhi	10,30,602
	Sindhi	16,79,246
	Others	40,007
20.	**TAMIL**	6,90,26,881
	Irula/Irular Mozhi	11,870
	Kaikadi	25,870
	Korava	10,421
	Tamil	6,88,88,839
	Yerukala/Yerukula	58,065
	Others	31,816
21.	**TELUGU**	8,11,27,740
	Telugu	8,09,12,459
	Vadari	1,98,020
	Others	17,261
22.	**URDU**	5,07,72,631
	Bhansari	22,806
	Urdu	5,07,25,762
	Others	24,063

1. Manipuri includes Meithai.
2. Nepali includes Gorkhali.

STATEMENT - 1
PART - B
LANGUAGES NOT SPECIFIED IN THE EIGHTH SCHEDULE (NON-SCHEDULED LANGUAGES)

	Name of Language & mother tongue(s) grouped under each language	Number of persons who returned the language (and the mother tongues grouped under each) as their mother tongue
	1	2
1.	**ADI**	2,48,834
	Adi	1,10,307
	Adi Gallong/Gallong	29,246
	Adi Miniyong/ Miniyong	13,344
	Talgalo	69,256
	Others	26,681
2.	**AFGHANI/ KABULI/PASHTO**	21,677
	Afghani/Kabuli/ Pashto	21,433
	Others	244
3.	**ANAL**	27,217
	Anal	24,301
	Others	2,916
4.	**ANGAMI**	1,52,796
	Angami	40,721
	Others	1,12,075
5.	**AO**	2,60,008
	Ao	1,19,549
	Chungli	70,782
	Mongsen	69,094
	Others	583
6.	**ARABIC/ARBI**	54,947
	Arabic/Arbi	54,871
	Others	76
7.	**BALTI**	13,774
	Balti	13,654
	Others	120

	Name of Language & mother tongue(s) grouped under each language	Number of persons who returned the language (and the mother tongues grouped under each) as their mother tongue
	1	2
8.	**BHILI/BHILODI**	1,04,13,637
	Baori	63,028
	Barel	9,91,257
	Bhilali	7,53,466
	Bhili/Bhilodi	32,06,533
	Chodhari	1,10,570
	Dhodia	49,097
	Gamti/Gavit	1,39,118
	Garasia	76,749
	Kokna/Kokni/Kukna	4,16,787
	Mawchi	98,486
	Paradhi	69,085
	Pawri	3,11,677
	Rathi	47,801
	Tadavi	52,347
	Varli	3,87,481
	Vasava	1,87,036
	Wagdi	33,93,991
	Others	59,128
9.	**BHOTIA**	2,29,954
	Bhotia	1,20,583
10.	**BHUMIJ**	27,506
	Bhumij	10,190
	Others	17,316
11.	**BISHNUPURIYA**	79,646
	Bishnupriya	
	Manipuri/Manipuri	
	Bishnupriya	74,069

	Others	5,577
12.	**CHAKHESANG**	19,846
	Chakhesang	19,846
13.	**CHAKRU/CHOKRI**	91,216
	Chakru/Chokri	91,216
14.	**CHANG**	66,852
	Chang	66,852
15.	**COORGI/KODAGU**	1,13,857
	Kodava	96,918
	Coorgi/Kodagu	16,939
16.	**DEORI**	32,376
	Deori	32,376
17.	**DIMASA**	1,37,184
	Dimasa	1,33,327
	Others	3,857
18.	**ENGLISH**	2,59,678
	English	2,59,678
19.	**GADABA**	40,976
	Gadaba	40,965
	Others	11
20.	**GANGTE**	16,542
	Gangte	16,542
21.	**GARO**	11,45,323
	Garo	11,25,359
	Others	19,964
22.	**GONDI**	29,84,453
	Dorli	47,701
	Gondi	28,56,581
	Kalari	26,769
	Maria/ Muria	15,864
	Others	37,538
23.	**HALABI**	7,66,297
	Halabi	7,65,464
	Others	833
24.	**HALAM**	38,915
	Halam	26,534
	Others	12,381
25.	**HMAR**	98,988
	Hmar	98,988
26.	**HO**	14,21,418
	Ho	14,10,996
	Lohara	10,422
27.	**JATAPU**	20,028
	Jatapu	19,990

	Others	38
28.	**JUANG**	30,378
	Juang	30,378
29.	**KABUI**	1,22,931
	Rongmei	68,706
	Kabui	54,220
	Others	5
30.	**KARBI/MIKIR**	5,28,503
	Karbi/Mikir	5,28,503
31.	**KHANDESHI**	18,60,236
	Ahirani	16,36,465
	Dangi	1,50,674
	Gujari	57,171
	Khandeshi	10,670
	Others	5,256
32.	**KHARIA**	2,97,614
	Kharia	2,93,665
	Others	3,949
33.	**KHASI**	14,31,344
	Khasi	10,37,964
	Lyngngam	11,586
	Pnar/Synteng	3,19,324
	War	51,558
	Others	10,912
34.	**KHEZHA**	41,625
	Khezha	36,383
	Others	5,242
35.	**KHIEMNUNGAN**	61,983
	Khiemnungan	61,968
	Others	15
36.	**KHOND/KONDH**	1,55,548
	Khond/Kondh	1,11,693
	Kuvi	43,855
37.	**KINNAURI**	83,561
	Kinnauri	83,427
	Others	134
38.	**KISAN**	2,06,100
	Kisan	2,06,100
39.	**KOCH**	36,434
	Koch	33,962
	Others	2,472
40.	**KODA/KORA**	47,268
	Koda/Kora	47,181
	Others	87

No.	Language / Mother tongue	Number
41.	**KOLAMI**	1,28,451
	Kolami	1,28,451
42.	**KOM**	15,108
	Kom	15,108
43.	**KONDA**	60,699
	Kodu	32,166
	Konda	24,987
	Others	3,546
44.	**KONYAK**	2,44,477
	Konyak	2,44,477
45.	**KORKU**	7,27,133
	Korku	6,88,053
	Muwasi	35,827
	Others	3,253
46.	**KORWA**	28,453
	Koraku	16,154
	Others	12,299
47.	**KOYA**	4,07,423
	Koya	4,07,423
48.	**KUI**	9,41,488
	Kui	9,41,377
	Others	111
49.	**KUKI**	83,968
	Kuki	82,049
	Others	1,919
50.	**KURUKH/ORAON**	19,88,350
	Kurukh/Oraon	19,76,920
	Others	11,430
51.	**LADAKHI**	14,952
	Ladakhi	14,952
52.	**LAHAULI**	11,574
	Lahauli	11,162
	Others	412
53.	**LAHNDA**	1,08,791
	Bahawal Puri	29,253
	Hindi Multani	61,722
	Others	17,816
54.	**LAKHER**	42,429
	Others	3,758
55.	**LALUNG**	33,921
	Lalung	33,921
56.	**LEPCHA**	47,331
	Lepcha	47,331
57.	**LIANGMEI**	49,811
	Liangmei	48,388
	Others	1,423
58.	**LIMBU**	40,835
	Limbu	38,067
	Others	2,768
59.	**LOTHA**	1,79,467
	Lotha	1,79,467
60.	**LUSHAI/MIZO**	8,30,846
	Lushai/Mizo	8,25,900
	Others	4,946
61.	**MALTO**	2,34,991
	Kulehiya	75,776
	Pahariya	1,52,814
	Others	6,401
62.	**MAO**	2,40,205
	Mao	97,195
	Paola	1,43,001
	Others	9
63.	**MARAM**	32,460
	Maram	32,460
64.	**MARING**	25,814
	Maring	25,814
65.	**MIRI/MISHING**	6,29,954
	Miri/Mishing	6,29,954
66.	**MISHMI**	44,100
	Mishmi	15,871
	Others	28,229
67.	**MOGH**	36,665
	Mogh	36,652
	Others	13
68.	**MONPA**	13,703
	Monpa	13,703
69.	**MUNDA**	5,05,922
	Kol	19,868
	Munda	4,64,817
	Others	21,237
70.	**MUNDARI**	11,28,228
	Mundari	11,28,050
	Others	178
71.	**NICOBARESE**	29,099
	Nicobarese	29,099
72.	**NISSI/DAFLA**	4,06,532
	Apatani	44,815
	Nissi/Dafla	2,89,166

	Tagin	62,897	**87.**	**TAMANG**	20,154
	Others	9,654		Tamang	20,154
73.	**NOCTE**	30,839	**88.**	**TANGKHUL**	1,87,276
	Nocte	29,810		Tangkhul	1,87,263
	Others	1,029		Others	13
74.	**PAITE**	79,507	**89.**	**TANGSA**	38,624
	Paite	79,443		Tutcha Tangsa	10,234
	Others	64		Others	28,390
75.	**PARJI**	52,349	**90.**	**THADO**	2,29,340
	Dhurwa	45,938		Thado	2,27,114
	Others	6,411		Others	2,226
76.	**PAWI**	28,639	**91.**	**TIBETAN**	1,82,685
	Pawi	28,639		Purkhi	93,500
77.	**PHOM**	54,416		Tibetan	83,779
	Phom	54,416		Others	5,406
78.	**POCHURY**	21,654	**92.**	**TRIPURI**	10,11,294
	Pochury	21,568		Kokbarak	9,17,900
	Others	86		Reang	58,539
79.	**RABHA**	1,39,986		Tripuri	33,138
	Rabha	1,39,985		Others	1,717
	Others	1	**93.**	**TULU**	18,46,427
80.	**RAI**	15,644		Tulu	18,41,963
	Rai	10,427		Others	4,464
	Others	5,217	**94.**	**VAIPHEI**	42,748
81.	**RENGMA**	65,328		Vaiphei	42,748
	Rengma	65,328	**95.**	**WANCHO**	59,154
82.	**SANGTAM**	76,000		Wancho	59,154
	Sangtam	75,684	**96.**	**YIMCHUNGRE**	83,259
	Others	316		Chirr	12,300
83.	**SAVARA**	4,09,549		Tikhir	11,071
	Savara	4,09,481		Yimchungre	56,538
	Others	68		Others	3,350
84.	**SEMA**	10,802	**97.**	**ZELIANG**	63,529
	Sema	10,802		Zeliang	63,529
85.	**SHERPA**	16,012	**98.**	**ZEMI**	50,925
	Sherpa	16,012		Zemi	50,923
86.	**SHINA**	32,247		Others	2
	Shina	32,069	**99.**	**ZOU**	26,545
	Others	178		Zou	26,545

Index

C

H

M

N

O

P

R

W

Y

Z